Organic Residue Analysis and the First Uses of Pottery in the Ancient Middle East

Organic Residue Analysis and the First Uses of Pottery in the Ancient Middle East

Michael W. Gregg

BAR International Series 2065
2010

Published in 2016 by
BAR Publishing, Oxford

BAR International Series 2065

Organic Residue Analysis and the First Uses of Pottery in the Ancient Middle East

ISBN 978 1 4073 0473 1

© MW Gregg and the Publisher 2010

The author's moral rights under the 1988 UK Copyright,
Designs and Patents Act are hereby expressly asserted.

All rights reserved. No part of this work may be copied, reproduced, stored,
sold, distributed, scanned, saved in any form of digital format or transmitted
in any form digitally, without the written permission of the Publisher.

BAR Publishing is the trading name of British Archaeological Reports (Oxford) Ltd.
British Archaeological Reports was first incorporated in 1974 to publish the BAR
Series, International and British. In 1992 Hadrian Books Ltd became part of the BAR
group. This volume was originally published by John and Erica Hedges Ltd. in
conjunction with British Archaeological Reports (Oxford) Ltd / Hadrian Books Ltd,
the Series principal publisher, in 2010. This present volume is published by BAR
Publishing, 2016.

Printed in England

PUBLISHING

BAR titles are available from:

        BAR Publishing
        122 Banbury Rd, Oxford, OX2 7BP, UK
EMAIL   info@barpublishing.com
PHONE +44 (0)1865 310431
FAX   +44 (0)1865 316916
        www.barpublishing.com

Abstract

In this book, I discuss the role of organic residue analysis in identifying economic activities and subsistence practices associated with the first uses of pottery in the Middle East, and present the results of my analyses of 280 potsherds recovered from 22 Neolithic and early Chalcolithic settlements dating between 7300 and 4300 cal BC. These analyses were undertaken as part of my doctoral research, and a thesis on which this volume is based was submitted in conformity with the requirements for the degree of Doctor of Philosophy to the Department of Anthropology at the University of Toronto in September 2009.

The adoption of pottery vessels in the early agricultural villages and pastoral encampments of the Middle East was not a uniform phenomenon, with this new technology not immediately of benefit, apparently, to all human groups. Results of my analyses have demonstrated that 'conventional' solvent extraction and alkaline hydrolysis techniques have limited utility in the recovery of diagnostic organic compounds from pottery from early ceramic horizons in the Middle East (Gregg et al. 2007), and that increased yields can be achieved through the use of a microwave-assisted liquid chromatography protocol (Gregg et al. 2009; Gregg and Slater in press). My research has established that there is greater diversity in the fractionation of stable carbon isotopes associated with the synthesis of fatty acids in domesticated animals than has previously been reported. In many instances, the ranges of modern isotopic values that have been used to categorize animal fats in archaeological potsherds in northern Europe cannot distinguish between the $\partial^{13}C$ ratios of ancient dairy residues and carcass fats of ruminant and non-ruminant species in central Europe or the Middle East (Gregg et al. 2009; Gregg and Slater in press).

In light of these results, I evaluate the diagnostic potential and limitations of different methodological approaches in the recovery and characterization of organic residues, and propose a series of measures that will allow more confident categorization of the substances early pottery vessels from the Middle East may have once contained. I also make a number of recommendations for archaeologists considering the use of organic residue analysis, and suggest some practical ideas on how to develop the degree of confidence necessary to assess the methods used in acquisition of molecular and isotopic data, and ultimately, to evaluate the adequacy of the analytical criteria used to address specific archaeological research questions.

Acknowedgements

I would like to thank the many people and organizations whose generous contributions, critical assessments and wealth of ideas have made my doctoral research project possible. Professors Michael Chazan, Edward Banning and Heather Miller of the Department of Anthropology at the University of Toronto have provided me with thoughtful advice and sound direction in the pursuit of my research goals. Dr. Chazan and Dr. Banning co-supervised the initial stages of my doctoral research, while Dr. Miller supervised the development of my research proposal, data collection and analytical strategy, and the writing, editing and completion of my dissertation. As my Masters advisor, Dr. Chazan instilled a fascination of prehistoric human behavior in me, and has pushed and cajoled me into investigating places, periods and topics I never dreamed I would explore. While I was completing my Masters degree, Dr. Banning introduced me to my research subject, and provided me with guidance in understanding the chronological sequence of cultural developments in the ancient Near East and the applicability of different archaeometric techniques in answering archaeological research questions. Dr. Banning also provided me with the opportunity to join his excavation team at the Late Neolithic site at al-Basatîn in northern Jordan. Details of Dr. Banning's contribution to our multi-authored published works are detailed in section 4.1.1. Dr. Banning and Dr. Miller have also made a large financial contributions towards the molecular and isotopic analyses of organic residues examined in this study from grants provided by the Social Sciences and Humanities Research Council of Canada.

While I was completing my Masters degree at the University of Toronto, Professor Matthew Collins and Dr. Oliver Craig offered me the opportunity to work on my doctoral research project under their joint supervision at the University of Newcastle. However, before the completion of my Master's degree, Dr. Collins and Dr. Craig took up positions at the Universities of York and Rome, respectively. Since the analytical equipment necessary to undertake my research was not yet available to them at either of these institutions, Dr. Collins introduced me to the head of the Department of Archaeological Sciences at the University of Bradford, Professor Carl Heron. Dr. Heron subsequently offered me the use of his laboratory and the analytical instrumentation at Bradford and provided me with instruction on the basic tenets of biomolecular archaeology and soil chemistry, and guidance in the interpretation of molecular compounds surviving in archaeological pottery. While at Bradford, Dr. Benjamin Stern instructed me on the recovery of organic residues from archaeological pottery and provided me with training in gas chromatography and mass spectrometry. Following my preliminary identification of molecular compounds in pottery fragments from two Neolithic sites in southwestern Iran, I collaborated with Dr. Stern and his laboratory assistant, Ms Rhea Brettell, on the subsequent molecular and isotopic analyses of these residues. Dr. Stern made a small financial contribution towards isotopic analysis of organic residues from a grant provided by the Natural and Environmental Research Council of the United Kingdom. Dr. Stern's and Ms Brettell's contribution to our multi-authored published work are detailed in section 3.1.

Professor Andrew Moore of the Rochester Institute of Technology was the first archaeologist to provide me with pottery fragments from his excavations of the late Neolithic occupation at the site of Abu Hureyra in northern Syria. As a result of Dr. Moore's support, many other excavators eagerly provided me with pottery fragments from early pottery horizons in the Middle East to examine. Dr. Bill Finlayson, Director of the British Council for Research in the Levant and Professor Ian Kuijt of Notre Dame University afforded me the opportunity to work with them on the excavation of the aceramic Neolithic settlement at Dhra' in central Jordan, and provided me with pottery from the nearby Late Neolithic occupation at the site.

Dr. Ehud Gallili of the Israel Antiquities Authority provided me with pottery fragments from his excavation of the submerged Late Neolithic settlement at Newe Yam in northern Israel, and welcomed me into the warmth and hospitality of his home. Professor Yossi Garfinkel of the Hebrew University in Jerusalem provided me with pottery from the Late Neolithic sites at Munhata and Sha'ar Hagolan in Israel. Professor Asli Erim of the University of Istanbul, provided me with pottery from Çayönü in southeastern Turkey. Professor Frank Hole of Yale University provided me with pottery fragments from the earliest pottery horizons at the sites of Ali Kosh and Chageh Sefid in southwestern Iran, and subsequently gave me advice on his excavations at nearby Tepe Tula'i. Professor Zeidan Kafafi of Yarmouk University provided me with pottery from the Late Neolithic site at Abu Thawwab in central Jordan. Professor Peder Mortensen at the Carsten Niebuhr Institute at the University of provided me with pottery fragments from the Initial Village period sites at Tepe Guran and Tepe Sarab in western Iran. Mr. Dan Rahimi, Director of the Royal Ontario Museum provided me with pottery from the Initial Village period site at Tepe Sarab in western Iran. Professor Steven Rosen at Ben-Gurion University of the Negev provided me with pottery fragments from the Chalcolithic sites of Abu Matar and Nevadim in southern Israel. Professor Mary Voigt of the College of William and Dr. Patrick McGovern of the Museum of Archaeology and Anthropology at the University of Pennsylvania endorsed my application to the museum's scientific testing committee for destructive testing of pottery fragments from the Neolithic sites at Hajji Firuz and Dalma Tepe. Professor Henry Wright of the University of Michigan provided me with pottery fragments from the sites of Kashkashok in Syria and Faruhkabad in Iraq.

Professors Kamyar Abdi of Dartmouth College and Reinhardt Bernbeck and Susan Pollock of the State University of New York – Binghamton provided me with the opportunity to join their excavations of the Late Neolithic site of Toll-e Bashi in southwestern Iran in 2003, and allowed me to recover potsherds from the earliest pottery bearing levels at the site specifically for organic residue analysis. Dr. Bernbeck provided me with guidance in the classification of clay fragments recovered from the site, and edited my contributions to two chapters in a volume on Toll-e Bashi. Dr. Bernbeck also collaborated with Dr. Abdi and I on publication of a brief report on two previously undiscovered Neolithic sites in southwestern Iran. Dr. Pollock provided me with guidance on excavating a circular mudbrick oven buried within sediments of similar consistency. Dr. Abdi also introduced me to Mr. Karim Alizadeh of the Iranian Cultural Heritage Organization in Tehran, who facilitated the export of pottery fragments to Canada for organic residue analysis. Mr. Alizadeh subsequently coordinated my reconnaissance of Neolithic sites in western and northern Iran with the provincial antiquities offices in 2005, and arranged for my examination and sampling of pottery fragments housed at the National Museum in Tehran. Ms Linda Godarzi of the Iranian Cultural Heritage Organization helped me locate the Neolithic sites of Ali Kosh, Chageh Sefid, and Tepe Tula'i in Khuzistan, and the nearby geological source of bitumen.

Professor Steve Weiner of the Weissman Institute in Rehovet allowed me to use the laboratory at the Kimmel Center for Archaeological Sciences in preparing pottery samples for export to Canada. Professor Tamar Dayan of the Department of Zoology at the University of Tel Aviv provided me with modern goat and wild boar fats from animals raised on lands adjacent to the Jordan Valley. Professor Füsun Ertug of the University of Istanbul introduced me to pastoralists Naci and Besime Kayan from Kizilkaya in central Anatolia who provided me with fragments of a ceramic vessel used in the manufacturing of dairy foods. Professor Yuval Goren allowed me to use laboratory space at the University of Tel Aviv for the preparation of modern animal fats for comparative purposes with organic residues recovered from archaeological pottery.

Professor Henry Schwarz of the School of Geography and Earth Sciences at McMaster University has given me advice on compound specific isotopic analysis of organic residues and introduced me to his colleague Dr. Greg Slater. Dr. Slater has subsequently provided me with advice on developing a new method to increase yields of organic residues from archaeological pottery, allowed me to use of his laboratory and analytical instrumentation. Dr. Slater has also made a financial contribution towards isotopic analysis of organic residues examined in this study from a grant provided by the Natural Sciences and Engineering Research Council of Canada. Dr. Slater's contribution to our multi-authored and jointly-authored published works are detailed in section 4.1. Dr. Slater's laboratory assistant, Ms Jennie Kirby has provided me with invaluable logistical support in my extraction of fatty acids surviving in pottery fragments and ensured the ongoing reliability and precision of the laboratory's analytical instrumentation. Dr. Kevin Gibbs of the Department of Archaeology at the University of Manchester collaborated on analysis and publication of pottery fragment recovered from the Late Neolithic site at al-Basatîn. Details of Dr. Gibbs' contribution to our multi-authored published work are detailed in section 5.1.

As members of my dissertation committee, Professor Max Friesen of the Department of Anthropology at the University of Toronto and Professor Mike Richards of the Department of Anthropology at the University of British Columbia, both closely examined my thesis and provided me with valuable feedback on my doctoral research and interesting questions and ideas for my postdoctoral research project.

The following institutions have provided financial or logistical support for this research project: The Social Sciences and Humanities Research Council of Canada (a doctoral research award, and contributions for isotopic analysis from the research awards of my doctoral advisor Dr. Heather Miller and my collaborator Dr. Edward Banning); the Natural Sciences and Engineering Research Council of Canada (a contribution for isotopic analysis from the research award of my collaborator Dr. Greg Slater); the University of Toronto; The University of Bradford; McMaster University; Andrea and Charles Bronfman Philanthropies; The Halbert Foundation; The Iran Heritage Foundation; The Iranian Cultural Heritage Organization; The Antiquities Department of Jordan, The Antiquities Authority of Israel; The Council for British Research in the Levant; The British Institute of Persian Studies, Tehran; The Canadian Union of Public Employees locals at Trent University and the University of Toronto.

My former marital partner Ms Diane Bracuk helped me recover my faculties following a traumatic head injury in 1995 and indulged my pursuit of Bachelor of Arts and Master of Arts degrees. Ms Elaine Wyatt has been both challenging student and engaging partner, and has lent her warm, whole-hearted support to my professional aspirations and my research goals.

M.W.G., December 17, 2009
Museum of Archaeology and Anthropology
University of Pennsylvania, Philadelphia

Table of contents

Abstract	i
Acknowledgments	i
Table of Contents	iii
List of Tables	vi
List of Figures	vi
List of Appendices	viii

Chapter 1

Organic residue analysis and the earliest uses of pottery in the ancient Middle East

1.1	Introduction	1
1.2	Background to my original research question	2
1.2.1	Chronological framework for the emergence of pottery in the Middle East	4
1.2.2	Early uses of pottery in the Middle East	7
1.2.2.1	Early use of pottery as storage and transport containers	7
1.2.2.2	Early use of pottery in serving and display of food, and as a medium for ritual practice	8
1.2.2.3	Early use of pottery in food preparation	9
1.2.2.4	Early pottery use in milk collection and processing of dairy foods	12
1.3	Research approaches	12
1.4	Summary of research findings and rationale for the broadening my research focus	13

Chapter 2

The task of extracting and identifying organic residues in archaeological pottery

2.1	Introduction	15
2.2	Early wet chemistry studies	15
2.3	Principles and of gas chromatography and mass spectrometry	16
2.4	The early use of gas chromatography and mass spectrometry in archaeology	17
2.5	Molecular characterization of vegetable oils and animal fats in more recent studies using gas chromatography and mass spectrometry (GC-MS)	18
2.6	Isotopic characterization of adipose and dairy fatty acids through the use of gas chromatography-combustion-isotope ratio mass spectrometry (GC-C-IRMS)	21
2.7	Molecular characterization of amino acids in animal proteins through use of acid digestion, and immunoassay techniques	25
2.8	Molecular characterization of animal fats and proteins through use of electrospray ionization mass spectrometry techniques	26
2.9	Molecular and isotopic characterization of plant sugars and starches through Fourier transform infrared spectroscopy, GC-MS, GC-C-IRMS, and high performance liquid chromatography (HPLC) techniques	26

2.10	Molecular and isotopic characterization of bitumen residues using GC-MS and elemental analyzer isotope ratio mass spectrometry (EA-IRMS)	28
2.11	Rationale for the choice of instrumental analytical techniques initially used in this study	28

Chapter 3
Use of 'conventional' solvent extraction techniques in recovery of organic residues from archaeological potsherds from 20 Neolithic sites in the Middle East

3.1.1	Preface: contributions of individual authors to the multi-authored paper on which this chapter is based	29
3.1.2	Introduction	29
3.2	'Conventional' solvent extraction	29
3.3	GC-MS analysis and preliminary molecular characterization of residues recovered through 'conventional' solvent extraction	30
3.4	Further molecular and isotopic characterization of bitumen residues	30
3.5	Molecular characterization of residues from the archaeological pottery, and archaeological and modern bitumen samples	31
3.6	Further $\partial^{13}C$ and ∂D isotopic characterization of the asphaltene fraction in bitumen residues	33
3.7	Further extraction of residues from four pottery fragments using saponification and BSTFA derivatization techniques	34
3.8	GC-MS analysis and molecular characterization of residues recovered through saponification and BSTFA derivatization techniques	34
3.9	'Conventional' solvent extraction and GC analysis of 164 additional pottery fragments	34
3.10	Assessment of my preliminary results and the efficacy of extraction methods	35

Chapter 4
A new method for increasing fatty acid yields: microwave-assisted extraction of organic residues from archaeological pottery

4.1.1	Preface: Contributions of individual authors to the multi-authored and jointly-authored papers on which chapters 4 and 5 are based	37
4.1.2	Introduction	37
4.2	Microwave extraction of lipids from archaeological pottery fragments	38
4.3	Liquid chromatography separation of free fatty acids in potsherd extracts	38
4.3.1	Silica gel columns	38
4.3.2	Aminopropyl columns	38
4.3.3	Transterification	38
4.3.4	Na_2SO_4 Columns	39
4.3.5	Secondary liquid chromatography separation of fatty acid methyl esters from potsherd extracts	39

4.4	Collection of modern animal fats for comparative purposes	39
4.5	Extraction of free-fatty acids from modern reference fats	39
4.6	GC-MS analysis	40
4.7	GC-C-IRMS analysis	40

Chapter 5

Results from use of microwave-assisted extraction techniques in recovery of free fatty acids from archaeological potsherds from nine Neolithic sites in the Middle East

5.1	The archaeological pottery fragments	41
5.2	GC-MS results from the al-Basatîn pilot study	41
5.3	GC-C-IRMS results of the al-Basatîn pilot study	41
5.4	Microwave extraction of organic residues from 55 additional pottery fragments from eight and GC-MS results of potsherd extracts	44
5.5	GC-C-IRMS characterization of residues from potsherds from eight additional Neolithic sites	45
5.6	Assessment of the diagnostic resolution of stable carbon isotopes in identifying ancient animal fats in archaeological pottery fragments from the earliest ceramic horizons in the Middle East	47

Chapter 6

Diagnostic potential and limitations of different analytical methods in identifying the earliest uses of pottery in the ancient Middle East

6.1	Overview	53
6.2	Likelihood for survival and identification of different substances in archaeological pottery	53
6.3	Efficacy of different extraction methods	54
6.4	Environmental, physiological, and anthropogenic factors affecting fractionation of stable carbon isotopes in early pottery vessels	54
6.5	Recommended measures for more confident categorization of organic residues from early ceramic horizons in the Middle East	55

Chapter 7

Summary of research findings and suggestions for archaeologists considering the use of organic residue analysis

7.1	Summary of research findings	57
7.2	Molecular and isotopic evidence of early pottery use in the Middle East	57
7.3	Suggestions for archaeologists considering the use of organic residue analysis	58
7.4	Conclusion	60

Bibliography		61
Appendices		77

List of Tables

1.2.1	Approximate dates of pottery bearing horizons from which archaeological potsherds examined in this study were recovered	7
3.3.1	Key to molecular compounds chromatograms in Figures 3.3.1 – 3.3.4	30
3.4.1	Details of the archaeological pottery, and archaeological and modern bitumen samples from southwestern Iran	31
3.5.1	Numerical values of ratios of diagnostic Ts to Ts terpanes and gammacerane to $C_{30}\alpha\beta$ hopane lipid species represented in Fig. 3.5.4.	32
3.6.1	Numerical values of the bulk $\partial^{13}C$ and ∂D isotopic values for the asphaltene fraction of bituminous materials examined in this study	33
5.3.1	Numerical $\partial^{13}C$ values plotted in Figure 5.3.1	44
5.4.1	Details of samples yielding measurable abundances of fatty acids using a microwave-assisted liquid protocol	45
5.5.1	Numerical $\partial^{13}C$ values plotted in Figure 5.5.1	50

List of Figures

1.2.1	Clay impression of a cylinder seal from the Diyala region of Mesopotamia Uruk III period circa 4400 calBC	3
1.2.2	Map showing location of archaeological sites from which organic residues were examined in this study and additional selected sites mentioned in text	5
2.3.1.	Schematic diagram of a gas chromatography column and chromatogram of the molecular compounds recovered from a modern butter fat sample	16
2.3.2	Mass spectrograph showing molecular weights and ion fragments of individual molecular components of modern butter fats	17
2.5.1	High temperature gas chromatograms of potsherd extracts with fatty acid ratios consistent with degraded plant oils and animal fats	19
2.6.1	Discrete ranges of $\partial^{13}C$ values of fatty acids of modern animal fats used to categorize potsherd extracts from prehistoric Britain	22
2.6.2	Observed $\partial^{13}C$ values of $C_{16:0}$ and $C_{18:0}$ fatty acids recovered from pottery fragments from Late Neolithic levels at Çatalhöyük	23
2.6.3	Plot the differences in $\partial^{13}C$ values of $C_{16:0}$ and $C_{18:0}$ fatty acids recovered from pottery fragments from Late Neolithic levels at Çatalhöyük	23
2.6.4	Observed $\partial^{13}C$ ratios of $C_{16:0}$ and $C_{18:0}$ fatty acids of modern reference fats from central Europe in context of the ranges of $\partial^{13}C$ values used to categorize organic residues in archaeological pottery from Great Britain	25
3.3.1- 3.3.4	Selected ion chromatograms (*m/z 191*) of potsherd extracts from Neolithic sites *at* Ali Kosh and Chagha Sefid in southwestern Iran	30

3.4.1	Bitumen-encrusted mudbrick and pottery fragment from Mohammad Jaffar phase at Ali Kosh	31
3.5.1-3.5.3	Partial ion chromatograms of terpanes (m/z 191) from archaeological bitumen samples from Ali Kosh and Tepe Tula'i and modern bitumen from the geological seep at Chershme Ghir	32
3.5.4	Plot of ratios of Ts to Tm terpanes to the ratio of gammacerane to C_{30} $\alpha\beta$ hopane from potsherd extracts and archaeological and modern bitumen	32
3.6.1	Plot of bulk $\partial^{13}C$ (‰ / PDB) v. ∂D (‰ / SMOW) isotopic values for the asphaltene fraction of bituminous materials examined in this study	33
3.8.1-3.8.3	Partial high temperature chromatograms of potsherd extracts exhibiting abundances of free fatty acids through the use of 'conventional' solvent extraction and saponification extraction techniques	34
4.1.1	Photographs of two pottery fragments with carbonized surface residues recovered specifically for chemical analysis from site at al-Basatîn	38
4.3.1	Schematic representation of liquid chromatography protocol for the recovery of free fatty acids from potsherd extracts	39
5.2.1-5.2.8	High temperature chromatograms of eight al-Basatîn potsherd extracts exhibiting fatty acid abundances consistent with degraded animal fats	42
5.3.1	Plot of $\partial^{13}C$ values of $C_{16:0}$ and $C_{18:0}$ fatty acids recovered from the al-Basatîn potsherds and modern reference fats	43
5.3.2	Plot the differences in $\partial^{13}C$ values of $C_{16:0}$ and $C_{18:0}$ fatty acids recovered from pottery fragments from al-Basatîn	43
5.4.1-5.4.17	High temperature chromatograms of 17 potsherd extracts yielding fatty acid abundances consistent with degraded animal fats	46-7
5.4.18-5.4.26	High temperature chromatograms of nine potsherd extracts yielding fatty acid abundances consistent with degraded plant oils	48
5.5.1	Plot of $\partial^{13}C$ values of $C_{16:0}$ and $C_{18:0}$ fatty acids recovered from 17 potsherds from eight Neolithic sites and modern reference fats	49
5.5.2	Plot of the differences in $\partial^{13}C$ values of $C_{16:0}$ and $C_{18:0}$ fatty acids recovered from 17 potsherds from eight Neolithic sites and modern reference fats	49
5.6.1	Plot of observed $\partial^{13}C$ values of $C_{16:0}$ and $C_{18:0}$ fatty acids from modern reference fats from central Europe, the Middle East and central Asia	51
5.6.2	Plot of observed $\partial^{13}C$ values of fatty acids from 25 potsherd extracts shown in the context of combined ranges of isotopic values for northern and central Europe, central Asia and the Middle East.	52
A.1.5	Modern pottery churn from central Anatolia	86
A.1.6.1	Drawings of profiles of 2 soft-ware bowl fragments from Tepe Guran and Tepe Sarab, western Iran	87
A.1.6.2.2	Drawing of profile of a bowl fragment from Farukhabad in western Iran	88
A.1.6.2.3	Drawing of profile of a bowl fragment from Toll-e Bashi in western Iran	88
A.1.6.3.1	Drawings of 2 'husking tray' fragments from Kashkashok in northern Syria	89

A.1.6.5.1	Drawings of a 'sieve' and bowl fragment from Çayönü in southeastern Turkey	90
A.1.6.6.1	Drawing of profiles of 9 Yarmoukian pottery fragments from Sha'ar Hagolan, Israel	91
A.1.6.6.2	Drawing of profiles of Jericho IX pottery fragments from Dhra', Jordan	92
A.1.6.6.1	Drawing of profiles of 25 Wadi Rabah pottery fragments from Newe Yam, Israel	92-5
A.1.6.7.1	Drawing of profiles of 3 shallow bowls from Tubna, Jordan	95
A.1.6.8.1	Drawing of profiles of 12 'churn' fragments from Abu Matar and Nevatim, Israel	96

List of Appendices

A.1.1	Pottery fragments initially examined at the Department of Archaeological Sciences, University of Bradford, using 'conventional' solvent extraction and saponification techniques	77
A.1.2	Pottery fragments subsequently examined at the Department of Chemistry, University of Toronto using 'conventional' solvent extraction technique	79
A.1.3	Pottery fragments examined at the School of Geography and Earth Sciences at McMaster University in the al-Basatîn pilot study using microwave-assisted solvent extraction and liquid chromatography separation technique	83
A.1.4	Pottery fragments subsequently examined at the School of Geography and Earth Sciences at McMaster University using microwave-assisted solvent extraction and liquid chromatography separation technique	83
A.1.5	Description of a pottery fragment from a churn obtained from pastoralists in a small farming and herding community in central Anatolia	86
A.1.6	Descriptions of the pottery fragments and the corresponding pottery assemblages of the 22 archaeological sites examined in this study	87
A.2	Detailed description of the standard operating procedures for the isolation of free fatty acids from marine sediments developed by Eglinton/Hughen Laboratories at Woods Hole Oceanographic Institution	97

Chapter 1
Organic residue analysis and the first uses of pottery in the ancient Middle East

"It will never be possible to assign specific functions to individual vessels, but the frequency with which open and closed-mouth vessels, for example, occur in several sizes can be suggestive."

Frederick Matson (1965: 204)

"The assignment of a specific source or constituent of a residue [in archaeological pottery] based on the presence of a particular biomarker or mixture of components demands a high degree of rigor, wherein consideration of the nature of other constituents may lead to the hypothesis of a putative source being rejected."

Richard Evershed (2008:899)

"It is quite possible that the earliest Near Eastern pottery operated in an entirely different sphere of activity than it did later on."

James A. Brown (1989:205)

1.1 Introduction

In the past fifty years a wide array of new scientific and archaeological approaches have contributed greatly to our understanding of the origins of humankind and the emergence of food-producing economies and complex social behavior in both the Old and New Worlds. Genetics, geochemistry, physics, botany, and zoology now play key roles in answering questions that have long puzzled archaeologists using more conventional methods of inquiry (Pollard and Heron 1996, 2008; Jones 2001; Pollard et al. 2007). The recovery and characterization of organic residues in archaeological pottery is becoming an increasingly effective means of identifying economic activities and subsistence practices associated with different prehistoric cultural and technological traditions (Pollard and Heron 1996, 2008; Jones 2001; Pollard et al. 2007; Evershed 2009). Residues imbedded in the clay matrix of pottery fragments can not only provide direct evidence of the uses of early pottery vessels, but also offer new prospects for answering myriad questions concerning the procurement and utilization of resources during the transition(s) from hunting and gathering to herding and farming following the last Ice Age. Archaeologists have long wondered whether new methods may one day come along to help resolve long-standing research questions about the first uses of pottery (Shepard 1957; Matson 1951; Hole 1989; DeAtley and Bishop 1991; Moore 1995; Rice 1999), and chemical analysis of residues surviving in archaeological potsherds has brought greater certainty to many interpretations than more traditional archaeological methods for assigning functions to prehistoric vessels (Evershed 2009). But because most archaeologists are generally unfamiliar with the instrumental techniques used in the categorization of organic residues, few have become directly involved in developing new analytical approaches themselves, and have relied on colleagues in the physical or biological sciences to recommend recovery procedures and methods for identifying substances pottery vessels may have once contained.

The origins of pastoralism and the emergence of pottery production are key themes in prehistoric archaeology, and much of my doctoral research has been focused on investigating whether there is a correlation between the first use of pottery and the domestication of milk-producing species in the Middle East during the early Holocene (Gregg 2003; Gregg in press, Gregg et al. 2009). There is no consensus today as to why late Pleistocene hunters and gatherers should have altered the way of life they had depended on for hundreds of thousands of years and began to cultivate cereal grains and herd animals following the last Ice Age. Additionally, just why pottery came to be used remains "among archaeology's most compelling issues" (Hoopes and Barnett 1995:1). In this research study, I hypothesized that invention of pottery by highly mobile pastoralists facilitated the widespread adoption of a new means of subsistence based on the herding of sheep and goats throughout the Middle East, and set out to test this supposition by obtaining direct evidence of the function of the earliest pottery vessels from the pottery itself. My analyses of extant residues in 280 pottery fragments from 22 Neolithic and Chalcolithic settlements has demonstrated that my initial premise is difficult to sustain, and that no single function can be ascribed to the earliest pottery vessels in this region. However, my research has also demonstrated that 'conventional' solvent extraction and alkaline hydrolysis techniques have limited utility in the recovery and identification of the first uses of pottery in the Middle East (Gregg et al. 2007), and that increased yields of diagnostic compounds can be achieved through the use of a microwave-assisted liquid chromatography protocol (Gregg et al. 2009; Gregg in press; Gregg and Slater in press). My results have also shown that, in many instances, the discrete ranges of modern isotopic values that have been used to categorize animal fats in archaeological potsherds from early ceramic horizons in northern Europe (Dudd and Evershed 1998; Evershed 2002; Copley et al. 2003, 2005a; Mukherjee et al. 2007) cannot distinguish between the $\partial^{13}C$ ratios of ancient dairy residues and those of adipose fats of ruminant and non-ruminant species in central Europe or the Middle East (Gregg et al. 2009; Gregg and Slater in press).

In light of these findings, I examine the role of organic residue analysis in answering archaeological questions about the first uses of pottery in the Middle East, and evaluate the diagnostic potential and limitations of the major instrumental analytical techniques used in identifying the different substances pottery vessels may have contained in antiquity. I outline the problems and opportunities associated with the extraction and identification of organic compounds from pottery fragments, and then generalize to discuss the implications of the use of organic residue analysis of archaeological pottery in interdisciplinary projects to produce complementary lines of evidence, to better address long-standing archaeological research questions.

In this chapter, I outline my reasons for examining organic residues in pottery fragments recovered from some of the earliest ceramic horizons in the Middle East, presenting the archaeological evidence that led me to arrive at my original research question, and summarizing the chronological framework for the emergence of pottery at different places and times in the region that James Breasted (1914) described as the Fertile Crescent. I then review the major studies that have examined the first uses of pottery in the Middle East using more conventional archaeological methods, paying particular attention to the possible connection between early pottery use and the processing of milk for human consumption. I conclude this chapter by describing my research approach designed to detect and explain regularities or variations in prehistoric economic activities and subsistence practices, summarizing the findings of this study, and providing a rationale for broadening my research focus to include a number of the many other uses that the earliest pottery vessels from the region may have served.

In chapter 2, I summarize the task of extracting and identifying organic residues in archaeological pottery fragments, and present a brief history of early studies examining the chemical composition of clay fabrics and extant residues in ancient pottery vessels. I also outline the major methodological issues associated with the recovery and diagnostic potential of the wide range of substances that may be preserved in archaeological pottery. In chapter 3, I put forward my rationale for choosing the instrumental analytical techniques used in this study, and present the results of my preliminary examination of 244 pottery fragments from 20 Neolithic sites using 'conventional' solvent extraction and saponification recovery techniques. This chapter also includes previously-published research, conducted in collaboration with Dr. Benjamin Stern and Ms Rhea Brettell of the Department of Archaeological Sciences at the University of Bradford, in which we identify the molecular and isotopic characteristics of bitumen residues recovered from two of the earliest agricultural villages in southwestern Iran and a late Neolithic pastoral encampment in nearby Khuzestan (Gregg et al. 2007). In chapter 4, I provide a detailed description of the first use for the recovery of organic compounds from archaeological pottery of a microwave-assisted liquid chromatography protocol initially developed for the isolation and concentration of free fatty acids in marine sediments. In chapter 5, I present molecular and isotopic evidence of subsistence practices and pottery use at the late Neolithic site of al-Basatîn in northern Jordan obtained using this protocol (Gregg et al. 2009), and results of my subsequent examination of 55 additional archaeological potsherds from eight other Neolithic sites in the Middle East using this method (Gregg in press; Gregg and Slater in press). This chapter includes in press research conducted in collaboration with Dr. Greg Slater of the School of Earth Sciences at McMaster University, and Dr. Edward Banning and Dr. Kevin Gibbs of the Department of Archaeology at the University of Manchester. These findings are presented in the context of the emerging debate concerning the efficacy of modern stable carbon isotope values in characterizing organic residues embedded in pottery fragments recovered from the earliest ceramic horizons in the Middle East and Europe (Spangenberg et al. 2006; Evershed et al. 2008; Gregg et al. 2009; Gregg and Slater in press). In chapter 6, I discuss the archaeological implications of the results of my doctoral research, and the potential and limitations of organic residues in providing direct evidence of the first uses of pottery in the Middle East. I also put forward a series of recommendations for archaeologists interested in using organic residue analysis to identify the use(s) of prehistoric pottery vessels, and outline a series of measures and future directions for research that will allow more confident categorization of organic residues recovered from early pottery vessels in the Middle East.

1.2 *Background to my original research question*
In the late 19th century, anthropologist Lewis Henry Morgan theorized that the invention of pottery was a consequence of farming (Morgan 1877), an idea that echoes strongly in archaeological explanations of the origins of pottery in the Middle East to this day (Frankfort 1927; Childe 1936; Rice 1987; Bar-Yosef and Khazanov 1992; Moore 1995; Aurenche et al. 2001; Haaland 2007). Discoveries of the use of pottery by pre-agricultural hunters and gatherers in the Americas, northern Europe, the Far East, and Central Asia have now decoupled the invention of pottery from the advent of food production (Barnett and Hoopes 1995, Kenrick 1995; Rice 1999; Zaretskaya et al. 2005; Dolukhanov et al. 2005; Coolidge 2005; Craig et al. 2007), yet the notion that pottery is a repercussion of the domestication of both plants and animals in the Middle East persists (Bar-Yosef & Khazanov 1992; Moore 1995; Rice 1999; Aurenche et al. 2001; Haaland 2007).

When and where sheep, goats, and cattle were first exploited for secondary products, such as milk, wool, and traction, rather than as an immediate food source, is crucial to our understanding of the symbiotic relationship that has developed between humans and domesticated animals (Payne 1973; Ingold 1980; 1984,1994, 2000; Sherratt 1981, 1983; Greenfield 1983, 2005; Rindos 1987; Zeder 1999, 2006; Copley et al. 2003; Craig et al. 205; Evershed et al. 2008). Iconographic representations (Fig.1.2.1) and cuneiform records bear witness to goats being milked and dairy fats being stored in pottery jars in the Diyala region of Mesopotamia by the Uruk III period, circa 4400 cal BC (Frankfort 1955; Englund 1995). However, archaeologists have long suspected that the profound change in the relationship between humans and milk-producing species came about in earlier periods in Near Eastern prehistory (Coon 1951a, 1951b, 1955; Payne 1973; Bökönyi 1977; Sherratt 1981, 1983; Davis 1982, 1984; Hole 1978, 1984, 1989, 1992; Voigt 1983; Ryder 1993; Zeder 1999, 2006; Zeder and Hesse 2000; Palmer 2002; Abdi 2003; Legge 2005; Tani 2005).

Figure 1.2.1
Clay impression of a cylinder seal from the Diyala region of Mesopotamia attests to goats being milked by the Uruk III period circa 4400 cal BC (Frankfort 1955; reproduced with permission of the Oriental Institute, University of Chicago)

In 1981, Andrew Sherratt subdivided Gordon Childe's (1928,1936) *Neolithic Revolution* into two fundamentally different stages. Sherratt (1981) hypothesized that farmers initially relied upon their own physical strength for the cultivation and harvesting of cereal grains, and herded animals exclusively as an immediate source of protein. In the second stage, that Sherratt termed the *Secondary Products Revolution*, cattle were employed as draught animals to plough fields and transport agricultural goods to the burgeoning urban centers of southern Mesopotamia, and were kept (along with sheep and goats) for the production of a continuously renewable food resource — milk. In his original paper, Sherratt did not identify the specific region or period where the use of secondary products first occurred. However, building on Simon Davis' (1982) assessment of changes in the ages that sheep and goats were killed at Neolithic and Chalcolithic settlements in western Iran, Sherratt (1983) soon hypothesized that his 'revolution' had occurred in the highland valleys adjacent to the fertile plains of Mesopotamia during the late Chalcolithic period. Nevertheless, direct evidence of the timing and location of the *Secondary Products Revolution* was lacking (Greenfield 1988), and it has been impossible to conclusively demonstrate from the mortality profiles of faunal assemblages that animals were being herded for the production of milk and wool rather than meat during the late Chalcolithic period (McCormick 1992). Similar mortality profiles have been observed for modern dairy herds with culling strategies that maximize the long-term security of the herd, as those of herds of sheep and goats that are being exploited primarily for meat (Zeder 1999). However, Sherratt's hypothesis resonates strongly in many explanations of the importance of secondary products to the adoption of domesticated animals and the intensification of economic activity in prehistoric Europe, the Middle East, and southern Asia (Bogucki 1984; Rosen 1988; Greenfield 1988, 2005; Shennan 1993; McCorriston 1997; Banning 1998; Fall et al. 2002; Fuller 2006). It has also been quite influential in leading researchers to look for chemical evidence of the processing of milk and milk byproducts in pottery vessels (Dudd and Evershed 1998; Craig et al. 2000; Copley et al 2003; Gregg 2003; Craig et al. 2005; Spangenberg et al. 2006; Mirabaud et al.2007; Evershed et al. 2008).

Frank Hole (1984) also reassessed Childe's *Neolithic Revolution* (1928,1936), and argued that two distinct subsistence strategies developed in the western and eastern regions of the Middle East at the beginning of the Holocene. Hole observed that cereal grains were cultivated in the lands adjacent to the Mediterranean coast thousands of years before there is any indication of either domesticated livestock or pottery containers, and sheep and goats were herded rather than hunted long before intensive cultivation of cereal grains in the highland valleys and fertile plains in or adjacent to the Zagros and Alborz mountains in western and northern Iran. Hole's argument for the eastern region is supported by two sets of data: (1) high frequencies of juvenile sheep and goat in the faunal assemblages of Belt and Hotu caves in northern Iran and Shanidar cave in northeastern Iraq, data that had previously led researchers to suspect that hunters were practicing some sort of incipient herding strategy during the late Epipalaeolithic period (Coon 1951a, 1951b; Perkins 1964, 1973); and (2) the absence of cereal grains and associated grinding technology in the basal levels of early Neolithic settlements in western Iran (Mortensen 1964, 1970; Young & Smith 1966; Hole & Flannery 1967; Hole 1974). More recent research supports Hole's model for the west, with three sets of data from the Levant clearly demonstrating that cereal grains were harvested and intensively processed before management of herd animals: (1) the presence of sickle elements and ground stone tools at many late Epipalaeolithic and PPNA sites (Bar-Yosef and Valla 1990; Bar-Yosef 1998, 2003; Moore et al. 2000; Bar-Yosef & Belfer-Cohen, 2002); (2) faunal assemblages from PPNB sites indicating increased reliance on goats and management of herds by the Middle PPNB circa 7500 cal BC (Garrard et al. 1988; Horwitz et al. 1999; Wasse 2001) and isolation from wild populations by the PPNC circa 6500 cal BC (Haber and Dayan 2004); and (3) paleo-DNA evidence obtained from bone collagen of morphologically "wild" goats at the PPNB site of Abu Ghosh in Israel indicates that the skeletal remains are intermediary between wild *C. aegagrus* and domesticated *C. hircus* species, and suggests that goats were domesticated within the region (Kahila Bar-Gal et al. 2003).

Unlike the relatively well-chronicled transition from hunting and gathering settlements to food-producing communities in the Levant, however, very little recent archaeological evidence informs our understanding of the processes giving rise to the herding of animals and cultivation of cereal grains in the eastern region of the Middle East. Due to political instabilities associated with the Islamic Revolution in Iran after 1979, only limited archaeological research on this subject has been undertaken in this region during the past thirty years (Alizadeh 1988; Bernbeck et al. 2003; Abdi 2003; Bernbeck, Abdi, and Gregg 2006; Bernbeck and Gregg in press; Gregg in press). As noted by archaeologists studying pastoralism, early cultural and economic developments in this region have not been taken into account in explanations asserting that the cultivation of cereal grains is an 'indispensable precondition' for the domestication of animals in the Middle East (Bar-Yosef and Khazanov 1992:4; Meadow 1993[1982]; Khazanov 1994: xl). Comprehensive investigations into the domestication of sheep and goats have been undertaken in Baluchistan, Israel, Lebanon, Syria, Turkey, and Jordan (Garrard et al. 1988; Horwitz 1989; Meadow 1993; Horwitz and Ducos 1998; Horwitz et al. 1999; Peters et al.1999; Wasse 2001;

Hesse and Wapnish 2002; Haber and Dayan 2004), but none provide compelling evidence for human control of milk-producing species predating the management of herds of goats at the site at Ganj Dareh in highland Iran between 8225 and 8000 cal BC (Smith 1974, 1978; Zeder 1999; Zeder and Hesse 2000). Part of this patterning may, in fact, stem from the way in which evidence has been collected at sites in southwestern and western Iran (Zeder 1999; Zeder and Hesse 2000), with the herding of goats inferred from the mortality profiles of faunal assemblages demonstrating none of the morphological changes that have traditionally been used as indicators of domestication. Researchers working in the Levant have rarely used culling patterns as early evidence of the management of goat herds, and have more conservatively only identified faunal remains with evidence of morphological change as those of domesticated animals (Horwitz 1989; Horwitz and Ducos 1998; Horwitz et al. 1999; Wasse 2001). A notable exception is a study combining analysis of kill off patterns and skeletal morphology of the faunal assemblage at Late Neolithic Hagoshrim by Haber and Dayan (2004), showing continuities in the management of goat herds between the PPNC and PN occupations of the site.

The basal level from Ganj Dareh not only provides us with faunal evidence suggesting the preferential culling of young male animals (Zeder 1999; Zeder and Hesse 2000) but also some of the earliest evidence of pottery vessels in the Middle East (Smith 1974, 1978; Le Mière and Picon 1987, 1999) possibly more than 1000 years before the appearance of pottery as a much more fully developed container technology in the southern Levant (Garfinkel 1999a; Banning 2007). Although there is no clear trajectory linking the adoption of pottery and the herding of milk-producing species in the Fertile Crescent, there appears to be increasing emphasis on the herding of sheep and goats accompanying the advent of the earliest pottery production at settlements of the Middle Euphrates and Balikh river valleys by approximately 6800 cal BC (Moore 2000; Akkermans and Schwartz 2003). The adoption of many different types of pottery containers at Yarmoukian villages in the southern Levant (Garfinkel 1999a; Banning 2007) also coincides with the introduction of sheep from southeastern Anatolia circa 6400 cal BC (Nissen 1993; Horwitz et al. 1999).

These coinciding phenomena and the advances that had been recently made in the identification of dairy residues in Late Medieval and Iron Age pottery from Great Britain (Dudd and Evershed 1998; Craig et al. 2000) sparked my interest in finding chemical evidence of a connection between the early use of pottery and the processing of milk for human consumption. In testing my hypothesis, I not only hoped to clarify whether the earliest pottery in the Middle East was used for single or multiple functions, but also to contribute to our understanding of the role of pottery in the exploitation of animals. I discuss the possible relation between pottery use and animal domestication further in section 1.2.2.4, but first outline the chronological framework of the emergence of pottery in the Middle East, and the potential uses of that pottery. The primary focus of this review is on uses that can be ascribed to vessels from sites of the Middle to Late Neolithic period in a broad geographic area in southwestern Asia bordered by the Caspian and Mediterranean basins in the east and west, and the Taurus mountains and Arabian desert in north and south (Figure 1.2.2). However, I also selectively draw on studies from other regions of the world to inform our understanding of the economic factors affecting developments in the first uses of pottery in this region.

1.2.1 *Chronological framework for the emergence of pottery in the Middle East*

The manipulation and intentional firing of clay objects is known to be as old as the Upper Palaeolithic period (Zimmerman and Huxtable 1971; Schmandt-Besserat 1974, Vandiver et al. 1990). However, awareness of the physical change that occurs when this moist, malleable material is exposed to high temperatures is not a sufficient precondition for the manufacture of pottery vessels (Brown 1989). Humans must first have acquired the know-how to make these tools (Braun 1983), and have also had some pressing economic, social, or spiritual need which could not be met by other types of containers. The adoption of pottery in the Middle East was not a uniform phenomenon, with this new technology not immediately of perceived benefit, apparently, to all human groups. Many of the peoples who settled in villages throughout the Fertile Crescent during the early Holocene continued to use other types of containers long after pottery was adopted at neighboring settlements (Akkermans and Schwartz 2003). Pottery was not uniformly embraced in its incipient forms, but in some communities or regions only as a more fully developed container technology (Akkermans and Schwartz 2003).

For the Middle East, the timing of the emergence of pottery has been a matter of much debate (Dyson 1965; Hole 1987a; Hedges et al. 1990; Akkermans 1991; Hours et al. 1994; Moore 1995; Tsuneki and Miyake 1996; Garfinkel 1999b; Hole 2000; Akkermans and Schwartz 2003; Aurenche et al. 2001). Recently, a greater sense of order has been brought to assessment of the Late Neolithic and Chalcolithic assemblages of the Levant, Anatolia, and northern Mesopotamia (Banning 2007; Campbell 2007; Cessford 2001; Gokturk et al. 2002; Biehl 2009). However, due to the political instability in southeastern Turkey, Iraq and Iran during the past thirty years, the chronological relationship(s) of assemblages from the aceramic and early pottery horizons of the eastern arm of the Fertile Crescent remain insufficiently dated and poorly understood. Aurenche et al. (2001) have asserted that there was a simultaneous appearance of pottery in various parts of the Middle East around 7000 cal BC. However, as Stuart Campbell (2007:107) points out, the Aurenche et al. (2001) study, and that of Hours et al. (1994) on which it is based, both accept the major ceramic groupings established for the region during the early to mid-20th century "without critical examination of their validity". Aurenche et al.'s (2001) statistical analysis of radiocarbon dates and subsequent grouping of chronological sequences, for instance, mistakenly classifies the early pottery-bearing occupations of Hotu and Belt Caves and Ganj Dareh in Iran as aceramic sites. Such an error could result in serious misunderstandings of the trajectories for the adoption of pottery by different proto-Neolithic and Neolithic cultures in the Middle East.

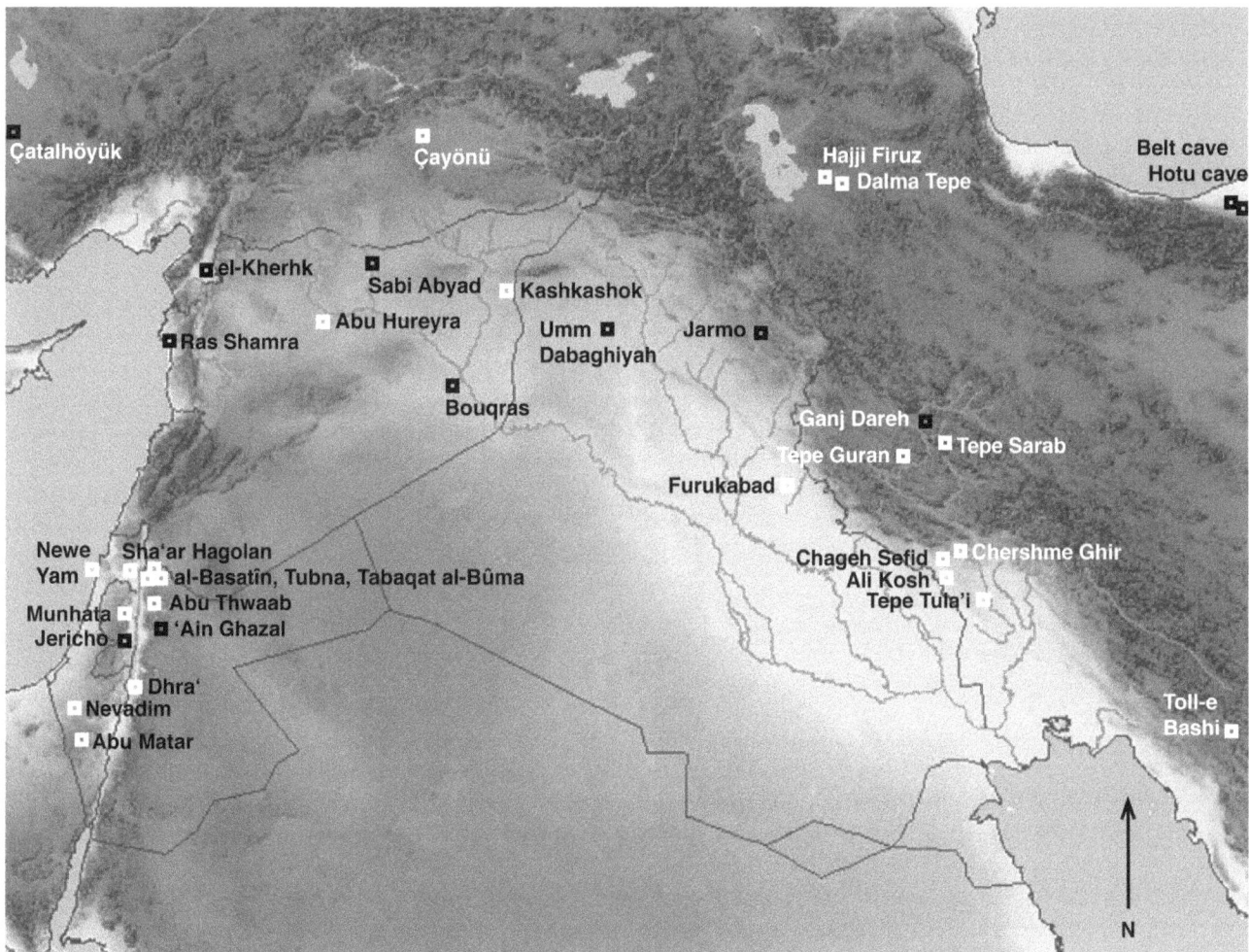

Figure 1.2.2
Location of archaeological sites from which organic residues were examined in this study (white boxes) and locations of additional selected sites mentioned in the text (black boxes).

Misunderstandings about the chronology of the first appearance of pottery in different regions of the Middle East can also result from many other factors. The wide range of statistical variability common with many older 'conventional' radiocarbon dates, such as the analyses undertaken by Dr. Willard Libby (1951), is often not specific enough to provide a reliable estimate of the actual age of the material examined, and due to the small number of radiocarbon samples from many Neolithic sites, the statistical significance of outliers has not often been assessed. A date obtained from charcoal in a fill deposit may have little relevance to the targeted occupation levels, such as is apparently the case with earliest pottery-bearing horizon at Jarmo (Libby 1951:71; Braidwood 1952). The later than expected dates at Jarmo may have been obtained from younger materials deposited through bioturbation or disturbance during excavation (Hole 1987b; Banning 2009, personal communication), or possibly from contamination from modern carbon (Banning 2000). Dates of a targeted occupation level may be overestimated due to 'old wood effect', with tree ring formation possibly having occurred hundreds of years before inclusion in the archaeological context we are interested in dating (Dean 1978). Such dates can often be in disagreement with those obtained from relatively short lived organic materials such as carbonized plant seeds (Banning 2000) or collagen from animal bone (Banning 2009, personal communication). With these caveats in mind, I outline the chronological framework for the emergence of pottery in the Middle East below. The radiocarbon dates for the pottery-bearing horizons from which organic residues were examined in this study are provided in appendices A.1.1 – A.1.4.

Among the earliest evidence of pottery that has been confidently dated in the Middle East are materials from Ganj Dareh (Figure 1.2.2), a small tell in highland Iran near Kermanshah suspected by its excavator, Philip Smith (1978), to have been initially inhabited by hunters or herders on a seasonal basis. Recovery of a single chaff-tempered potsherd from level (E) at the site indicates that pottery may have been in use from its earliest occupation (Smith 1978; Le Mière and Picon 1999). AMS radiocarbon analysis of faunal remains has placed this level between 8225 and 8000 cal BC (Zeder and Hesse 2000; OxCal 2009, 68% confidence). In the immediately overlying stratum (D), dated between 8250 and 7500 cal BC (Zeder and Hesse 2000; OxCal 2009, 68% confidence), hundreds of pottery fragments from thick, chaff-tempered soft-ware bowls, small pots, and miniature vessels were found (Smith 1978:539). Soft-ware is the term first used by Robert Dyson (1965) to describe the lightly-fired, chaff-tempered, clay vessel fragments that are crumbly in texture, and have been recovered from early pottery horizons throughout northern, western and southwestern Iran.

Lightly fired, chaff-tempered, soft-ware pottery similar to that found at Ganj Dareh has also been recovered from Hotu and Belt caves in northern Iran with the most common form being "a deep bowl resembling a beaker, with slightly concave sides and rounded rim" (Dyson 1991:266). Based on the relative position of the overlying Late Neolithic deposits of painted Djeitun and Cheshmeh Ali wares (Voigt and Dyson 1992), Robert Dyson (1991) has conservatively placed dates of this soft-ware horizon at the two caves between 6200 and 5900 BC. However, my calibration of Willard Libby's conventional radiocarbon dating of charred wood (8,085 BP ± 720) using OxCal 4.0 (2009) places the pottery-bearing level at Belt cave between 7962 and 6238 cal BC (Libby 1952:72; OxCal 2009, 68% confidence). A single soft-ware fragment, suspected by excavator Carlton Coon to have fallen from previously-excavated levels, was also recovered from a late Epipalaeolithic level at Belt Cave dated by Libby (1952:72) to 10,560 BP ± 610, calibrated to 11,116 and 9460 cal BC (OxCal 2009, 68% confidence).

The earliest pottery recovered from immediately above aceramic occupations at Jarmo in northeastern Iraq and at Tepe Guran in western Iran includes lightly-fired, chaff-tempered soft-ware consisting of circular or oval bowls or beakers (Dyson 1965; Mortenson 1992). Bases of larger, chaff-tempered vessels were also found embedded in house floors at Jarmo (Braidwood et al. 1960; Matson 1965). However, the majority of fragments recovered from early ceramic levels at both of these sites are more highly-fired, and have typological and stylistic parallels with decorated and undecorated vessels from a broad geographic area adjacent to the foothills of the Zagros mountains during the Middle to Late Neolithic periods (Braidwood 1962; Dyson 1965; Hole et al. 1965; Levine and McDonald 1977; Dyson 1992; Voigt 1992; Mortensen 1992; Voigt and Dyson 1992; Bernbeck, Abdi, and Gregg 2006). A single radiocarbon date obtained using conventional radiocarbon dating methods places the earliest pottery horizon at Jarmo between 4650 and 3540 cal BC (Libby 1955; OxCal 2009, 68% confidence), but much earlier conventional radiocarbon dates were obtained from early pottery horizons yielding both soft-wares and more highly-fired pottery fragments at Tepe Guran and at the nearby Pottery Neolithic site at Tepe Sarab. Dates for this horizon range between 6811 and 6445 cal BC at Tepe Guran (Tauber 1969; OxCal 2009, 68% confidence) and 7031 to 6392 cal BC at Tepe Sarab (Stuckenrath 1963; OxCal 2009, 68% confidence).

Although soft-ware pottery may be a relatively long-lived and persistent tradition at a number of early settlements adjacent to the Zagros mountains, it is not found at all aceramic to ceramic sites from the Initial Village period in western Iran. Pottery from the earliest ceramic phases of Ali Kosh and Chageh Sefid in Khuzistan greatly resembles the more highly-fired pottery at Jarmo, Tepe Guran and Tepe Sarab (Hole et al. 1965:106). Most pots are small to medium open bowls, both plain and painted with geometric chevron designs, but there are also plain, medium-sized, closed, globular, hole-mouth vessels. Two relatively new AMS radiocarbon dates from the Mohammad Jaffar phase at Ali Kosh place this early pottery horizon between 7313 and 7040 cal BC (Zeder and Hesse 2000; Hole 2000; OxCal 2009, 68% confidence).

The timing of the first appearance of chaff-tempered, undecorated pottery in southeastern Turkey, northern Syria, and central Anatolia broadly corresponds with Aurenche et al.'s (2001) argument regarding the simultaneous adoption of pottery throughout the Middle East circa 7000 cal BC. Pottery fragments from thick, simple bowls or jars with large flat bases had been recovered from an undated ceramic horizon directly overlying the earlier aceramic occupation at Çayönü (Ozdogan and Ozdogan 1993:95). However, only later pottery bearing levels at the site have been dated, with two conventional radiocarbon dates placing the appearance of closed forms with a dark, burnished surface between 5500 and 4650 cal BC (Çambel 1981; Thissen 2002; OxCal 2009, 68% confidence). A limited range of small to medium, chaff-tempered, undecorated bowls from the first pottery-bearing level (XI) at Çatalhöyük dated to approximately 7000 cal BC (Last 2005; Hodder 2006; Hodder et al. 2007). Although conventional radiocarbon dates for the pottery-bearing levels at Abu Hureyra date between 7400 and 6200 cal BC (Moore et al. 2000; OxCal 2009; 68% confidence), pottery does not become traditional at most settlements built alongside the Middle Euphrates and Balikh river valleys until approximately 6800 cal BC (Akkermans and Schwartz 2003). These chaff-tempered vessels include hole-mouth jars, and rounded and straight-walled bowls (Le Miere 1983; Moore 1995). Most pottery fragments from these sites are crumbly in texture, undecorated, and beige in color (Moore 1995), but a small percentage is burnished, or has fugitive red wash or linear geometric patterns, similar to potsherds recovered from the earliest Proto-Hassuna pottery levels at Umm Dabaghiyah and Sabi Abyad in upper Mesopotamia. There are some similarities in decoration to the more highly-fired vessels from the early pottery horizon at Jarmo, but vessels from these horizons are also known to have more forms and greater proportions of decorated vessels (Le Miere 1983; Cauvin 2000; Akkermans and Schwartz 2003). Yoshihiro Nishiaki and Marie Le Miére (2005) have recently identified a distinctive earlier pottery type termed the Pre-Proto-Hassuna at the site of Seker al Aheimar in the Khabur basin. This undecorated ware is characterized by simple closed or vertically-sided forms, and hole-mouth jars with convex bodies and flat bottoms. Unlike the chaff and mineral tempered pottery from the overlying Proto-Hassuna levels at the site, the Pre-Proto-Hassuna ware is exclusively mineral-tempered. Eight radiocarbon dates from the stratigraphic levels containing this pottery type cluster between 7000 and 6500 cal BC while nine dates from the overlying Proto-Hassuna levels cluster between 6500 and 6000 cal BC.

In the northern Levant (lands adjacent to the Mediterranean in present day northern Lebanon, Syria and Turkey), chaff and mineral-tempered pottery appear together above aceramic occupations of PPNB sites in horizons that have been variously dated to 7543 - 7315 and 7062 - 6707 cal BC at Ras Shamra (Stuckenrath 1963; Contenson 1977; OxCal 2000, 68% confidence), and 8232 - 7329 cal BC and 7344 - 6659 cal BC at Tell el-Kherhk 2 (Tsuneki and Miyake 1996; OxCal 2000, 68% confidence). Four sub-groupings of Dark-Faced Burnished Ware (DFBW) were first reported by Robert and Linda Braidwood (1960) from a survey of the Amuq plain in western Syria with test excavation of a number of sites. All DFBW vessels are small-to-medium-

Site, location	Approximate dates	Dominant types of pottery
Tepe Guran, Iran	6800 - 6450 cal BC	Soft ware circular or oval bowls, beakers,open bowls, plain and painted, hole-mouth jars
Tepe Sarab, Iran	7000 - 6300 cal BC	Soft ware circular or oval bowls, beakers,open bowls, plain and painted, hole-mouth jars
Ali Kosh, Iran	7300 - 7040 cal BC	Open bowls, plain and painted, hole-mouth jars
Chageh Sefid, Iran	8170 - 6700 cal BC	Open bowls, plain and painted, hole-mouth jars
Toll-e Bashi, Iran	6000 - 5750 cal BC	Open bowls, plain and painted, hole-mouth jars
Hajji Firuz, Iran	6150 - 5750 cal BC	Open bowls, plain and painted, hole-mouth jars
Dalma Tepe, Iran	5000 - 4800 cal BC	Open bowls, plain and painted, hole-mouth jars
Jarmo, Iraq	4650 - 3550 cal BC	Soft ware circular or oval bowls, beakers,open bowls, plain and painted, hole-mouth jars
Farukhabad, Iraq	4750 - 4400 cal BC	Open bowls, plain and painted, hole-mouth jars
Kashkashok, Syria	6600 - 4400 cal BC	Open bowls, plain and painted, hole-mouth jar, 'husking tray'
Abu Hureyra, Syria	7450 - 6200 cal BC	Hole-mouth jars, and rounded and straight-walled bowls, crumbly in texture, most undecorated
Çayonu, Turkey	5500 - 4650 cal BC	Chalcolithic pottery recovered from above aceramic Neolithic levels with dark burnish
Sha 'ar Haogolan, Israel	6500 - 5800 cal BC	Yarmoukian developed container industry
Newe Yam, Israel	5527-4996 cal BC	Wadi Rabah, cups, bowls and hole mouth jars
Munhata, Israel	6500 - 5800 cal BC	Yarmoukian developed container industry
Nevatim, Israel	4500 - 3700 cal BC	Ghassulian developed container industry, 'butter churns'
Abu Matar, Israel	4500 - 3700 cal BC	Ghassulian developed container industry, 'butter churns'
al-Basatîn, Jordan	5700 - 5200 cal BC	Wadi Rabah, cups, bowls and hole mouth jars
Tubna, Jordan	5000 - 4800 cal BC	Chalcolithic ceramic industry without distinctive Ghassulian coronets or churns
Tabaqat al-Bûma, Jordan	5700 - 5100 cal BC	Wadi Rabah, cups, bowls and hole mouth jars
Abu Thwaab, Jordan	4500 - 4250 cal BC	Wadi Rabah, cups, bowls and hole mouth jars
Dhra, Jordan	6000 - 5700 cal BC	Jericho IX developed container industry

Table 1.2.1
Approximate dates for early pottery horizons of archaeological sites from which organic residues were examined in this study. References for radiocarbon dates from these horizons are provided in Appendices A.1.1 – A.1.4. Brief descriptions of the pottery fragments and relevant assemblages are provided in Appendix A.1.6. Uncalibrated published dates were calibrated using OxCal 4.0 (68% confidence). Much of the variation in dating these early pottery horizons can be attributed to differences in dating methods. For instance, two relatively new AMS radiocarbon dates from the Mohammad Jaffar phase at Ali Kosh place this early pottery horizon between 7313 and 7040 cal BC (Zeder and Hesse 2000; Hole 2000; OxCal 2009, 68% confidence), while the two available conventional radiocarbon dates of the Mohammad Jaffar phase at nearby Chagha Sefid provide a range between 8170 and 6700 cal BC; 68% confidence (Hole 1977; Hole 1987a; OxCal 2009, 68% confidence).

sized shallow and deep bowls, or medium-sized globular, hole-mouth vessels with subsequent divisions of ware groupings based predominantly on differences of mineral and organic temper (Tsuneki and Miyake 1996). This pottery is burnished to a glossy finish, with incised decoration common on many bowls (Akkermans and Schwartz 2003). Fragments of large, chaff-tempered, Simple Coarse Ware vessels have also been recovered from DFBW horizons in the northern Levant, but no vessel profiles have been identified, nor have any vessel shapes been reconstructed (Tsuneki and Miyake 1996). Akira Tsuneki and Yukiko Miyake (1996:122) have argued that small, undecorated, burnished bowls with slightly incurving rims mixed in with Dark Faced Burnished Ware and Simple Coarse Ware from earliest pottery-bearing levels at Tell el-Kherhk 2 are a "direct ancestor" of the DFBW pottery identified by the Braidwoods. However, this chronological relationship is not confirmed by the stratigraphy, and this issue is further clouded by radiocarbon dates obtained using conventional methods that are inverted relative to their stratigraphic position. An older date falling between 8232 - 7329 cal BC was obtained from charcoal in pottery-bearing layer 5, whereas a younger date between 7344 - 6659 cal BC was obtained from an aceramic context in level 10 (Tsuneki and Miyake 1996; OxCal 2000, 68% confidence)

In contrast to many other regions in the Middle East (with assemblages dominated by rounded and straight-walled bowls, beakers, and hole-mouth jars), when pottery emerges in the southern Levant (present day Israel and Jordan), it appears as a more fully developed container technology. Crude pottery fragments, perhaps representing early experimentation with clay (Banning 1998), were recovered from an Middle PPNB aceramic horizon dated to about 7500 cal BC at 'Ain Ghazal (Rollefson and Simmons 1985). A large, fragmented, unfired clay vessel was also recovered along with a small quantity of sherds with blackened exterior surfaces from a Middle to Late PPNB horizon dated between 7550 and 7050 cal BC at Basta (Nissen et al.1987; OxCal 2009, 68% confidence). However, no study has directly linked these fragments to incipient pottery forms at these or any other pre-pottery Neolithic village. Pottery did not become traditional in the southern Levant until nearly a thousand years later in the Yarmoukian period (Rollefson et al. 1992) beginning between 6527 and 6376 cal BC (Banning 2007; 68% confidence). Yarmoukian vessels come in a full range of shapes and sizes, in decorated and undecorated forms: finewares, coarsewares, with and without handles, with mineral and vegetable tempers, both painted and incised (Garfinkel 1999a).

1.2.2 *Early uses of pottery in the Middle East*
Whatever the additional uses to which a pottery vessel is put, almost all pottery vessels are used as containers, with the only exception being their exclusive use as a display item, which is relatively unusual. Prudence Rice (1987: 208) asserts that functions of pottery containers fall into three broad realms, "storage, transformation or processing, and transfer or transport". My review examines the early use of pottery in the Middle East using slightly different categories:
  storage and transport containers;
  utensils for serving and display of food and a medium for ritual practice;
  appliances for the cooking of food by direct and indirect methods;
After discussing these categories, I conclude with a more in-depth discussion of vessel use for the collection of milk and processing of dairy foods for human consumption as a subset of food processing.

1.2.2.1 *Early use of pottery as storage and transport containers*
The use of other types of containers predate the emergence of pottery in many regions of the world, including the Middle East, with the form and decoration of many early pottery vessels mirroring the physical or stylistic aspects of containers made from gourds, stone, wood, reeds, animal skin, or lime plaster (Childe 1936; Garstang and Garstang

1940; Amiran 1965; Matson 1965; Rice 1987; Kingery et al. 1988; Brown 1989; Mortensen 1992). V. Gordon Childe (1936:89) suggested that pottery in the Middle East might have "originated in the accidental burning of a basket plastered with clay to make it water-tight", and the forming of bowls with the aid of basketry is attested by impressions on exterior surfaces of lime plaster fragments recovered from early aceramic villages in southwestern Iran (Hole and Flannery 1962; Hole et al. 1965; Hole 1977). Open linear motifs "reminiscent of basketry" are also painted on software pottery bowls and beakers from the earliest ceramic horizons in this region (Mortensen 1992:177). Basket fragments, many coated with bitumen, have been recovered from a wide range of pre-pottery contexts in the Middle East, including Nahal Hemar, Netiv Hagud and Gilgal in the southern Levant and Ali Kosh and Chageh Sefid in southern Khuzestan (Hole and Flannery1967; Hole et al. 1969; Bar-Yosef 1985; Noy 1989; Shick 1997). However, whether bitumen was used to waterproof basketry or whether baskets were used to collect and transport bitumen for other uses remains unclear. This viscous substance also appears to have been used as a roofing sealant and adhesive for mud bricks at Ali Kosh and Chageh Sefid (Hole and Flannery1967; Hole et al. 1969), and for decorative and symbolic purposes at Nahal Hemar (Bar-Yosef 1985). Pottery fragments recovered from the Mohammad Jaffar levels at Ali Kosh and Chageh Sefid also exhibited evidence of a thin layer of a dark substance assumed by the excavators to be bitumen adhering to their interior surfaces, but no additional evidence was obtained during excavation about the potential use of pottery in the transport of bitumen from the nearest geological seep (Hole and Flannery1967; Hole et al. 1969).

Lime and gypsum plaster vessels have also been reported from pre-pottery villages throughout the Fertile Crescent, including sites at Jericho, Tell Ramad, Abu Hureyra, 'Ain Ghazal, Beidha, Jerf el Ahmar, Çayönü, Tepe Guran, Ali Kosh and Chageh Sefid (Kenyon 1957, 1960; Hole and Flannery1967; Hole et al. 1969; Contenson 1971; Maréchal, 1982; Simmons et al. 1984; Noy et al. 1980; Noy 1989; Kingery et al. 1988; Rollefson et al. 1992; Moore 2000). Many of these plaster vessels appear to be small bowls and pans during the PPNB period (Maréchal, 1982), but larger, unfired clay and plaster bins built into PPNA and PPNB domestic structures have been interpreted as permanent food storage facilities. Included in these is a large unfired clay vessel found partially blocking the doorway of a LPPNB house at 'Ain Ghazal (Rollefson et al. 1992) and "a basin scooped in the earth and lined with a coat of marl or limey earth" (Garstang and Garstang 1940: 54) from the PPNB occupation at Jericho. Botanical or faunal remains have only rarely been recovered in direct association with storage features in houses in pre-pottery villages (Noy et al. 1980; Rollefson 1984; Simmons et al. 1984; Noy 1989; Wright 2000; Atalay and Hastorf 2006), and food storage has been argued to have been managed at the village level rather than that of individual households as early as the PPNA period (Stordeur 2000; Scarre 2005). However, as Andrew Moore (2000) has noted in an extensive report on excavations at Abu Hureyra, in the absence of a more compelling explanation, the function of these large clay and plaster containers was likely for storage of food and protection from rodents.

Moore (1995) has also argued that, following the adoption of pottery in the Levant, plaster storage bins were gradually replaced by coarse, pottery containers that *may* have been used for storage of cereal grains and pulses, but notes that the overall strength and density of fabric of some vessels would also have allowed them to hold water.

Assessments of the physical attributes of vessel form have been frequently used to infer the suitability of uses and predict the function of early pottery containers, as in the example above (Matson 1965; Vitelli 1989; Perles 2001; Tomkins 2007; Mee 2007), but this practice has not been widely accepted because total vessel profiles are only rarely recovered from Neolithic deposits (Morris 2002). Prudence Rice (1990:4-8) also points out that "it is a dubious strategy to predict use from form... The relationships between use and form are better considered as hypotheses to be tested, rather than as empirical givens". Moore's suppositions about the early use of pottery for storage of grains are highly plausible for Yarmoukian assemblages from the southern Levant, where vessels come in a full range of shapes and sizes (Garfinkel 1999a), or at Jarmo where bases of large pottery vessels were found imbedded in the floors of houses (Braidwood et al. 1960; Matson 1965). However, for other regions in the Middle East where the earliest ceramic assemblages are almost exclusively dominated by small and medium-sized bowls or medium-sized globular vessels, only recovery of large quantities of botanical remains from inside a vessel or adjacent to broken pottery fragments is likely to verify the exclusive use of vessels for storage rather than some other purpose.

Similarly, Frederick Matson (1965:204-5) originally stressed the likely importance of early pottery vessels for "procuring, conserving, and storing of water" throughout the Middle East. However, in his assessment of the early ceramic assemblage from Tepe Sarab, Matson (1965:205) concludes that "the absence of large vessels that might have been water jars carried on the heads of women, could suggest that water was transported in other ways", such as the animal skin bags used by herders in Afghanistan and Iran during the early 20th century. Vessels with narrow necks are most ergonomically well-suited to the transportation and serving of liquids (Tomkins 2007), but these types of vessels have not been recovered from the overwhelming majority of the earliest pottery horizons in the Middle East, with tapered vessel openings first appearing in Hassunan assemblages of the Middle Euphrates and Balikh River Valleys (Akkermanns and Schwartz 2003) circa 6500 cal BC, and shortly thereafter in the southern Levant as part of the more fully-developed Yarmoukian ceramic industry (Garfinkel 1999a; Banning 2007).

1.2.2.2 Early use of pottery in serving and display of food, and as a medium for ritual practice

The social and symbolic importance of the early use of pottery in serving and displaying food has been stressed in a theoretical model developed by Brian Hayden (1995). In Hayden's paradigm, great gains in social status are realized by self-aggrandizing 'big men' in complex hunter-gatherer or early agricultural societies through an ongoing cycle of reciprocal feasts. By means of the display and distribution of prestige foods and drink at these celebratory gatherings, *economic capital* is transformed into *symbolic capital* (in the sense of Bourdieu 1977), and this transformation consequently results in increased prestige and social status of the 'big man' hosting the event. Hayden (1995) suggests that serving plates and bowls, and beakers and cups would be among the dominant forms in the earliest pottery assemblages, along with larger vessels used in the boiling of prestige foods or brewing of beverages. Hayden's ideas have subsequently been applied to interpretations of the early use(s) of pottery in the Middle East (Twiss 2008) and the Aegean (Vitelli 1999; Tomkins 2007).

In a brief assessment of uses of early pottery technology in the southern Levant, Cathy Twiss (2008: 430-31) has concluded that the large proportion of cups, bowls, and of decorated vessels in Yarmoukian assemblages indicate their involvement in the "sphere of food distribution, consumption, and enjoyment", and strongly suggest "display in the context of hospitality or feasting". Peter Tomkins (2007) sees even greater symbolic significance than either Hayden or Twiss in the display of food in pottery vessels at reciprocal feasting. In his analysis of breakage patterns from the fragmentary remains of the ceramic assemblage at Early Neolithic Knossos on Crete, Tomkins (2007:190) interprets the recovery of pottery containers consistently missing part or all of their bases as the ritual killing of vessels in a "deliberate act of conspicuous consumption." Tomkins further suggests that rendering the pottery as functionally useless may have acted as "cues for self-aggrandizement narrative, such as illustrious vessel biographies or daring stories of acquisition, that translated symbolic capital into status" (Tomkins 2007:193). Based on the low levels of production at Early Neolithic sites in Greece such as at Franchthi cave and Nikomedia, Karen Vitelli (1999) has also argued for the early use of pottery by ritual specialists competing with one another through reciprocal feasting. The knowledge of certain materials and transformation processes "may have been restricted to certain individuals such as shamans", and "open firing is potentially full of symbolism and possibilities for divining" (191). A number of researchers (Schmandt-Besserat 1974; Cauvin 2000; Meskell 2008) have examined the ritual use of clay in the manufacture of figurative representations in early villages the Middle East, but none have addressed the issue of whether the earliest pottery vessels were used as a medium of ritual practice. Peder Mortensen (1992) has speculated that miniature vessels from the early levels at Ganj Dareh (Smith 1978) may have had some ritual function, but has also suggested that these small vessels were as likely to have been used as children's toys.

Tomkins (2007:175) suggests that there is "common agreement that early ceramic vessels functioned to serve, display, but not cook food". Tomkins cites researchers working on the analysis of pottery primarily from Early to Middle Neolithic sites in southeastern Europe (Gardner 1978, Kotsakis 1983; Vitelli 1993; Bjork 1995; Youni 1995, 1996) as those who have reached consensus on the subject, but also names Andrew Moore (1995:47) as concurring with this commonly-held view. However, as I note below, traces of soot on many hole-mouth jars recovered from some of the earliest pottery horizons in the Middle East did, in fact, lead Moore (1995:47) to conclude that these vessels were "apparently used in cooking". Undoubtedly, the early uses of pottery in the Middle East include the serving and presentation of food, but no single use can currently be ascribed to the first appearance of pottery throughout the region. Large numbers of undecorated hole-mouth vessels that were likely used in cooking, as discussed in the next section, were recovered from the earliest pottery horizons in southwestern Khuzestan along with significant quantities of small-to-medium-sized decorated bowls (Hole and Flannery 1962; Hole et al. 1965; Hole 1977) likely used in the serving and display of food.

1.2.2.3 *Early use of pottery in food preparation*

In a journal entry for August 15, 1773, Scottish lawyer and diarist James Boswell noted that "other species had toolmaking and rationality, but only humans were cooking animals" (as cited by Solomon Katz, 2003: 458). This view was echoed 200 years later by Claude Lévi-Strauss in the first volume of his *Science of Mythology: The Raw and the Cooked* (1970:164): "Not only does cooking mark the transition from nature to culture, but through it and by means of it, the human state can be defined with all its attributes". Numerous studies have sought to explain the first appearance of pottery as a result of changes in food preparation and cooking practices (Childe 1936; Linton 1944; Amiran 1965; Matson 1965; Caneva 1983; Brown 1989; Goodyear 1991; Pearson 1991; Roosevelt 1991; Haaland 1992; Sassaman 1993; Payne 1994; Aikens 1995; Moore 1995; Roosevelt 1995; Kenrick 1995; Harris 1997; Zhang 2002a, 2002b; Kobayashi 2004; Last 2005; Atalay 2005; Kuzmin 2006; Haaland 2007). There is growing consensus that different methods may have been used in cooking different types of foods in early pottery vessels in many regions of the world. However, these issues have not received sufficient consideration in explanations about the first uses of pottery in the Middle East. Nor have they been examined in anywhere near the same detail as have other prehistoric food-processing technologies that emerged in southwest Asia during the early Holocene, such as sickle elements and ground-stone tools used in the harvesting and grinding of cereal grains.

For hundreds of thousands of years, humans have used tools to make foods more edible, with the digestive process, more often than not, beginning outside the human body through the cutting and tenderizing of meats, or the removal of shells, seed casings, or pelts from plant and animal foods (Katz 2003). Developments in food-processing technologies can be linked to changes in human population dynamics and the evolution of culture (Wrangham 1999; Bar-Yosef 2002; Katz 2003), with the benefits realized through the cooking of food providing human groups in many different regions of the world with adaptive advantages during the late Pleistocene and early Holocene, and facilitating intensified use of both plant and animal resources. By releasing nutritive elements in some foods, or detoxifying others and making them safe to eat (Stahl 1986, Wright 1994. 2000, Katz 2003, Wollstonecroft et al. 2008), new cooking technologies greatly increased the effective carrying capacity of different ecological niches (Ikawa-Smith 1976). Although cooking makes meat easier to digest, much of its nutritive value is lost by roasting cuts over an open fire (Reid 1989). Boiling or simmering meats in a stew in a watertight container, on the other hand, prevents the loss of nutrients, by conserving high-caloric dietary fat in the broth (Myers 1989). Prolonged simmering of animal bone is the most effective means of extracting marrow by turning it into grease (Sassaman 1993), while sustained boiling breaks down difficult-to-digest seeds into a gelatin, and ultimately into a palatable starch (Braun 1983; Brown 1989). The boiling of shellfish, such as clams or oysters, causes them to open quickly, greatly reducing the labor investment in extracting the meat from the shell, and making short work of preparing for dinner.

The first appearance of pottery in many regions of the world has been linked to the cooking of shellfish (Caneva 1988; Clark 1989; Pearson, 1991; Roosevelt et al. 1991; Haaland 1992; Roosevelt 1995; Kenrick 1995; Zhang 2002b; Kobayashi 2004). In East Asia, where pottery emerges separately in southern China, Japan, and the Russian Far East between 14,500 and 13,700 cal BC (Kuzmin 2006; OxCal 2009, 68% confidence), large quantities of clam and oyster shells have been recovered from middens and stratigraphic sequences yielding small, fired clay containers with rounded or conical bottoms. At Dayan cave in China's Guangxi province, clamshells appear to have no longer been cracked or pried open following appearance of pottery around 14,000 cal BC. Shells were found to be consistently more fragmentary and heavily damaged in earlier levels of the cave (Zhang 2002b). The presence of rice phytolith remains in later pottery-bearing levels from two nearby cave sites at Xianrendong and Diaotonghuan dating between 8000 and 6000 cal BC has also led to suggestions of the use of pottery in cooking rice prior to its appearance in domesticated form (Zhang 2002a). However, whether these early pottery vessels from southern China could have sustained the high temperatures required in the preparation of starchy grains (Braun 1983; Brown 1989) has not been confirmed. This issue is discussed further in the context of the preparation of cereal-based porridges in the Middle East. Similarly, shellfish only began to be consumed in large quantities by prehistoric peoples in Japan after the advent of small, thin-walled vessels with rounded or conical bottoms (Kobayashi 2004). Shellfish also appear to have been processed in medium-sized, globular, pottery vessels at three Mesolithic sites in the Upper and Middle Nile Valley as part of the intensive exploitation of aquatic resources that included 22 fish species and large quantities of mollusks (Caneva 1988; Clark 1989; Haaland 1992). Isabel Caneva (1983) has suggested that the globular jars, wide-mouth bowls, and beakers (all with rounded bases) recovered at these sites were *probably* used for the storage of fats or oils. However, like many authors who have speculated about the early uses of pottery, Caneva does not provide direct evidence for vessel use, nor does she acknowledge the different methods that could have been used in the recovery of fats and oils through heating in pottery or other types of containers.

There are both direct (over fire) and indirect (stone boiling, steam oven) methods of cooking in pottery containers. The methods used in heating liquids and cooking foods in various types of containers (including pottery, animals skins, baskets and boats) have been extensively discussed in North America by both archaeologists and ethnographers. The use of heated rocks to boil liquids and cook foods in water-tight baskets, wooden or bark containers, skin-lined pits or buried boats is well attested in the journals of Western explorers in North America (Thoms 2008), and late 19th - and early 20th - century ethnographic accounts of First Nations cooking practices (Jones 1873; Harrington 1942; Gayton 1948; Driver and Massey 1957; Krause 1956; Johnson 1969), with stone boiling persisting in some regions even long after pottery cooking vessels had been adopted throughout much of the New World (Ebeling 1983).

However, up until quite recently (Last 2005; Atalay 2005; Atalay and Hastorf 2006; Hodder 2006; Haaland 2007), the subject has received scant attention in the study of late Pleistocene and early Holocene communities in the Middle East. In 1965, Ruth Amiran (1965: 242) suggested that large, clay basins sunken into floors of PPNB houses at Jericho (Kenyon 1957, 1960), may have been transformed from clay mud to pottery following "some accidental firing", and were possibly used in "stone boiling". The use of heated rocks in cooking during the Pre-Pottery Neolithic A period in the Levant has subsequently been inferred from the recovery of fire-cracked rocks from PPNA sites (Bar-Yosef 1998), but no study has associated their possible use with any of the container technologies that are known from the pre-pottery Neolithic or earlier Epipalaeolithic periods in the Middle East. There has been a little more discussion in the Middle Eastern literature on the use of pottery vessels in direct cooking over a fire. In 1965, Matson speculated that the "probable" first uses of pottery in the Middle East included the cooking of "gruels or mush" (205), but that "stewing meats and other items have not been clearly identified so far in terms of fire stains on exterior surfaces or animal bones in the vessels" (209). Ofer Bar-Yosef has stated that there is no proof that early pottery was used for cooking (as cited in Bellwood 2005: 283), a view echoed by Randi Haaland (2007: 176) who claims there is "no evidence in the published material of traces of fire". However, as Moore (1995: 47) notes in a paper on the inception of pottery in the Middle East (cited by Haaland 2007), hole-mouth jars from early pottery horizons in the Middle East have "traces of soot on their sides". The absence of sooting has often been taken as evidence that a pot has not been placed directly on or over an open fire, but experimental studies have shown that there is little or no sooting produced on the sides of pottery vessels when placed in large, very hot fires, or on a bed of hot embers (Hally 1983; Sassaman 1993).

Moreover, microwear studies of teeth from human skeletal remains recovered from aceramic and pottery-bearing occupations at Abu Hureyra also support the idea that at least some early pottery vessels were used for cooking of cereal-based porridges. Studies by Molleson and Jones (1991) and Molleson et al. (1993) have shown that there is a marked reduction in tooth wear during the periods coinciding with and following the first appearance of pottery. This reduction in tooth wear is hypothesized to have resulted from a shift from a reliance on gritty, uncooked cereal grains to softer, cereal-based porridges cooked in pottery that had recently been adopted at sites along the Middle Euphrates. Although

Abu Hureyra's excavator Moore does not suggest the cooking method used in preparation, the sustained high temperatures required to transform cereal grains into edible starches are unlikely to have been consistently achieved through stone boiling in a pottery vessel or a non-ceramic alternative (Braun 1983; Cordell 1984; Myers 1989). In addition to having a relatively high degree of stability when placed in the coals of a fire, pottery containers with rounded bases, such as hole-mouth jars, distribute heat uniformly and are more resistant to thermal stress than flat-bottomed vessels made of a similar clay fabric (Linton 1944; Sinopoli 1991; Sassaman 1993), and are better able to withstand the high temperatures necessary for cooking cereal grains (Brown 1989: 220).

Lower temperatures are required for preparing stews and soups or rending fats or oils from animal bones or oily seeds, and can be achieved either through the immersion of heated rocks in a water-tight container, placement of the container in a pit containing heated rocks, or by simmering in a fireproof vessel placed directly on the coals of fire (Goodyear 1988; Sassaman 1993). Temperatures of 85°-88°C are ideal for the extraction of marrow from bone, with collagen being released into the simmering liquid in a gelatinous form (Sassaman 1993). The efficiency of turning marrow into grease decreases as temperatures approach the boiling point. Marrow proteins coagulate, toughen and shrink at 100°C, with yields greater from a simmering rather than a boiling liquid because the grease is easier to skim off (Sassaman 1993). Firecracked rock has been recovered from numerous sites in North America, including many from as early as the Late Archaic period (Goodyear 1988), but ethnographic accounts attest to the failure of baskets in stone boiling, and the difficulty in sustaining high temperatures in large volume of liquid in wooden or skin containers for prolonged periods of time (Gayton 1948; Myers 1989). Pottery vessels, on the other hand, can be placed directly in the coals of a fire, and cooking or rending of grease undertaken in conjunction with other tasks or social activities (Schiffer and Skibo 1987; Brown 1989; Haaland 1992). Albert Goodyear (1988) has called attention to the importance of pottery containers in the extraction of grease from bone during the Early Woodland period in the Midwestern United States, and has hypothesized that the shift from indirect to direct cooking methods may have occurred during the Late Archaic, circa 600 cal BC. However, pottery vessels from these periods did not exhibit the thermal shock resistance necessary to withstand high temperatures of an open fire until shell became the dominant tempering agent in the Mississippi basin during the Late Woodland period, circa 900 - 950 cal AD (Braun 1983).

In the Middle East, a shift from cooking with heated clay balls in watertight baskets to cooking by direct placement of pottery vessels on an open fire is hypothesized to have occurred circa 6500 - 6400 cal BC at Çatalhöyük (Atalay 2005; Last 2005: Hodder 2006; Atalay and Hastorf 2006). A team led by Ian Hodder has found no evidence that the chaff-tempered, undecorated bowls from the earliest pottery-bearing levels from the east mound of the site dating to approximately 7000 cal BC were used in cooking (Last 2005; Hodder 2006). But drawing on a number of the ethnographic studies mentioned above, Çatalhöyük team member Sonya Atalay (2005) has concluded that the most tenable hypothesis for the use of the great numbers of fired-clay balls found in close association with hearths was for heating of liquids and cooking of food. Many baskets and wooden vessels were recovered from early pottery levels XI -VII, but their number and that of clays balls diminishes with the appearance of mineral-tempered, fire-sooted, hole-mouth vessels that dominate the subsequent Neolithic ceramic assemblage beginning in level VI (Last 2005). In a subsequent paper on food preparation practices at Çatalhöyük, written in collaboration with Christine Hastorf, and citing evidence obtained through analysis of organic residues (Copley et al. 2005e), Atalay subsequently contends that grease and oils were extracted from animal bones and oil-rich seeds through the use of clay balls and basketry, and vessels from the earliest pottery bearing levels were used in the storage of animals fats (Atalay and Hastorf 2006). Although the evidence marshaled by Last (2005), Atalay (2005) and Hodder (2006) for change in cooking practices associated with the appearance of hole-mouth vessels at Çatalhöyük is quite compelling, the results of Copley et al.'s (2005e) study (examined in detail in section 2.6.) do not, in fact, substantiate Atalay's and Hastorf's claim of use in the extraction of grease or oils. Molecular or isotopic evidence of a substance in a pottery container or fragment is confirmation of its existence, not necessarily of exclusive vessel use. The absorption of animal fats in archaeological pottery (as has been reported in Copley et al. 2005e study) can result from use in cooking, serving, transportation, as well as storage (Evershed 1993; Heron and Evershed 1995). Atalay's and Hastorf's (2006:310) contention that the chaff-tempered, undecorated bowls from the early pottery-bearing levels at Çhatalhöyük were used exclusively for food storage is not supported by empirical evidence, but only by the assumption that because no pottery was recovered from contexts associated with human burials in early levels of the east mound of the site that "pottery initially was not for presentation or for cooking, but for food storage".

The prehistoric technologies associated with the fermentation and brewing of wine and beer have been of great academic and popular interest for many years (Lutz 1922; Huber 1926; Oppenheim and Hartman 1950; Lucas 1948; Braidwood et al. 1953; Katz and Voigt 1986). In light of the preliminary results from his excavations at Jarmo (Braidwood 1952), and questions raised by botanist Jonathan Sauer about the relationship between bread making and the domestication of cereal grains, Robert Braidwood convened a symposium examining the issue "Did Man Once Live by Beer Alone?" (Braidwood et al. 1953). Many eminent anthropologists, Assyriologists and botanists of the day participated in these discussions, including Braidwood, Sauer, Hans Helbaek, Paul Mangelsdorf, Hugh Cutler, Carleton Coon, Ralph Linton, Julian Steward and Leo Oppenheim. Braidwood acknowledged that none of the container technologies made by early agriculturalists were likely to have been used exclusively in the sprouting of barley and brewing of beer but, among the containers mentioned by symposium participants as possible contenders for the earliest vessels were clay and plaster basins, stone vessels, and bitumen-coated basketry from PPNA and PPNB villages in the Levant, and pottery from the earliest pottery horizons at

Jarmo and Jericho. Solomon Katz and Mary Voigt (1986:33) subsequently proposed that "the technology of brewing" developed accidentally from sprouting cereal grains fermenting in a cooked porridge or gruel after coming into contact with wild yeasts, perhaps as early as 9000 BC in Natufian villages in the Levant. More recent studies using wet chemical spot test and a number of different instrumental analytical techniques in attempts to identify evidence of winemaking and brewing in pottery are evaluated in section 2.9.

Besides beer and wine, there are many other ways that early pottery could have been used in food processing. The possible collection of milk and processing of dairy foods for human consumption in early pottery vessels from the Middle East is discussed in the next section, in light of the timing and location of the earliest exploitation of milk-producing species, and recent advances that have been made in characterizing and categorizing organic residues in archaeological pottery as part of my doctoral research project.

1.2.2.4 Early pottery use in milk collection and processing of dairy foods

The use of prehistoric pottery vessels for the collection of milk and the manufacturing of dairy products has long been inferred from 'functional' descriptions of ceramic artifacts, such as Chalcolithic 'butter churns' in the Levant (Mallon et al. 1934; Dalman 1938; Kaplan 1954, 1965) and Linearbandkeramik (LBK) 'cheese strainers' in Europe (Curwen 1938; Boguki 1984). However, direct evidence has yet to be recovered in Europe or the Middle East linking the functional attributes of these 'butter churns' and 'cheese strainers' to the processing of milk or milk byproducts. As I have previously noted, the basal level from Ganj Dareh in western Iran provides us with some of the earliest evidence of pottery vessels in the Middle East (Smith 1974, 1978; Le Mière and Picon 1987, 1999) and faunal evidence suggesting the preferential culling of young male goats (Zeder 1999; Zeder and Hesse 2000). Elizabeth Henrickson and Mary McDonald (1980) speculated that the shape and size of large carinated vessels from the nearby Initial Village period site at Tepe Sarab would have been well suited to the fermenting and manufacture of yogurt, as Mary Voigt (1983) has also suggested for medium and large closed bowls from the Late Neolithic site of Hajji Firuz in northwestern Iran. Frank Hole and his colleagues Kent Flannery and James Neeley (1965) have interpreted the increase in faunal remains of sheep and goat and the apparent decline in the cultivation and processing of cereal grains accompanying the emergence of pottery at the sites of Ali Kosh and Chageh Sefid in Khuzestan as a preference for pastoralism over agriculture by the inhabitants of the Deh Luran plain. An increasing emphasis on the herding of sheep and goats accompanies the advent of the earliest pottery production at settlements of the Middle Euphrates and Balikh river valleys approximately 6800 cal BC (Moore 2000; Akkermans and Schwartz 2003), and the appearance of many different types of pottery containers also coincides with the introduction of sheep in the southern Levant circa 6400 cal BC (Nissen 1993; Horwitz et al. 1999).

1.3 Research approaches

In light of the advances that had been made in the categorization of animal fats in archaeological pottery discussed in the following chapter, I set out to obtain direct evidence of the uses of pottery recovered from some of the earliest ceramic horizons throughout the Middle East. In order to address my initial research questions, I decided that it would be necessary to improve my understanding of the processes affecting the preservation and identification of different substances that pottery vessels may have once contained, and undertook courses in biomolecular archaeology and soil chemistry at the Department of Archaeological Sciences at the University of Bradford in the United Kingdom. Working under the guidance of Dr. Carl Heron and Dr. Benjamin Stern at Bradford, I received training in gas chromatography and mass spectrometry and began my examination of organic residues imbedded in pottery fragments from Neolithic and Chalcolithic settlements in the Middle East.

During the course of my doctoral research, I have attempted to extract (or have been successful in extracting) organic residues from nearly 300 pottery fragments recovered from 22 early agricultural villages or pastoral encampments in the Fertile Crescent. The majority of fragments were obtained from the collections of excavators, but I have also excavated 30 potsherds specifically for organic residue analysis at the late Neolithic site at al-Basatîn in northern Jordan and the Initial Village period site at Toll-e Bashi in southwestern Iran. Twenty-two (22) pottery fragments from Dr. Edward Banning's excavation the late Neolithic site at Tubna were also recovered specifically for organic residue analysis by one of his former graduate students, Ms Alicia Beck. Tables with sample numbers, site locations, site references, and approximate dates of the pottery horizons from which these fragments were recovered can be found in Appendices A.1.1 to A.1.4. Because the majority (77%) of pottery fragments examined in this study are body sherds, I did not consider any possible correlation between pottery use and vessel size and form. I have included 65 vessel profiles I was able to identify along with brief descriptions of the pottery fragments and characteristic pottery assemblages recovered from the corresponding ceramic horizons of the archaeological sites in Appendix A.1.6. Summaries of the extraction protocols and instrumental analytical techniques used in the recovery and categorization of organic residues in these pottery fragments are presented in chapters 3 and 4.

My primary research objective has not been to develop a generalizing law of human behavior concerning the emergence of social, technological and economic complexity in the Binfordian sense (1962). Rather, I have looked for regularities in subsistence practices and pottery use at early agricultural villages and pastoral encampments throughout the Middle East using organic residue analysis to place these patterns in the context of our current understanding of the diversity of human responses to the oscillating environmental conditions that occurred during the late Pleistocene and early Holocene (Hole 1984,1989; Bottema 1986; Zeist and Bottema 1991; Bar-Matthews et al. 1999; Wick et al. 2003). My secondary goal has been (and remains) somewhat more teleological, in that I hoped to obtain new evidence from Initial Village period sites in western Iran that would better inform our understanding of the interaction between hunting and gathering and herding and farming populations in the Middle East during the early Holocene.

Before undertaking this research, I familiarized myself with the broad outlines of human prehistory, and the worldwide shift in human subsistence practices and settlement patterns that occurred following the last Ice Age. The great variations in technological innovations that have been observed in many regions during the late Pleistocene and early Holocene led me to conclude that human behavioral responses are constrained by, rather than determined by, environmental pressures. Drawing upon a group of interrelated ideas from high-level theories explaining the shift from hunting and gathering to the emergence of village life in the Middle East at the end of the Pleistocene (Childe 1928, 1936; Braidwood 1952; Sherratt 1981,1983; Hole 1984), I developed a working hypothesis contending that the invention or early adoption of pottery by mobile pastoralists facilitated the widespread acceptance throughout the Middle East of a new means of subsistence based on the herding of sheep and goats and the manufacture of dairy foods during the early Holocene. I then began to collect data through analysis of organic residues embedded in pottery fragments to determine whether, in fact, my tentative explanation corresponded to the molecular and isotopic evidence and my low-level observations about early pottery use. My theoretical framework has neither a particularizing nor a generalizing view of prehistoric human behavior, but makes the assumption that the past is knowable and that there is an objective reality separate from any philosophical perspective, or means of observing and interpreting the world. The 'biomarker' methodological approach that I use in this study builds on the *methodological uniformitarianism* that is integral to a rationalist scientific approach. Conceived of by geologist James Hutton (1794), refined by John Playfair (1802), and elaborated on by Charles Lyell (1830), this paradigm contends that processes observed in the modern world can be used to explain and account for unobserved causes in the past. Archaeological 'biomarkers' are specific unique compounds or a known distribution of compounds that have been observed and identified in modern substances or physiological processes that can be used as evidence of past human activity (Pollard et al 2007; Evershed 2008). Archaeologists of many different theoretical stripes have long drawn on the rationalist scientific approach and its *methodological uniformitarianism* to confirm or disprove existing theories (Childe 1928; 1936; Sahlins 1972; Hodder 1978; Rindos 1987; Robb 1998; McGhee 2008), and continue to use inductive reasoning to make "genuinely new discoveries about aspects of human behavior" (Trigger 2006:36).

1.4 *Summary of research findings and rationale for the broadening of my research focus*

I have been successful in recovering organic residues from 38 of 280 pottery fragments I have examined (Appendices A.1.1 – A.1.4; Gregg et al. 2007; Gregg in press; Gregg et al. 2009; Gregg and Slater in press). My preliminary examination of 244 of these pottery fragments from 20 Neolithic and Chalcolithic sites used 'conventional' solvent extraction techniques that yielded evidence for the survival of diagnostic organic compounds in only five (2%) potsherds. I was able to identify molecular compounds characteristic of bitumen in four of these fragments from the sites of Ali Kosh and Chageh Sefid in southwestern Iran. Subsequent analyses of the stable carbon and hydrogen isotopic composition ($\partial^{13}C$ and ∂D) of these residues revealed the geological source lies within the Deh Luran region of Khuzestan, and confirmed the earliest recorded presence of bitumen in pottery vessels in the Middle East (Chapter 3; Gregg et al. 2007). A single potsherd from Çayönü in central Anatolia yielded saturated fatty acids with relative abundances consistent with degraded animal fats through use of this 'conventional' solvent extraction method.

The poor recovery of organic compounds in the preliminary stages of my doctoral research led me to seek the advice of geochemist Dr. Greg Slater of the School of Geography and Earth Sciences at McMaster University. Dr. Slater suggested that increased lipid yields might be realized through use of a microwave-assisted liquid chromatography protocol initially developed for the isolation and concentration of free fatty acids in marine sediments. Together we undertook a pilot study examining residues in 10 pottery fragments from the late Neolithic site at al-Basatîn in northern Jordan. My extraction of residues from a total of 65 pottery fragments from 9 Neolithic sites using this protocol yielded measurable concentrations of free fatty acids from 34 potsherds (52%). 27 of the 65 potsherds from which residues were extracted using the microwave-assisted recovery protocol had previously produced no measurable results through 'conventional' solvent extraction. 16 of these 27 potsherds (59%) yielded measurable concentrations of free fatty acids through the use of the microwave-assisted extraction technique.

Our subsequent isotopic analyses of residues from 25 potsherds yielding fatty acids consistent with degraded animal fats revealed $\partial^{13}C$ ratios consistent with those of adipose fats of ruminant and non-ruminant animals pastured on lands adjacent to the Jordan Valley (Chapter 5; Gregg et al. 2009; Gregg and Slater in press). However, our comparison of isotopic values of modern adipose and dairy fats obtained in Israel, Palestine, Jordan, and Turkey with those previously used to categorize potsherd extracts (Evershed et al. 2002; Copley et al. 2003, 2005a,b; Mukherjee et al. 2007) also established that the ranges of isotopic values from the Middle East differ substantially from those in northern Europe, and demonstrated that the previously reported ranges from northern Europe must be applied with caution in the categorization of organic residues from archaeological sites in the Middle East (Chapter 5; Gregg et al. 2009; ; Gregg and Slater in press).

I have found no conclusive proof to substantiate my working hypothesis that the invention or early adoption of pottery by mobile pastoralists facilitated the widespread acceptance throughout the Middle East of a new means of subsistence based on the herding of sheep and goats and the manufacture of dairy foods during the early Holocene. The archaeological, molecular and isotopic evidence recovered from the charred remains adhering to the interior surfaces of eight pottery fragments from the site at al-Basatîn suggests that ceramic vessels were used for cooking of meats or extraction of marrow from both ruminant and non-ruminant animals during the Late Neolithic period in the southern Levant. However, because the isotopic values of these residues also plot between or near observed values for modern dairy foods in central Europe (Spangenberg et al. 2006) and Middle East (Gregg et al. 2009), the use of this pottery in the processing of dairy foods for human consumption cannot be ruled out.

In light of these findings and the findings of other researchers that are discussed in the next chapter, I shifted the focus of my research study to include an evaluation of the diagnostic potential and limitations of the major instrumental analytical techniques used in identifying the different substances that the earliest pottery vessels from the Middle East may have contained. In addition to detailing my findings and outlining the problems and opportunities associated with the extraction and identification of organic compounds in pottery from the earliest ceramic horizons in the Fertile Crescent in subsequent chapters, I put forward a number of suggestions for archaeologists considering the use of organic residue analysis. These include some practical ideas on how to develop the degree of confidence that is necessary to assess the methods used in acquisition of molecular and isotopic data and, ultimately, the adequacy of the analytical criteria used to address specific archaeological research questions. I also discuss future directions for the study of the uses of early pottery vessels from the Middle East and propose a series of measures for more confident characterization of organic residues they may contain.

Chapter 2
The task of extracting and identifying organic residues from archaeological pottery

2.1 Introduction

Over the past thirty years, many different extraction methods and analytical techniques have been used in attempts to identify the diverse range of proteins, fats, oils, starches, alcohols, resins, and pigments that may survive in archaeological pottery — many with ambiguous or misleading results (Jones 2001; Pollard et al. 2007). This chapter outlines the wet chemistry extraction protocols and instrumental analytical methods employed in key studies isolating the molecular 'biomarkers' of organic compounds adhering to the surfaces or embedded in the fabric of archaeological pottery. I begin by providing a brief history of early studies examining the chemical composition of pottery fabrics and extant residues in vessels from museum collections, and then outline the methods and results of more recent analyses of archaeological pottery fragments recovered from sites of the Mesolithic to Medieval periods in the Middle East and Europe. This chapter will also examine the differential recovery and diagnostic potential of different organic compounds but, due to the preferential survival of lipids in archaeological pottery, it will focus primarily on the analytical instrumentation techniques most often used to analyze lipids and employed in the current study: gas chromatography (GC); gas chromatography-mass spectrometry (GC-MS); and gas chromatography-combustion-isotope ratio mass spectrometry (GC-C-IRMS).

2.2 Early wet chemistry studies

Researchers have been investigating the chemical properties of ancient ceramic vessels for more than 150 years, with most early studies attempting to identify the chemical elements of pottery fabrics and clay sources, rather than isolating the organic compounds vessels may have once contained. In 1844, French geologist and chemist Alexandre Brongniart (1844) included lists of the chemical components of pottery vessels from many different periods in his historical survey of pottery production techniques around the world. Nobel laureate Theodore William Richards (1895:153) later used a series of wet chemistry spot tests to quantify the chemical elements in the "finely powdered" clay fabric of four Athenian ceramic vessels, in an attempt to establish their origin for Boston Museum of Fine Art curator Edward Robinson. Richards provides detailed percentages of different chemical components, such as silica, iron oxides, and aluminum oxides, but does not outline the procedures used in his spot tests or describe his analytical methods. He also does not compare the chemical composition of the Athenian vessels to that of other Greek city states within the region, but concludes the vessels were probably of local origin due to the "singularly small range" of chemical elements when compared to vessels from Europe, Asia, Africa, and North and South America recorded by Brongniart fifty years earlier (Richards 1895:153). Analyses of the chemical composition of pottery fabrics proliferated, and are a major subject of archaeological study. Summaries of the major early-to-mid-20th century studies examining the chemical composition of pottery fabrics and related provenance of component elements can be found in Caley (1951, 1967), Rice (1987), Pollard and Heron (1996), and Pollard et al. (2007).

In contrast to many studies comparing the elemental composition of pottery fabrics and original sources, organic residues associated with pottery vessels were rarely analyzed until the last quarter of the 20th century. French chemist Marcellin Berthelot (1906) realized limited success in his characterization of dregs in two Gallo-Roman vessels from the Musée de Reims through separation of the solid and liquid portions by blotting paper filtration and application of alkali and alcohol solvent protocol. Berthelot (1906:128-129) claimed to have quantified the stéarique ($C_{16:0}$), palmitique ($C_{18:0}$) and oléique ($C_{18:1}$) free fatty acids surviving in the solid and liquid fractions of the residue, but, unfortunately, the specific methods used in his recovery and quantification of these compounds remain unclear. As we now know, fatty acid concentrations can serve as evidence of both degraded animal fats and degraded plant oils in archaeological ceramics, and his identification of these fatty acids as matching those of a vegetable oil is ambiguous. An unauthored research item in a 1930 issue of Nature noted that "charred grease" had been used as a glaze in shell-tempered earthenware burial urns ascribed to peoples of the Choctaw cultural tradition, from sites adjacent to the Talapoosa and Alabama Rivers excavated by Mr. P.A. Brennan in central Alabama (Nature 1930:147). The chemical composition of this glaze was not confirmed by chemical analysis. In notable works by Hackford et al. (1931) and Forbes (1936), petroleum chemists assisted Sir Leonard Wooley in identifying bitumen residues at the ancient city of Ur in southern Mesopotamia. Through application of different organic solvents to solid bitumen, Hackford et al. (1931) and Forbes (1936) separated organic petroleum carbon compounds from the asphaltene mineral fraction and imbedded plant remains such as reed and rushes, and measured these different components by both weight and volume.

No further progress was made in the characterization of residues in archaeological pottery until advances in computer technology and analytical instrumentation in the late 1970s brought a more systematic approach to the classification of ancient organic compounds. An overview of the major instrumental analytical techniques currently in use and their application to archaeology can be found in Pollard et al. (2007), but a brief summary of the principal techniques used in gas chromatography and mass spectrometry will inform the following discussion of early developments in the extraction and instrumental analysis of organic residues in archaeological pottery.

2.3 Principles of gas chromatography and mass spectrometry

Gas chromatography (GC) separates and measures the molecules in a compound on the basis of their physical behavior. Gasses, liquids, and solids can all be separated on a GC column but, before solid residues from potsherds can be analyzed, preserved compounds must be released from the fabric of the pottery fragment to which they are bound. This is accomplished through a variety of recovery protocols that will be discussed in subsequent chapters. All compounds are introduced into the GC column dissolved in an organic solvent solution (such as hexane or dichloromethane) that is vaporized as it is injected into a carrier gas (such as hydrogen or helium) known as the mobile phase (Figure 2.3.1). The carrier gas then passes the components of the vaporized solution into a long, coiled, silica-lined, narrow-diameter, metal column inside a temperature-controlled oven where organic compounds 'stick' in what is known as the stationary phase. Temperatures are programmed to rise in the oven at very controlled rates, and compounds are released, or eluted, into the carrier gas again as temperatures rise and their volatility increases. The retention times, elution orders, and relative abundances of the different molecules in the compound are then measured and recorded as they are released and combusted in a device known as a flame ionization detector. Components with lower molecular weights and polarities elute before those with higher weights and polarities, and are thus are retained in the column for longer periods (Pollard et al. 2007). Comparisons of the retention times, elution orders, and relative abundances of molecules in the unknown samples are then made to those of known compounds, generally through the use of a chromatogram, a graphic representation of the measured values of molecular components in the separated organic compound (Figure 2.3.1).

Figure 2.3.1

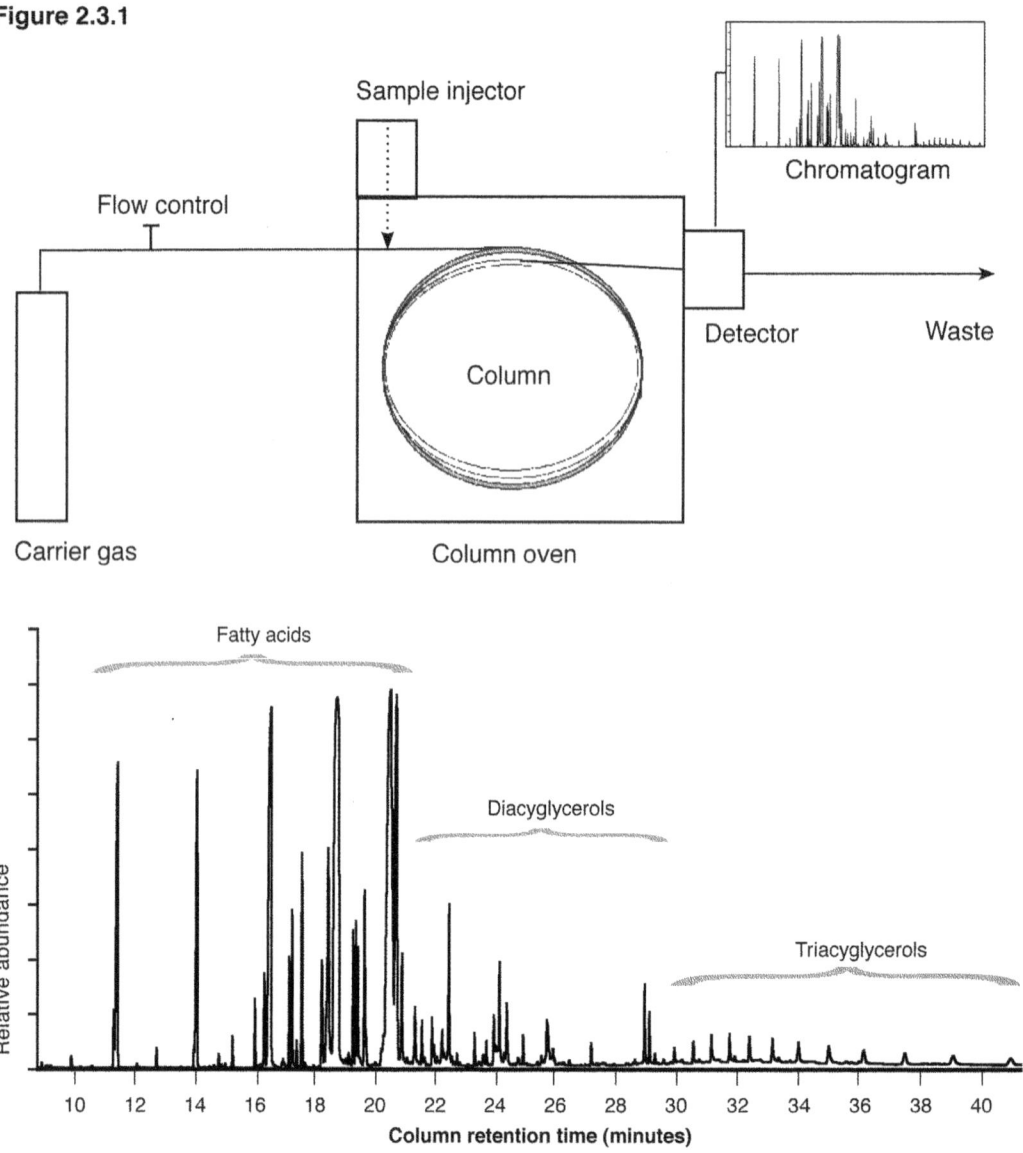

Figure 2.3.1
Schematic diagram of a gas chromatography column and a chromatogram of the molecular compounds recovered from a modern butter fat sample. The retention times, elution orders, and relative abundances of different molecular components in unknown samples can be matched to the observed values of known organic compounds. Retention times of shorter carbon chain fatty acids are less than those of longer carbon chain molecules, such as covalently-bonded diacyglycerols, and triacyglycerols bonded to three or more fatty acids (Mirabaud et al. 2007; Daintith 2008).

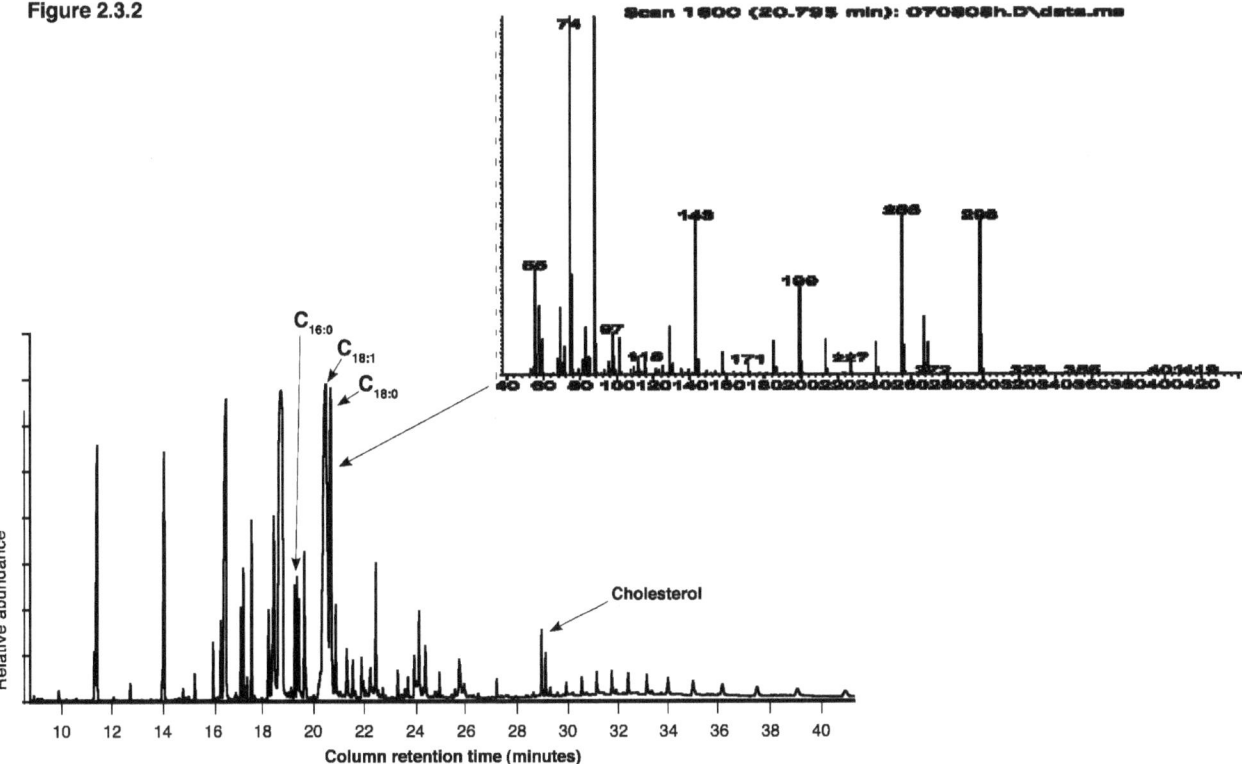

Figure 2.3.2
The molecular weights and ion fragments of individual molecular components in a compound can be statistically matched to those of known compounds through a computer database attached to the mass spectrometer. The mass spectra of compounds can be measured separately including closely eluting fatty acids, such as $C_{18:0}$ and $C_{18:1}$.

A mass spectrometer is often coupled to the output port of a GC in order to match the molecular weights and ion fragments of the components in a compound. As molecules are released from the gas chromatography column, the mass spectrometer generates a shower of high-energy electrons that removes an electron from each molecule, and creates a stream of charged particles that is subsequently bent by a powerful magnetic or electrical field. The positive molecular ions in the stream of charged particles are separated from one another on the basis of their atomic masses (Pollard et al 2007), with lighter ion fragments bending more readily than ions of heavier masses. The ion fragments of individual molecular components of a potsherd extract can then be statistically matched to those of known organic and inorganic compounds through an attached computer database (Figure 2.3.2). Because different compounds often share many molecular components that vary only to a small degree, mass spectrometry also provides corroboration of the identification of compounds through the use of gas chromatography, and increased efficiency and reliability in the identification of complex mixtures.

2.4 *The early use of gas chromatography and mass spectrometry in archaeology*

The first detailed examination of organic residues in archaeological pottery using gas chromatography and mass spectrometry was published in Archaeometry in 1976 by French researchers from the University of Lyon (Condamin et al. 1976). Jacques Condamin and his colleagues examined residues from twenty amphora and a Gallo-Roman lamp using gas chromatography in their analysis of all samples, and mass spectrometry on an unspecified number of samples. These researchers very clearly describe the steps taken in the preparation of samples, extraction and analysis of archaeological residues, and comparison of their results with a reference chromatogram of pure olive oil. In preparing the samples, large amphorae fragments between 250 and 300g were sawn into sections with a diamond disc cutter and ground into a fine ceramic powder with the aid of a mechanical crusher. Residues were extracted from 100g subsamples of the ceramic powder through continuous application and recovery of methanol in a Soxhlet extraction apparatus for six hours. Details of the Soxhlet extraction procedure can be found in Jensen (2007). The methanol extract was then evaporated to dryness through the use of a rotary evaporator, and organic compounds surviving in the dry extraction residue converted to the corresponding methyl esters through catalyzation in an unspecified methanolic medium, treatment of extract salts in a sodium methylate solution, and subsequent neutralization through addition of a small quantity of hydrochloric acid. This solution was then evaporated to dryness through the use of a rotary evaporator and reanimated in 1 ml of chloroform in preparation for analysis by gas chromatography and mass spectrometry (GC-MS).

The instrumental analytical techniques used in this study were outlined in a very straightforward manner, but a great deal of ambiguity remains in the presentation and interpretation of results. This report presents chromatograms from three of the 21 archaeological vessels examined, but neglects to note the number of vessels in which fatty acid concentrations were recorded. No direct comparison is made between the relative abundances of extant fatty acids in potsherd extracts and the modern olive oil sample, nor with any other vegetable oils that are now known to have similar fatty acid concentrations (Pollard et. al. 2007:151). The authors suggest that potsherd extracts obtained from the Gallo-Roman lamp also display evidence of "the presence of fatty acids characteristic of olive oil" (Condamin et al. 1976:201). However, the relative abundance of $C_{18:0}$ from this vessel is markedly greater than that of the amphorae, and much more indicative of the relative abundance of degraded animal fats than vegetable oils (Evershed et al. 1992; Heron and Evershed 1995). The authors also provide no contextual information about the provenance of the vessels that were examined other than that the amphorae were recovered from "ground or sea excavations" within the Mediterranean basin (Condamin et al. 1976:197), compounding their difficulties in substantiating the claim that "it is possible, even after thousands of years, to reveal the presence of olive oil in an amphora by detecting traces in its porous wall" (Condamin et al. 1976:201).

Rottländer and Hartke (1982) also extracted and examined organic residues surviving in an unspecified number of Gallo Roman potsherds recovered from the large settlement at Noreia near Klagenfurt, Austria. Residues were extracted by soaking pottery fragments in a mixture of benzene and methanol and alteration, and fatty acids recovered were transformed into corresponding fatty acid methyl esters to increase their detectability during GC analysis. The alteration or replacement of specific groups of atoms within molecular compounds surviving in potsherd extracts to increase detectability will be discussed in section 6.3. Rottländer and Hartke acknowledge the difficulties arising in the analysis and identification of oils and fats in archaeological samples due to decomposition, but nevertheless categorize organic residues recovered from three samples as those of pig fat, and olive and poppy seed oils. Although the relative abundance of fatty acids surviving in the potsherd extract identified as pig fat is consistent with those of animal origin, and the fatty acids surviving in the potsherd extract identified a olive oil is consistent with a plant oil, neither of these ratios are, in fact, species specific as Rottländer and Hartke contend. The ratio of fatty acids surviving in the potsherd extract identified as poppy seed oil are also not distinctive enough to determine whether the extant organic remains are of plant or animal origin (Evershed et al. 1992; Heron and Evershed 1995). However, in spite of these critiques, the results of both the Condamin et al (1976) and Rottländer and Hartke (1982) studies are noteworthy in that they encouraged other researchers to attempt to characterize organic compounds recovered from ancient vessels during an early period of residue analysis in archaeology.

Molecular characterization of tree resins was also the focus of early gas chromatography studies. In 1977, as part of a report published in Studies in Conservation, National Gallery of Britain conservators John Mills and Raymond White identified "resinous adhesive material" recovered from a 3rd century BC Carthaginian shipwreck submerged off the coast of Sicily near Marsalla as pine tree resins through the use of gas chromatography (Mills & White 1977b: 24). In this study, the solvents or acids used in their extraction protocol are not specified, but the authors acknowledge the addition of an alkyl functional group to the surviving organic compounds through "methylation of the acid components with diazomethane" and conversion to the corresponding methyl esters (Mills & White 1977: 23-24). Mills and White present high-temperature gas chromatograms, matching the elution orders and abundances of diterpenoid methyl esters to those of pine resins from their previous analyses of plant resins used in fine art painting (Mills 1966; Mills and White 1977a,b).

John Mills' subsequent characterization of the 'resinous crust' of pottery fragments of storage jars recovered during the excavation of a 6th century AD Byzantine fort at En Boqeq in Israel for Myra Shackley of the University of Leicester is reported in a similar manner (Shackley 1982:306). In this first citation of the use of gas chromatography in the Journal of Archaeological Science, Mills identifies these residues as a "highly oxidized diterpenoid Pinus-type resin" (Shackley 1982:306). Unfortunately, the Shackley paper provides no summary of the extraction protocols or instrumental methods used in Mills' study, nor any chromatograms or quantitative molecular data. However, Shackley does acknowledge that, without additional chemical or archaeological evidence, the presence of diterpenoid compounds is insufficient to identify the specific purpose of the pottery vessel, and puts forward three competing hypotheses for the potential use of pine resins in antiquity as fragrant unguents, caulking or waterproofing for boats, or a preservative in resinated wine.

Three other small studies were conducted during the early 1980s using solvent and acid extraction protocols and gas chromatography techniques to examine organic residues in pottery fragments from Neolithic settlements in Denmark and Britain (Evans & Hill 1982; Needham & Evans 1987) and an open air Late Stone Age pastoral encampment in the southwestern cape of South Africa (Patrick et al. 1985). These studies demonstrated that some fatty acids could survive burial in the moist soils of northern Europe and exposure to the variable coastal conditions of South Africa for extended periods of time. Due to preferential degradation of individual molecular components in potsherd extracts however, none of these studies was able to confirm whether the extant fatty acids came from plant or animal sources.

2.5 Molecular characterization of vegetable oils and animal fats in more recent studies using gas chromatography and mass spectrometry (GC-MS)

In two studies conducted in 1990-91 by Richard Evershed and Carl Heron of the Department of Chemistry at the University of Liverpool, preserved organic residues were extracted from archaeological pottery fragments through repeated applications of chloroform and methanol to a fine ceramic powder that had been removed from the interior surface of each fragment with a high-speed modeling drill. The major classifications of lipids (free fatty acids, monoacylglycerols, diacylglycerols, and triacylglycerols) were separated from one another through gas chromatography (GC), and the relative abundances of each of these compounds was then measured and compared against modern reference samples associated with particular foodstuffs (Evershed et al. 1990; Heron et al. 1991). In one of these studies, the presence of animal fats was identified in vessels recovered from a Roman

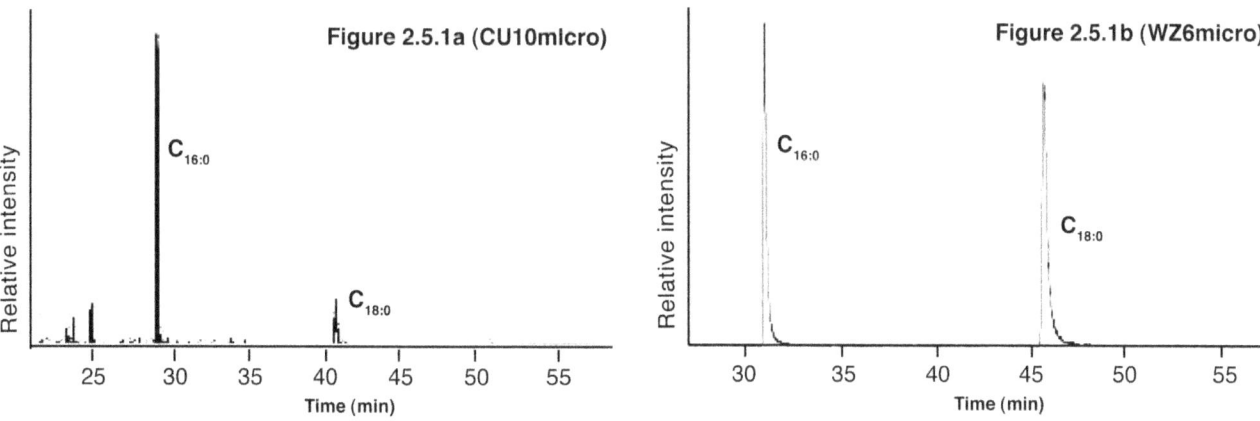

Figure 2.5.1
$C_{16:0}$ and $C_{18:0}$ saturated fatty acids are often the only lipids recovered from archaeological pottery from very early ceramic horizons, but can still provide useful information about whether residues are of plant or animal origin. Chromatograms of potsherd extracts from Late Neolithic occupations at the sites of Çayönü in Turkey and al-Basatîn in Jordan exhibit relative abundances of extant $C_{16:0}$ and $C_{18:0}$ fatty acids consistent with degraded plant oils (left) and animal fats (right).

villa and a medieval Saxon hamlet in Great Britain through detection of small amounts of cholesterol (cholest-5-en-3ß-ol -7E-diol, and cholest-5-en-7-one-3ß-ol) in addition to high abundances of n-hexadecanoic ($C_{16:0}$) and n-octadecanoic ($C_{18:0}$) fatty acids (Heron et al. 1991). Both studies noted that the interpretation of fatty acid distributions could be impaired by microbial degradation during burial, but suggested that the decomposition of lipids may have been minimized by absorption into the ceramic matrix of the pottery fabric (Evershed et. al 1990; Heron et al. 1991). Heron and Evershed subsequently noted that "although fatty acids can provide useful information on the origins of residues, their diagnostic potential is limited when considered in isolation" from other recognizable lipid distribution patterns (Heron & Evershed 1995: 260). Relative abundances, elution orders, and retention times of specific lipid classes, such as long-chain n-alkanes and n-alkenes in beeswax and broad leaf vegetables, or triacylglycerols (TAGs) in dairy foods and animal fats, need to be identified before organic residues in archaeological pottery can be confidently categorized.

Distributions of saturated and unsaturated fatty acids and longer chain lipid classes diagnostic of animal fats, plant oils, waxes, and tree resins have now been identified in archaeological pottery from a wide range of archaeological contexts in both the Old and the New Worlds. These include an adhesive used to repair a Roman jar (Charters et al. 1993); fish oils in vessels from late pre-contact sites in western Canada (Malainey et al. 1999); and beeswax surviving in a late Neolithic vessel from Great Britain (Heron et al. 1994). However, diagnostic triacygliceride distributions are rarely preserved in pottery from early ceramic horizons, and TAGs are often "completely hydrolyzed to their free fatty acid components" (Dudd and Evershed 1998:1481). Chromatographic distribution patterns are greatly affected by variations in the water solubility and oxidation of different lipid species, with hydrophobic $C_{16:0}$ and $C_{18:0}$ fatty acids or free fatty acid components of hydrolyzed triacyglycerols often the only lipids to survive microbial degradation and abiological hydrolysis over very long periods of time (Heron and Evershed 1995; Evershed et al. 1997; Evershed and Dudd 1998). That is, both unsaturated fatty acids and long-chain lipid moieties are depleted at a much quicker rate than saturated fatty acids. While $C_{16:0}$ and $C_{18:0}$ can attest to the presence of either animal fats or vegetable oils in archaeological ceramics, the relative abundance of these saturated fatty acids to one another provide useful information about whether residues are of plant or animal origin (Evershed et al. 1992; Heron and Evershed 1993; Evershed et al. 2001; Copley et al. 2005). Our knowledge of the degradation processes affecting the preservation of $C_{16:0}$ and $C_{18:0}$ fatty acids is incomplete, but the relative water solubility of $C_{16:0}$ is well-attested in comparison to the more hydrophobic $C_{18:0}$ (Copley et al. 2005e). Chromatograms of potsherd extracts below show the relative abundances of $C_{16:0}$ and $C_{18:0}$ saturated fatty acids consistent with degraded vegetable oils (Figure 2.5.1a) and animal fats (Figure 2.5.1b).

Diagnostic lipids other than fatty acids have been identified in only a small number of pottery fragments recovered from Neolithic sites, most of these in Europe or the Middle East (Heron et al. 1994; Connan et al. 2004; Mirabaud et al. 2007; Gregg et al. 2007). Long carbon chain lipids identified as beeswax have been reported as surviving in pottery vessels from a Neolithic site in Great Britain (Heron et al. 1994) and three Chalcolithic sites in Israel at En-Gedi, Moringa, and Grar (Namdar 2007). Triacylglycerols (TAGs) indicative of dairy foods have also been recovered from carbon-encrusted potsherds from a submerged lakeside Neolithic settlement at Clairvaux XIV in France (Mirabaud et al 2007). However, diagnostic lipid distributions such as these are only known to survive in Neolithic pottery under exceptional circumstances, such as the relatively anaerobic conditions at Clairvaux XIV (Mirabaud 2008, personal communication). Secure identification of these compounds also requires use of electrospray ionization mass spectrometry techniques (described below in section 2.9) in order to distinguish TAGs of mammalian body fats from those of dairy foods. Modern milk fats contain high abundances of short-chain saturated fatty acids in the C_4 - C_{14} carbon number range that make them distinguishable from adipose fats of the same animal (McDonald et al. 1988), but these compounds very rarely survive in archaeological pottery, and interpretation as evidence of dairy foods needs to be substantiated by additional triacylglycerol distributions or isotopic data (Evershed et al. 2001).

In a comparison of 5 extraction methods that had previously been used in the recovery of lipids from archaeological pottery, Stern et al. (2000), subsampled pottery fragments from Canaanite amphorae recovered from a continuously desiccated context dated to approximately 1500 BC at the Egyptian capital at Amarna by grinding portions into a fine powder as described in section 3.2. Sherd powders (0.1 g) from each pottery fragment and their extracts were then subjected to the five following protocols for the recovery of and derivitazation of lipids. Derivatization of carbon compounds surviving potsherd extracts involves the alteration or replacement of specific groups of atoms within a molecule responsible for the characteristic chemical reaction of that molecule to increase the molecule's volatility during instrumental analysis, thereby improving its detectability (Pollard et al. 2007). Summaries of the techniques used in the Stern et al. (2000) are as follows:

a. TMTFTH extraction and derivatization:
0.1g of ceramic powder was heated to 60° in .1 ml of toluene and .1 ml of trimethylammonium hydroxide (TMTFTH) in a 5% concentration in methanol for three hours, and organic compounds recovered through sequential rinsing with 3 aliquots of DCM:MeOH (1:1,v/v).

b. Conventional solvent extraction, diazomethane derivitazation:
0.1g of ceramic powder was immersed in three 0.5 ml aliquots of MeOH/DCM and subjected to high frequency sound waves as described in section 3.2, and then derivatized with diazomethane.

c. TMTFTH extraction and derivatization following conventional solvent extraction:
0.1g of ceramic powder was immersed in three 0.5 ml aliquots of MeOH/DCM and subjected to high frequency sound waves as described in section 3.2. This extract was subjected to the TMTFTH extraction and derivatization described above in (a).

d. Saponification and diazomethane:
0.1g of ceramic powder was subjected to the alkaline hydrolysis process described in section 3.7 to induce a reaction in which fatty-acid methyl esters yield carboxylic acid salts. These salts were then derivatized with diazomethane.

e. Acidic extraction:
0.1g of ceramic powder that has previously been extracted using methods (a) and (c) were immersed in 0.5 ml of deionized water, acidified using an unspecified quantity of HCl, and organic compounds recovered through sequential rinsing with 3 aliquots of hexane. This was then derivatized with diazomethane.

Stern et al. (2000) observed that the highest yields of fatty acids were achieved through saponification and diazomethane derivitization, but that conventional solvent extraction and diazomethane derivitization resulted in more highly resolved triacylglycerol distributions. However, none of the five recovery methods yielded diagnostic molecular distributions of lipids from the materials examined in the Stern et al. (2000) study. Due to the presence of odd-numbered and branch-chained fatty acids in potsherd extracts, known from both fatty acid synthesis in ruminant animals and bacterial degradation of vegetable oils (Evershed et al. 1997), Stern et al. (2000) were unable to identify the remnant lipid species unambiguously, or to confirm the long-suspected use of the amphorae for the transport and storage of olive oil (Lucas and Harris 1962).

A comprehensive geographic survey of the survival of lipids in archaeological pottery has yet to be undertaken but, based on published studies conducted on materials recovered from the earliest ceramic horizons in the Middle East (Shimoyama and Ichikawa 2000; Sauter, et al. 2003; Connan et al. 2004; Copley et al. 2005e, Gregg et al. 2007; Evershed et al. 2008; Gregg et al. 2009; Gregg in press), lipids appear to be less well preserved in the Middle East than in Europe. The poor recovery of diagnostic compounds may result from a combination of factors, including the greater antiquity of pottery in the Middle East, the range of seasonal variation in temperatures, the calcareous soil conditions characteristic of many Pottery Neolithic sites, and the differing efficacy of the extraction protocols and instrumental methods used to identify residues.

Free fatty acids have been previously observed in three pottery fragments from the late Neolithic village at Tell el-Kherkh in northwestern Syria (Shimoyama & Ichikawa 2000) and two pottery fragments from the Chalcolithic settlement at Yarikkaya in central Turkey (Sauter et al. 2003). Japanese researchers Akira Shimoyama and Ayumi Ichikawa used both gas chromatography and mass spectrometry in their examination of potsherd extracts but unfortunately did not report the number of pottery fragments or quantity of material examined, nor did they provide a detailed description of their extraction procedures or instrumental methods. The relative abundance of $C_{18:0}$ in two strainer fragments indicates these fatty acids are of animal origin, but fatty acid distributions alone are of little diagnostic value in differentiating between the major classifications of mammalian fats — those from subcutaneous adipose tissue and residues of dairy products (Heron & Evershed 1993). Without characteristic triacylglycerol (TAG) distributions, their interpretation of 'milk as a possible candidate for the strainers' (Shimoyama & Ichikawa 2000:36) remains highly conjectural. This is also the case with Sauter et al.'s (2003) report of the two pottery fragments from Yarikkaya. Although the extraction procedures and instrumental methods used in this study are much more clearly defined, the analysis of extant compounds relies solely on gas chromatography in its characterization of fatty acids as those of dairy foods. Sauter et al. (2003) acknowledge that triacylglycerols (TAGs) are preserved in the two pottery fragments, but do not present this data, nor attempt to match the TAG compositions of the ancient extract to corresponding TAGs of modern adipose or dairy fats. Because diagnostic molecular distributions have been observed in only a small number of pottery fragments from the earliest ceramic horizons in Europe and the Middle East (Heron et al. 1994; Connan et al. 2004; Mirabaud et al. 2007; Gregg et al. 2007), many researchers have come to rely on compound-specific isotopic analysis of $C_{16:0}$ and $C_{18:0}$ fatty acids for the categorization of the substances early pottery vessels once contained (Evershed et al. 1997; Dudd and Evershed 1998; Evershed et al. 2002; Copley et al. 2003, 2005a; Craig et al. 2005, 2007; Spangenberg et al. 2006; Mukherjee et al. 2007; Evershed et al. 2008; Gregg et al. 2009; Gregg and Slater in press).

2.6 Isotopic characterization of adipose and dairy fatty acids through the use of gas chromatography-combustion-isotope ratio mass spectrometry (GC-C-IRMS)

Distinctive microbial lipid species were isolated in the rumen of dairy animals as early as 1963 (Katz & Keeney 1963), but it was not until 1988 that the differential routing of dietary carbon and fatty acids was discovered to produce distinguishable $\partial^{13}C$ signatures for subcutaneous body fats and dairy fats in ruminant species (Byers and Schelling 1988). The mammary glands of dairy animals are unable to synthesize $C_{18:0}$ (one of the principal components of all animal fats) and must obtain it from the unsaturated fatty acids ($C_{18:1}$, $C_{18:2}$, and $C_{18:3}$) of the plants they consume, which are partially hydrogenated by bacteria in their rumen (Copley et al. 2003). The differential routing of dairy and adipose body fats is traceable through measurement of the ratio of two stable carbon isotopes involved in this biological process. ^{12}C and ^{13}C both have 6 protons in their nuclei and 6 orbital electrons, but the less abundant ^{13}C isotope has an additional neutron, and consequently a different and measurable atomic weight (Pollard et. al 2007). Detectable amounts of ^{12}C and ^{13}C in a compound are measured and reported using the following formula:

$$\partial^{13}C = \frac{R_{sample} - R_{PD}}{R_{PDB}} \times 1000 \, ^0/_{00}$$

where R_{sample} is the ratio of detectable amounts of ^{13}C in the sample divided by the detectable amounts of $\partial^{12}C$ in a sample, and R_{PDB} is the ratio of detectable amounts of ^{13}C in the agreed international standard divided by detectable amounts of ^{12}C in the same international standard. $\partial^{13}C$ values are reported relative to the ratio of $^{13}C/^{12}C$ in the PDB (Pee Dee Belemnite) carbonate formation (Kendall and Caldwell 1998). By convention, the lower case letter delta in the Greek alphabet (∂) is used to denote the infinitesimally small nature of the changes in these values, and the upper case letter delta in the Greek alphabet (Δ) is used to denote subsequent comparison of ∂ values (Fauer 1986).

In 1997, a group led by Richard Evershed at the University of Bristol established new criteria for the identification of animal fats preserved in archaeological ceramics based on the measurement of $\partial^{13}C$ values of individual fatty acids surviving in potsherd extracts. Employing gas chromatography and combustion isotope ratio mass spectrometry (GC-C-IRMS) as analytical techniques, Evershed et al. (1997) measured the ratio of $\partial^{13}C$ ratios of $C_{16:0}$ and $C_{18:0}$ fatty acids in uncooked adipose and dairy fats from sheep, cattle, and pigs in Great Britain. By plotting the $\partial^{13}C$ values of these fatty acids against one another, Evershed et al. (1997) established that there were discrete ranges for adipose fats and dairy fats from ruminant species and adipose fats from non-ruminant species. Evershed and colleague Stephanie Dudd later measured the $\partial^{13}C$ ratios of $C_{16:0}$ and $C_{18:0}$ fatty acids surviving in potsherd extracts from early medieval and late Iron Age vessels in the United Kingdom and, through comparison with the discrete ranges of modern values categorized residues as those of dairy fats or adipose fats from milk-producing animals, or adipose fats of non-ruminant species. Isotopic values falling between the discrete modern ranges were attributed to the mixing of animal fats in antiquity (Dudd & Evershed 1998). The discrete ranges of modern isotopic values of ruminant and non-ruminant adipose fats and ruminant dairy fats from northern Europe first published by Dudd and Evershed (1998), and subsequently used by Dudd et al. (1999), Evershed et al. (2002), Copley et al. (2003, 2005a-d), and Mukherjee et al. (2007) to categorize potsherd extracts from Great Britain are illustrated by the ellipses in Figure 2.6.1.

Using these same techniques for characterizing $\partial^{13}C$ values of $C_{16:0}$ fatty acids in potsherd extracts pioneered by Evershed and Dudd (1998), other researchers have identified a range of animal fats in archaeological pottery from early ceramic horizons in Europe and the Middle East. Most of these studies have been conducted by the research group at the University of Bristol led by Richard Evershed (Evershed et al., 2002, Copley et al. 2003, 2005a-e, Mukherjee et al., 2007; Evershed et al. 2008), with smaller contributions from Craig et al. (2005, 2007), Spangenberg et al. (2006), Gregg (in press), Gregg et al. (in press), Gregg et al. (submitted). The Evershed group's work initially focused on identifying the uses of pottery at Neolithic through Iron Age sites in Great Britain, but this group has recently turned its attention to uncovering molecular and isotopic evidence of subsistence practices originating in the 'Fertile Crescent' of the Middle East (Copley et al. 2005; Evershed et al. 2008).

In 2003, Copley et al. (2003; 2005a) established that dairying in Great Britain was an already well-developed agricultural practice that was introduced with farming from mainland Europe circa 4400 cal BC. They have also demonstrated the importance of milking to the agricultural economies of later periods in Great Britain (Copley et al. 2005b,c,d). A team led by Oliver Craig subsequently pushed the date and location of the earliest evidence of dairy foods in pottery vessels back to 5940 - 5500 cal BC at two Linearbandkeramik settlements in the Danube basin (Craig et al. 2005). In an examination of pottery used by Mesolithic coastal populations living on lands adjacent to the Baltic Sea, Craig et al. (2007) have also shown that hunters and fishers continued to rely on marine resources for more than 1000 years after the introduction of farming practices into northern Europe.

In 2005, Copley et al. (2005e) found residues sufficiently preserved in five of 28 pottery fragments and 10 clay balls from Late Neolithic Çatahöyük to measure $\partial^{13}C$ values of extant $C_{16:0}$ and $C_{18:0}$ fatty acids. Copley et al. reported that four pottery fragments yielded isotopic values consistent with adipose fats from modern ruminant animals from northern

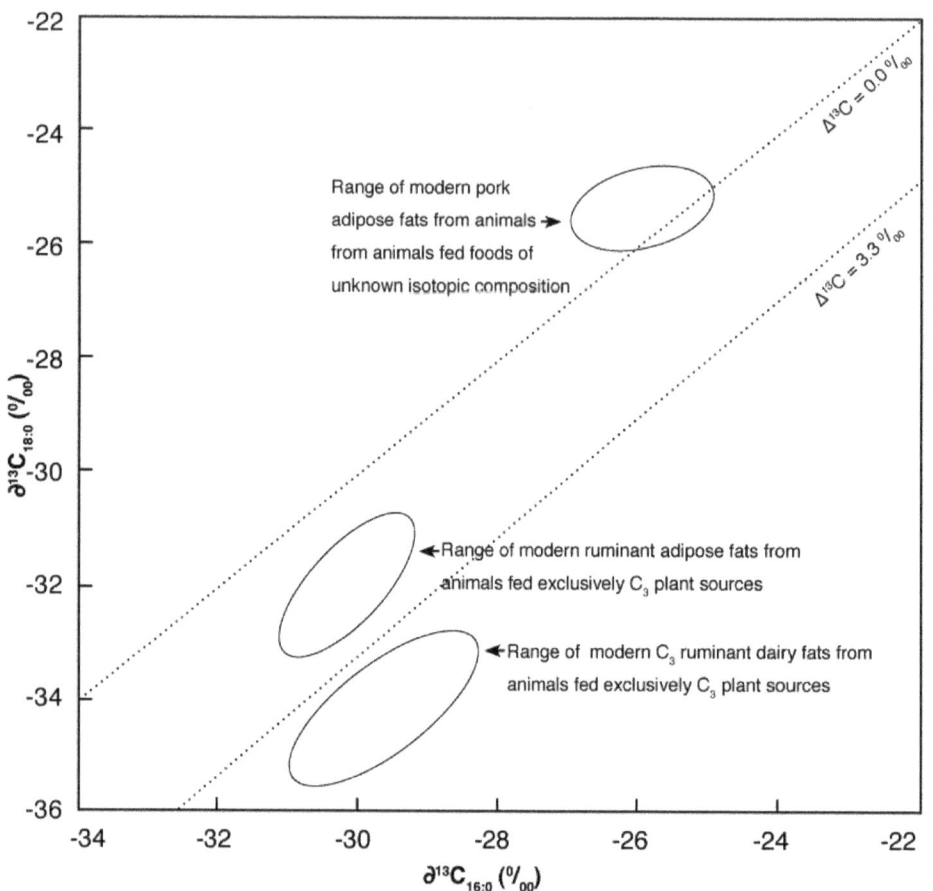

Figure 2.6.1
The discrete ranges of $\partial^{13}C$ values of $C_{16:0}$ and $C_{18:0}$ fatty acids of modern reference fats used to categorize potsherd extracts of late Iron Age to early Neolithic vessels from Great Britain by Dudd and Evershed (1998), Dudd et al. (1999), Evershed et al. (2002), Copley et al. (2003, 2005a-d;) Mukherjee et al. (2007) are shown in the ellipses in this diagram.

Europe, while one potsherd exhibited values consistent with a mixture of subcutaneous fats of ruminant and non-ruminant species. None of the materials from Çatalhöyük exhibited evidence of the processing or consumption of dairy products, nor did any of the clay balls yield verification of Atalay's and Hastorf's (2006) hypothesized use as pot boilers in grease and seed oil extraction. Of particular interest in Copley et al.'s (2005e) report, only 18% of pottery fragments yielded measurable quantities of lipids through use of previously established solvent extraction and saponification protocols (Evershed et al. 2002; Copley et al. 2003). This proportion is significantly below the 50 to 60% recovery rates members of this research group 'routinely' detected in Neolithic pottery from Great Britain (Copley et al. 2005a-d), and would be much lower still (13%) had the clay balls been included in their calculations.

A great deal of ambiguity also remains in the categorization of potsherd extracts from Çatalhöyük due to uncertainties about the relative contributions of C_3 and C_4 plants to animal diets in central Anatolia during the early Holocene (Richards et al. 2003; Pearson et al. 2007). Variations in the fractionation of carbon isotopes in plants having different photosynthetic pathways produces a shift in the $\partial^{13}C$ values of fatty acids in the animals that consume them (O'Leary 1981; Lee-Thorpe 2008). You are what you eat. Animals exclusively consuming C_3 grasses or cereals in regions of the world with temperate climates such as Europe, have more negative $\partial^{13}C$ values than animals consuming large quantities of C_4 plants, such as corn, sorghum, and millet, or the tropical grasses or chenopods that are abundant in many parts of the Middle East (O'Leary 1981). Copley et al. do not compare their results from Çatalhöyük with those of fatty acids from animals pastured in central Anatolia, but rather with ruminant animals exclusively fed a diet of C_3 plants in northern Europe and an unspecified group of non-ruminant animals (Figure 2.6.2). This same range of modern values for non-ruminant adipose fats had been previously assigned to domesticated pigs consuming foods of unknown isotopic composition by Copley et al. (2005a-d) working on related projects in Great Britain (Figure 2.6.1).

Due to uncertainties about the proportions of C_3 and C_4 plants in ancient animal diets at Çatalhöyük, Copley et al. (2005e:173) use a mathematical proxy to remove the influence of different photosynthetic pathways on the $\delta^{13}C$ values of fatty acids surviving in the potsherd extracts (Figure 2.6.3). In a previous study, Copley et al. (2003) had proposed to account for differences in the ^{13}C values of fatty acids and carbohydrates in plants that animals consume by plotting the differences in the ^{13}C values of $C_{16:0}$ and $C_{18:0}$ fatty acids against the ^{13}C values of $C_{18:0}$ alone [$\Delta^{13}C_{18:0 - 16:0}$ (‰) : $\delta^{13}C_{18:0}$ (‰)]. This proxy is intended to produce numeric values that more directly reflect the biochemical and physiological origins of animal fats recovered from archaeological pottery. Unfortunately, there is no clear division between C_3 and C_4 dietary input in this proxy, and therefore, no means of directly assessing the extent of impact of different photosynthetic pathways on animal diet solely from the differences in $\partial^{13}C$ values of individual fatty acids. The efficacy of this proxy is also not substantiated by direct comparison of $\delta^{13}C$ values of $C_{16:0}$ and $C_{18:0}$ fatty acids from animals known to have consumed a range of plants with different photosynthetic pathways, and its use is discussed critically in section 5.6.

Of relevance to this problem is an isotopic study subsequently conducted on bone collagen from sheep and goats from

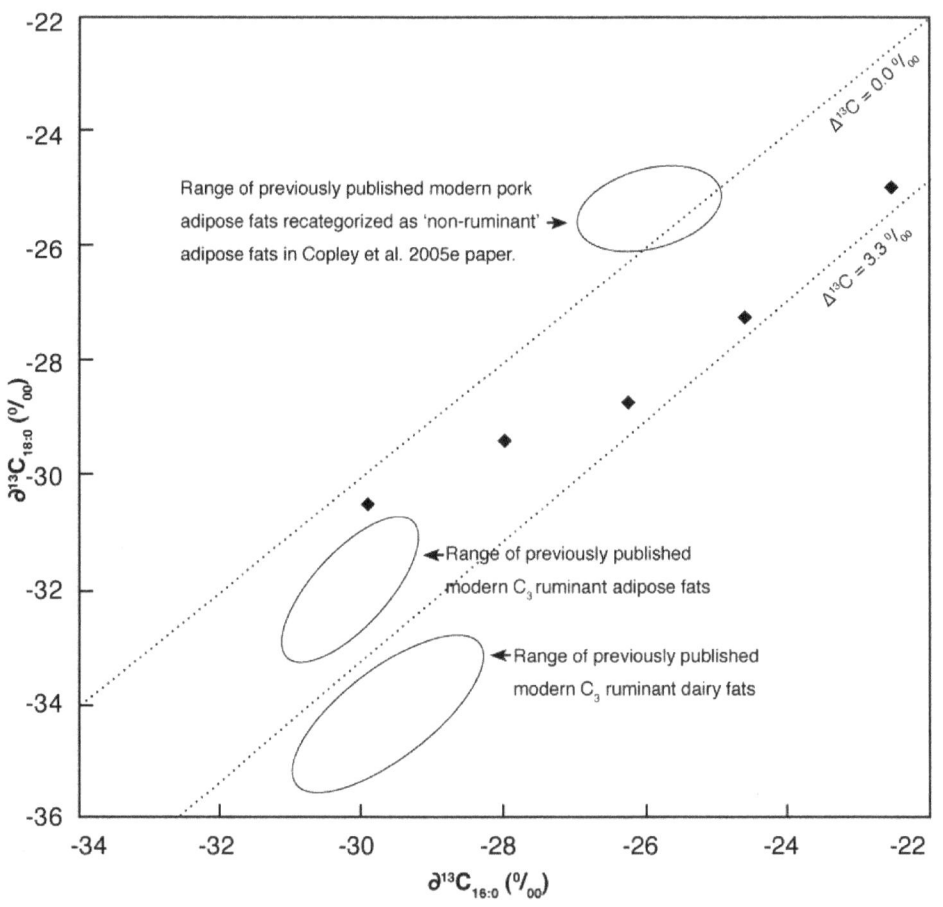

Figure 2.6.2
The observed $\partial^{13}C$ values of $C_{16:0}$ and $C_{18:0}$ fatty acids recovered from pottery fragments from Late Neolithic levels at Çatalhöyük do not fall within the ranges of modern reference fats previously used to categorize potsherd extracts in northern Europe.

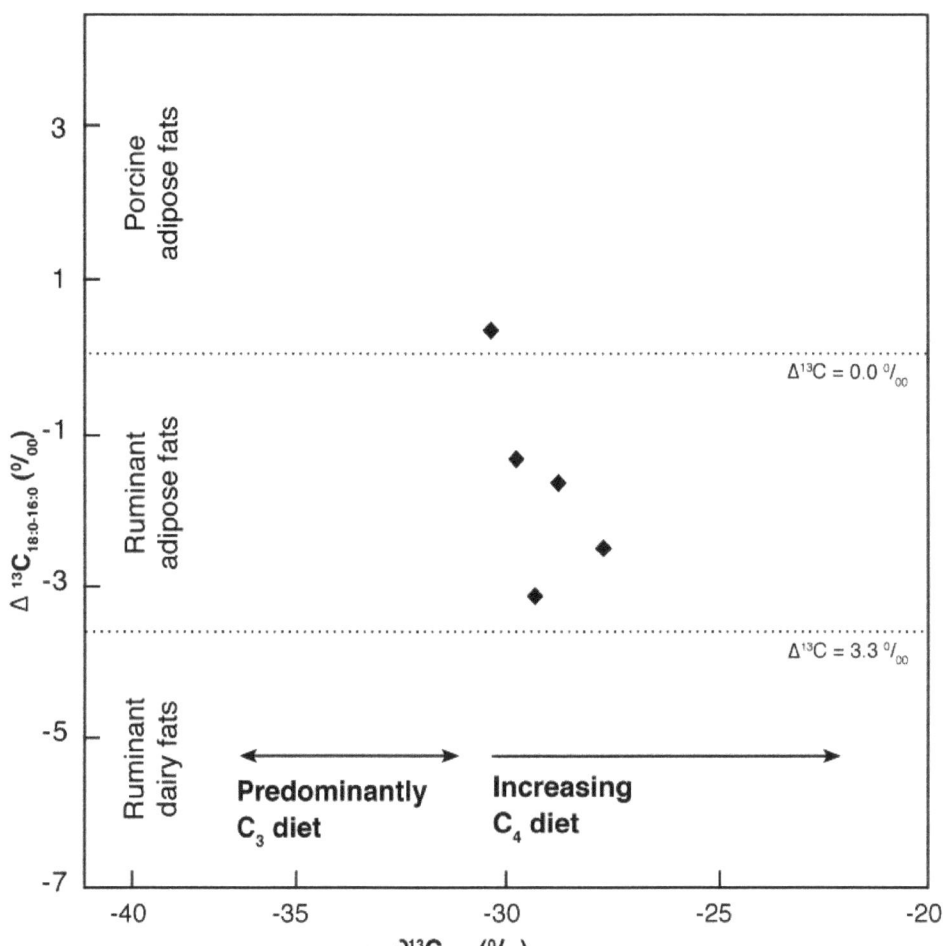

Figure 2.6.3
Copley et al. (2005e:173) plot the differences in $\partial^{13}C$ values of $C_{16:0}$ and $C_{18:0}$ fatty acids against the values of $C_{18:0}$ alone [$\Delta^{13}C_{18:0 - 16:0}$ (‰): $\partial^{13}C_{18:0}$ (‰)] to demonstrate the relative contribution of C_3 and C_4 plants to the $\partial^{13}C$ values of $C_{16:0}$ and $C_{18:0}$ fatty acids surviving in potsherd extracts. The efficacy of this proxy is not substantiated by direct comparison of $\delta^{13}C$ values of $C_{16:0}$ and $C_{18:0}$ fatty acids from animals known to have consumed a range of plants with different photosynthetic pathways, and its use is discussed critically in Chapter 5 (Section 5.6)

Çatalhöyük. Pearson et al. (2007) have observed a high degree of variability in $\partial^{13}C$ values in the faunal remains, and suggest that the isotope values reveal different herd-management strategies at the site, with some animals feeding exclusively on C_3 grasses and others consuming a substantial proportion of C_4 plants from a much wider geographic range.

A team led by Jorge Spangenberg has also raised many questions concerning the efficacy of modern GC-C-IRMS data obtained from animals pastured in northern Europe to categorize organic residues in archaeological pottery from other regions of the world. Spangenberg et al.'s (2006) comparison of potsherd extracts from a Late Neolithic site in Switzerland with modern adipose and dairy fats from central Europe has demonstrated there is greater diversity in the fractionation of carbon isotopes (the division of carbon into relative amounts of ^{12}C and ^{13}C) associated with the synthesis of $C_{16:0}$ and $C_{18:0}$ fatty acids in ruminant and non-ruminant animals than previously reported (DeNiro and Epstein 1977, 1978; Dudd and Evershed 1998; Evershed et al. 2002; Copley et al. 2003; Craig et al. 2005; Copley et al. 2005a-e). In the Spangenberg et al. study, stable carbon isotope values of modern pig fat, sheep adipose, cow's milk, and goat cheese all overlap the discrete range of ruminant adipose values from northern Europe used to categorize potsherd extracts by the Evershed group. As can be seen in Figure 2.6.4, the $\delta^{13}C$ values for both raw milk and processed dairy foods have been observed to plot above the $\Delta^{13}C = -3.3$ line, while the $\delta^{13}C$ values for pig fats fall within the range of values previously observed for body fats of ruminant animals, and $\delta^{13}C$ values for ruminant body fats within the range previously observed for pig fats.

This variability in the fractionation of carbon isotopes cannot be attributed to the photosynthetic pathway of plants in animal diet, as the animals in both northern and central Europe are reported to have been exclusively fed a diet of C_3 forage grasses (Copley et al. 2003, 2005a-e; Spangenberg et al. 2006). Spangenberg et al. have shown that the overlap in stable carbon isotope values of dairy foods and adipose fats of ruminant and non-ruminant species can result from a wide range of other factors that affect fractionation, not only in the synthesis of fatty acids in the animals themselves, but also during the subsequent preparation and storage of fermented milk byproducts. For example, the $\partial^{13}C$ ratios of $C_{16:0}$ and $C_{18:0}$ fatty acids from adipose fats from suckling calf and lamb plot between the values of adult pig adipose in the study from central Europe, an inconsistency that Spangenberg et al. (2006) ascribe to the high ratio of glucose carbon from mother's milk in the diet of young ruminant animals (Vernon 1981). In addition to the natural variability in isotopic values of dairy fats from the different milk-producing species, Spangenberg et al. (2006) have also reported more positive $\partial^{13}C$ values for goat and sheep cheese than whole milk from the same animals. Through a series of experiments, Spangenberg et al. (2006) have shown that $\partial^{13}C$ values of $C_{16:0}$ and $C_{18:0}$ fatty acids in milk become enriched as isotopically-lighter compounds are preferentially released through the increased temperatures of the manufacturing process and bacterial degradation during storage.

The complexities in differentiating the isotopic values of dairy foods from those of adipose fats have a major effect on the interpretation of archaeological data. In an extensive examination of 2218 pottery fragments from 23 Neolithic and Chalcolithic sites in southeastern Europe, the Levant, and Anatolia, Evershed et al. (2008) have recently reported finding the earliest date for milk use in the Near East and southeastern Europe. In this study, Evershed et al. recovered free fatty acids from 11.5% of the materials they examined, with approximately 8% of potsherds yielding relative abundances of $C_{16:0}$ and $C_{18:0}$ fatty acids indicative of animal fats rather than plant lipids. Further stable carbon analyses of these compounds yielded $\partial^{13}C$ values consistent with those of modern reference values of dairy foods, ruminant adipose fats and pig fats from northern Europe. Evershed et al. acknowledge that the range of observed $\partial^{13}C$ values of $C_{16:0}$ fatty acids from potsherd extracts "is somewhat wider than seen for northern European sites" (Evershed et al. 2008:2), but do not directly compare the isotopic values of ancient residues with those of modern reference fats obtained from within the region. These researchers instead chose to "emphasize the biosynthetic and metabolic characteristics of the fat source" by mathematically removing the implied "contribution of C_4 and water-stressed plants" to animal diet (Evershed et al. 2008:3), using the same mathematical proxy as in the Copley et al. studies (2003; 2005e) mentioned above. However, much like the previous work, Evershed et al. do not substantiate the efficacy of this mathematical proxy by direct comparison of $\delta^{13}C$ values of $C_{16:0}$ and $C_{18:0}$ fatty acids from animals known to have consumed a range of plants with different photosynthetic pathways. Use of the proxy in categorizing fatty acids in archaeological pottery is discussed critically in section 5.6.

Although the isotopic evidence presented by Evershed et al. (2008) indicates that pottery was being used in the processing or consumption of dairy foods by 6500 cal BC in southeastern Europe and western Anatolia, Edward Banning, Kevin Gibbs, Greg Slater and I have subsequently demonstrated that, in many instances, the $\partial^{13}C$ ranges for dairy and adipose fats for northern Europe cannot distinguish the $\partial^{13}C$ values of ancient dairy residues from those of adipose fats of ruminant and non-ruminant species in the Middle East (Gregg et al. 2009; Gregg and Slater in press). Our comparison of $\partial^{13}C$ values of modern adipose and dairy fats obtained in Israel, Palestine, Jordan, and Turkey with those previously used to categorize potsherd extracts (Evershed et al. 2002; Copley et al. 2003, 2005a-e; Mukherjee et al. 2007) establishes that the ranges of isotopic ratios for adipose and dairy fats in the Middle East differ substantially from those in northern Europe. These data show an even greater diversity in the fractionation of carbon isotopes associated with the synthesis of $C_{16:0}$ and $C_{18:0}$ fatty acids in ruminant and non-ruminant animals than reported by Spangenberg et al. (2006), and demonstrate that the previously reported empirical ranges of isotopic values of animal fats from northern Europe have limited applicability in categorizing organic residues from archaeological sites in the Middle East. The findings of the Gregg et al. (2009) study and archaeological data from eight additional Neolithic sites in the Fertile Crescent are presented in chapter 5 in the context of the overlapping and contradictory ranges of $\partial^{13}C$ values that have been

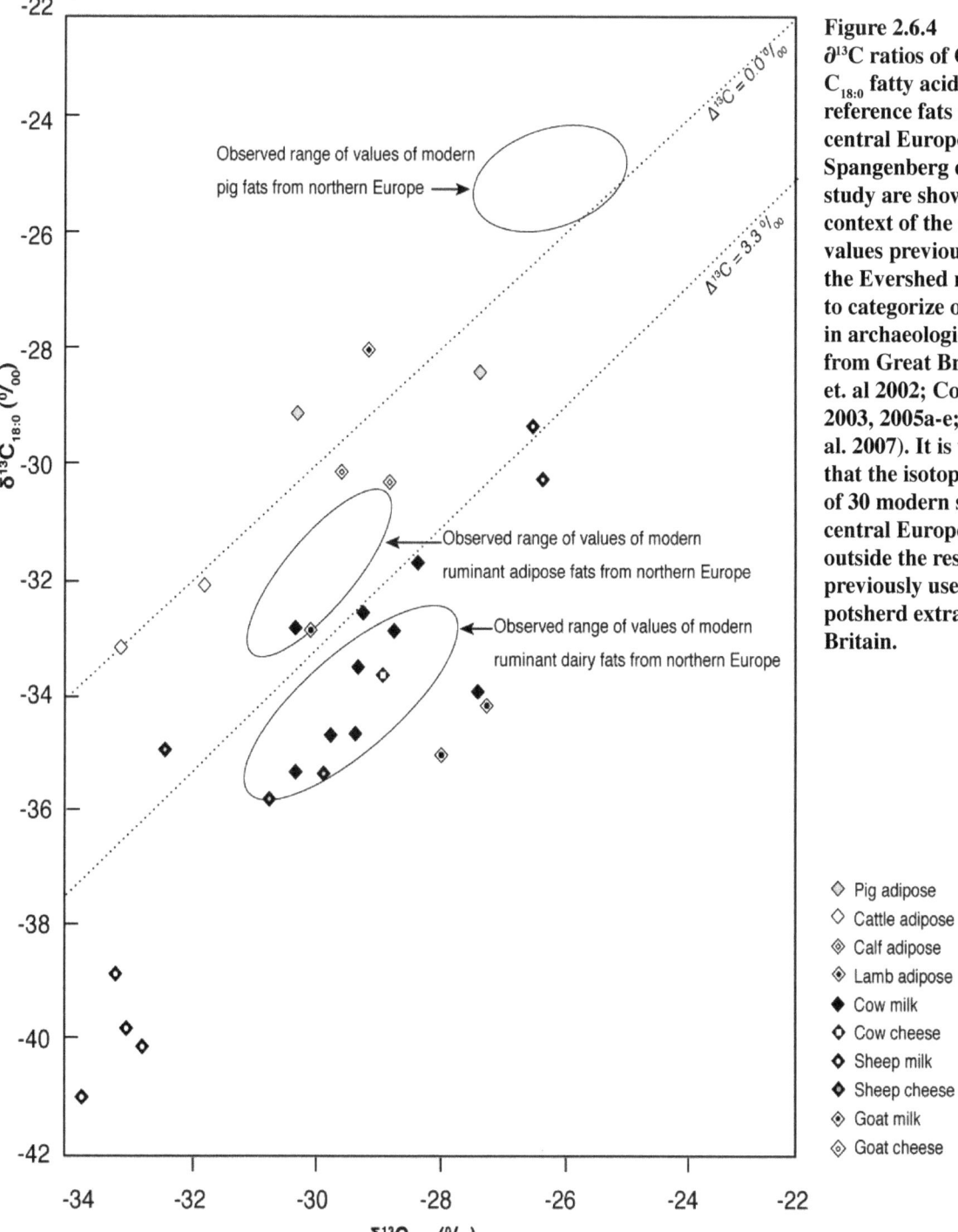

Figure 2.6.4
$\delta^{13}C$ ratios of $C_{16:0}$ and $C_{18:0}$ fatty acids of modern reference fats from central Europe from the Spangenberg et al. (2006) study are shown in the context of the ranges of $\delta^{13}C$ values previously used by the Evershed research group to categorize organic residues in archaeological pottery from Great Britain (Evershed et. al 2002; Copley et al. 2003, 2005a-e; Mukherjee et al. 2007). It is worth noting that the isotopic values of 6 of 30 modern samples from central Europe (20%) plot outside the respective ranges previously used to categorize potsherd extracts in Great Britain.

observed for dairy foods and adipose fats. In chapter 6, I will discuss the implications of these findings for the identification of organic residues preserved in archaeological pottery from the earliest ceramic horizons in the Middle East, and reassess the criteria used to evaluate the fractionation of carbon isotopes in fatty acid synthesis and subsequent processing of animal fats for human consumption.

2.7 Molecular characterization of amino acids in animal proteins through use of acid digestion and immunoassay techniques

Due to the preferential survival of animal fats and vegetable oils in most archaeological contexts, the overwhelming majority of studies examining extant organic residues in pottery have focused on the identification of molecular and isotopic biomarkers of lipids rather than proteins. However, when proteins do survive, they can provide species-specific identification of organic residues (Barnard et al. 2007). Unlike lipids, proteins will induce an antibody response when injected into a host organism, and identification can be undertaken with a wide range of immunological testing methods (Newman et al. 1993; Smith & Wilson 2001; Barnard et al. 2007). But many researchers have questioned the merit of attempting to characterize them in archaeological ceramics. The peptide bonds holding these long chains of amino acids together break down rapidly under highly acidic or alkaline soil conditions, and protein concentrations are often below the detectable limits of conventional chromatography biomarker techniques (Evershed and Tuross 1996). Proteins appear to be $1/10,000$th as abundant as lipids in archaeological fragments where animal fats are known to be present (Charters et al. 1993).

Uncertainties concerning the diagnostic potential of proteins in archaeological pottery have been aggravated by the ongoing controversy surrounding the detection of blood residues on the surfaces of prehistoric stone tools and alleged identification of species (Loy 1983). Material scientists, biochemists, immunologists, and archaeologists (Gurfinkel and Franklin 1985; Custer et al. 1988; Smith and Wilson 1992, 2001; Downs and Lowenstein 1995; Manning 1995; Gernaey et al. 2001; Pollard et al. 2007) have all questioned the validity of the discovery of haemoglobin on stone tools based on the use of chemical test strips for the detection of haemoglobin in urine (Loy 1983; Loy and Wood 1989), or the visual recognition of crystalline structure of salts allegedly formed through the precipitation of proteins from a solution in which the tools were soaked (Loy 1983; Loy and Wood 1989; Loy and Hardy 1992). The selectivity of chemical test strips is not only limited to haemoglobin, with consistent false positive results produced through the presence of manganese oxide, hypochlorite, and microbial peroxidases in archaeological soils (Custer et al. 1988; Downs and Lowenstein 1995; Manning 1994). Researchers have also not been able to replicate the crystalline structures allegedly attesting to the presence of haemoglobin using the methods put forward by Loy (Smith and Wilson 2001).

Despite the improbabilities associated with identification of proteins in archaeological pottery, researchers from the University of Newcastle suspected that mineral-bound amino acids were not poorly preserved, but only poorly characterized due to difficulties in extracting them from archaeological materials (Craig and Collins 2000, 2002). Matthew Collins and Oliver Craig met with some initial success in identifying bovine a_{s1}-casein in storage vessels from an Iron Age site in the Hebrides employing their hydrofluoric acid digestion-and-capture immunoassay (DACIA) method (Craig et al. 2000), but were unable to replicate their results in their examination of suspected proteins in 80 pottery fragments from three Neolithic sites in the Danube basin (Craig et al. 2005). Due to poor preservation of proteins, Collins and Craig subsequently abandoned the DACIA process and adopted the lipid recovery protocols and GC-IRMS techniques developed by the Evershed group and outlined above. Using these methods, Craig et al. (2005) recovered fatty acids from 10 of 49 pottery fragments from two of these sites, and have reported $\partial^{13}C$ values in these residues consistent with milk fats from ruminant species.

2.8 Molecular characterization of animal fats and proteins through use of electrospray ionization mass spectrometry techniques

Recent innovations in electrospray ionization mass spectrometry (ESI-MS) have allowed archaeological researchers to resolve the molecular structures of animal fats and proteins preserved in archaeological pottery that are otherwise unable to be characterized through use of conventional mass spectrometry techniques (Mirabaud et al. 2007; Sallazo et al. 2008). In electrospray ionization mass spectrometry, a small amount of substances being analyzed are dissolved in a volatile mixture of solvents such as acetonitrile, water, methanol, or l-proponol, and introduced into a chamber where a charged field at the tip of a hypodermic needle disperses the mixture into a fine spray of charged droplets (Fenn et al. 1990; Gross et al. 2002). The volatile solvents rapidly evaporate through a sequence of small Coulomb explosions, with individual ions from the substance being released into the ambient gas of the chamber before being sent to a mass analyzer (Fenn et al. 1990). Electrospray instrumental methods are particularly well suited to the analysis of proteins because they compensate for the tendency of macromolecules, such as triacyglycerides in animal fats and amino acids in animal proteins, to fractionate when they are ionized (Gross et al. 2002).

Mirabaud et al. (2007) have used electrospray ionization mass spectrometry to more highly resolve triacyglyceride (TAG) distributions of body and dairy fats from modern ruminant animals than those of TAGs previously provided by conventional mass spectrometry techniques. TAG distributions of ruminant body fats and dairy foods become indistinguishable from one another following burial for prolonged periods of time (Heron & Evershed 1995), but Mirabaud et al. (2007) have been able to match TAG distributions of milk fats from modern European cattle to those of potsherd extracts from a long submerged Neolithic settlement at Clairvaux XIV in France. Mirabaud (2008) admits that TAG distributions such as these are only known to survive in Neolithic pottery under exceptional circumstances, such as the relatively anaerobic depositional environment at Clairvaux XIV, and that this instrumental technique may have little applicability in characterizing organic residues in pottery fragments recovered from most early agricultural or pastoral settlements.

A team of French and American researchers has also recently used electrospray ionization mass spectrometry to identify protein peptide sequences of seal muscle and whale blubber in the clay matrix of an 800-year-old Inupiat potsherd from Point Barrow in northern Alaska (Sollazo et al. 2008). Proteins were extracted from the pottery fragment through acid digestion of a small quantity of ceramic powder, with amino acids separated from one another through hydrolysis with a hydrolase enzyme. Through the use of ESI-MS, myoglobin of seal muscle tissue and hemoglobin in whale blubber were identified in potsherd extracts through comparison with modern reference samples with the aid of a protein-matching database (Sollazo et al. 2008).

Undoubtedly, electrospray ionization mass spectrometry holds great promise for identification of organic compounds in archaeological pottery recovered from burial environments that have remained frozen or oxygen-free for prolonged periods. Much like mammoths from northern Siberia (Michel 1998), the 'Iceman' from the Austrian Alps (Gostner 2002), or 'bog bodies' from the northern Europe (Stankiewicz et al. 1997), frigid or anaerobic conditions are likely to protect residues in archaeological pottery from biodegradation processes prevalent at archaeological sites throughout much of the rest of the world.

2.9 Molecular and isotopic characterization of plant sugars and starches through Fourier transform infrared spectroscopy, GC-MS, GC-C-IRMS, and high performance liquid chromatography (HPLC) techniques

Attempts to identify fruit sugars and starchy grains in archaeological pottery through chemical analysis have not proven to be particularly successful (Reber and Evershed

2004a, Evershed 2008). Many researchers have questioned whether carbohydrates are able to survive burial for prolonged periods as discrete entities, retaining their diagnostic potential in reconstructing subsistence behaviors of prehistoric populations (Atchinson and Fullagar 1998; Piperno et. al 2000; Perry 2001; Haslam 2004; Reber and Evershed 2004a, Evershed 2008). The importance of not oversimplifying the identification of starch grain components in organic residues has been stressed by Elanora Reber and Richard Evershed (2004a: 409) "since false positive identification of these components will lead to serious misunderstandings in the archaeological record". Michael Haslam also points out that "once a component such as starch has entered the soil and begun to be broken down, it is rarely possible to determine just how much was present, owing to biochemical similarities in the make-up of all living things" (Haslam 2004:1720). The poor preservation of complex carbohydrates in most soil conditions is further aggravated by the lack of any known species-specific lipid biomarkers for starch grains (Reber & Evershed 2004a), and the masking of starch lipids by those from foods such as meat, milk, fish, and oily seeds that the ancient vessel may have also once contained (Gunstone et al. 1994; Reber and Evershed 2004a;). Reber and Evershed (2004a: 400) note this masking often "leads to the underestimation of starchy staple lipids present in a residue," making it difficult, if not impossible, to confirm evidence of starchy grains through molecular criteria alone.

However, Reber and Evershed (2004b) have been able to demonstrate a chronological progression of the processing of maize in pottery vessels that may have been used for additional purposes during the early Mississippian period in southern North America, ca. 800 – 1100 cal AD. Through adaptation of the GC-MS and GC-IRMS instrumental analytical techniques described above, Reber and Evershed (2004b) characterized the isotopic values of long chain carbon compounds surviving in 16 of 130 potsherds recovered from 16 pre-contact sites along the Mississippi Valley. Isotopic analysis revealed a change in $\partial^{13}C$ values of this compound coinciding with botanical evidence for the introduction of maize, a C_4 plant, into the American Bottom region from the Lower Mississippi Valley between 1000 and 1100 cal AD (Reber and Evershed 2004b).

A number of studies of organic residues embedded in pottery vessels have focused on evidence of winemaking and brewing during a number of different periods in antiquity by targeting specific trace organic compounds associated with the conversion of sugars and starches to alcohol. Patrick McGovern of the University of Pennsylvania's Museum of Archaeology and Anthropology has led projects looking to find direct chemical evidence of the manufacture or storage of alcoholic beverages in pottery vessels from the Middle East, China, and Central America (Michel et al. 1992, 1993; McGovern et al. 1996; McGovern et al. 1997, 2003, 2004; Cavalieri et al. 2003; Henderson et al. 2007). However, a number of researchers have questioned the reliability of the Fourier transform infrared spectroscopy (FT-IR) and wet chemistry "spot tests" used in McGovern's studies from the Middle East (Boulton and Heron 2000; Gauche-Jané et al. 2004; Pollard et al. 2007; Stern et al. 2008), and the identification of trace amounts of beeswax associated with honey in 'mixed fermented beverage' from the Early Neolithic period in China (Evershed 2008).

There also remains a great deal of uncertainty as to whether the biomarkers recovered from potsherd extracts in McGovern's studies can be interpreted as conclusive proof that the vessels ever contained beer or wine rather than other plant foods or fruit beverages (Lev-Yudin 2000; Hornsey 2003; Stern et al. 2008).

Using a solvent recovery protocol involving the boiling of potsherds in acetone and FT-IR instrumental analytical techniques, McGovern and his colleagues have detected trace amounts of calcium oxalate (a degradation product known from modern industrial brewing processes) in a vessel from the Uruk period site of Godin Tepe in highland Iran (Michel et al. 1992). However, this compound is not inextricably linked with the brewing process, as Michel et al. have argued, and cannot be interpreted as a biomarker of beer. A report in Modern Brewery Age by Dana Johnson (1998) notes that the presence of calcium oxalate residues in vats and piping of modern breweries is largely due to a reaction between caustic alkaline cleaners, calcium and magnesium in water, and amino acids in proteins in hops and barley. Residual calcium oxalate is also known to be present in a wide range of other biological systems (Lev-Yadun 2000; Hornsey 2003), with possible sources including any number of roots, tubers, legumes, nuts, or grains that flourished in the Middle East during the early Holocene (Lev-Yadun 2000), or calcium oxalate-rich soils in post-depositional contexts (Hornsey 2003).

McGovern and his colleagues have also reported the first chemical evidence of winemaking through the use of the same instrumental analytical methods (Michel et al. 1993; McGovern et al. 1996), citing the presence of salts of tartaric acid in a vessel recovered from Godin Tepe and another from the late Neolithic site of Hajii Firuz in northwestern Iran as confirmation of the survival of trace amounts of phenolic compounds from red grapes. In an assessment of McGovern's early results, however, Neil Boulton and Carl Heron have pointed out: the degree to which qualitative spot tests can be used with confidence in archaeological investigations is debatable. One problem is the cross-reactivity leading to 'false positive' results. Although the spot test employed by McGovern and his co-workers is claimed to be sensitive to 10 μg of tartaric acid, a possible cross-reaction is with malic acid, a common acid in many fruits (Boulton & Heron 2000:601).

Boulton and Heron (2000) also suggest that the FT-IR and liquid chromatographic instrumental techniques used in the molecular characterization of these residues lack the selectivity and sensitivity of other combined molecular separation and characterization methods, such as gas chromatography/ mass spectrometry (GC/MS), or high performance liquid chromatography/mass spectrometry (HPLC/MS). In a further assessment of methodologies available for the identification of biomarkers of wine, Stern et al. (2008) re-examined residues in vessels that McGovern et al. (1997) had previously identified as those of wine, impregnated with Pistacea tree resins and recovered from a Late Bronze Age shipwreck off the southwest coast of Turkey at Ullaburn. Stern et al. were unable to replicate McGovern et al.'s results through the use of spot tests or FT-IR instrumental techniques to confirm the presence of wine in these vessels. However, their GC-MS analysis of residues of red and white wines obtained from experimental pottery vessels established the necessity of identifying both calcium tartrate and tartaric acid to determine whether an ancient vessel once contained wine. Stern et al.'s detection of trace amounts of syringic acid in both the ancient vessel and modern pistachea fruit has also shown that the use of this compound as a unique biomarker of red wines, as has been suggested by Guasch-Jané et al. (2004, 2006), may lead to false positive results.

McGovern's instrumental analytical methods have included GC-MS, HPLC-MS and GC-IRMS in more recent reports of chemical evidence of wine in a Late Bronze Age vessel from the Egyptian capital at Amarna (Cavalieri et al. 2003), a 'mixed fermented beverage' from the Early Neolithic site at Jiahu, China (McGovern et al. 2004), and the earliest cacao beverages from the late Archaic site, Puerto Escondido, in Honduras (Henderson et al. 2007). These reports are more circumspect in their characterization of potsherd extracts, acknowledging that direct chemical evidence of alcohol is lacking, but inferring its presence from a biomarker of wine yeast in the Amarna and Jiahu vessels (Cavalieri et al. 2003; McGovern et al. 2004), and a fruity pulp in vessels from Puerto Escondido similar to that of the alcoholic beverage chicha known in the region from much later periods (Henderson et al. 2007). The GC-MS, HPLC-MS and GC-IRMS methods used more recently by McGovern are widely viewed as trustworthy analytical techniques (Pollard et al. 2007). However, as Richard Evershed (2008) has pointed out, McGovern et al.'s (2004) identification of long-chain carbon compounds in residues from an Early Neolithic vessel from Jiahu "do not unambiguously derive from beeswax", as McGovern et al. have claimed. The relative abundance of and distribution of C_{23}, C_{25}, C_{27}, C_{29}, C_{31}, and C_{33} n-alkanes in the chromatographic profile of residues (McGovern et al. 2004) are also characteristic of petroleum (Killops and Killops 2005). Although petroleum is not likely to be the source of these compounds during the Early Neolithic period in China, " the assignment of a specific source or constituent of a residue based on the presence of a particular biomarker component or mixture of components demands a high degree of rigor, wherein consideration of the nature of other constituents of the residue may lead to the hypothesis of a putative source being rejected" (Evershed 2008:898-899).

2.10 *Molecular characterization of bitumen residues from pottery vessels in recent studies using GC-MS and elemental analyzer isotope ratio mass spectrometry (EA-IRMS)*

Using the GC-MS analytical techniques outlined above, two studies by Connan et al. (2004) and Gregg et al. (2007) have identified molecular biomarkers of bitumen in absorbed or surface residues adhering to archaeological pottery fragments at Neolithic sites in northeastern Syria and southwestern Iran. As part of a long-term study of the use and trade of bitumen in antiquity, Elf-Aquitane geochemist Jacques Connan isolated steranes (m/z 217) and terpanes (m/z 191) characteristic of bitumen in pigments used to decorate pottery from Late Neolithic Tell Sabi Abyad in northern Syria (Connan et al. 2004). Gregg et al. (2007) have subsequently confirmed the earliest recorded presence of bitumen in pottery vessels in the Middle East (7100 cal BC) in four pottery fragments from the Initial Village period sites at Ali Kosh and Chageh Sefid in southwestern Iran. Using isotopic characterization techniques pioneered by Connan (∂D, EA-IRMS and $\partial^{13}C$, IRMS), Gregg et al. (2007) have also shown that the bitumen source lies within geological formations near Susa and Deh Luran in Khuzestan. Details of these findings and an assessment of the instrumental analytical techniques used in the Gregg et al. study (2007) are presented in the next chapter in the context of my preliminary extraction of organic residues from pottery fragments from early agricultural villages in the Middle East using 'conventional' solvent recovery techniques.

2.11 *Rationale for the choice of instrumental analytical techniques initially used in this study*

Given the poor preservation of complex carbohydrates, proteins, and DNA in archaeological sediments, the absence of species-specific lipid biomarkers for starch grains, and false positive results of previous efforts that targeted biomarkers associated with alcohol, potential identification of direct chemical evidence for these substances in archaeological pottery is quite limited through the use of current molecular or isotopic approaches. Although a number of the extraction protocols and instrumental analytical methods outlined above can possibly be used in the identification of organic residues in archaeological pottery, the most successful studies conducted to date have been those using gas chromatography and mass spectrometry (GC-MS) and gas chromatography and combustion isotope ratio mass spectrometry (GC-C-IRMS) instrumental techniques (Dudd and Evershed 1998; Evershed et al. 2002; Copley et al. 2003, 2005a-d; Craig et al. 2005; 2007). In light of their apparent success in the characterization of animal fats from the earliest pottery horizons in Europe, and the scope of my doctoral research question, I made a decision to use these analytical techniques in my examination of pottery fragments recovered from 20 Neolithic sites in the Middle East.

In subsequent chapters, I present the results of my preliminary examination of 244 pottery fragments from 12 Neolithic sites using 'conventional' solvent extraction and saponification recovery techniques, and provide a detailed description of the first use of a microwave-assisted liquid chromatography protocol (initially developed for the isolation and concentration of free fatty acids in marine sediments) in the recovery of organic compounds from archaeological pottery. These chapters include research identifying the molecular and isotopic evidence of bitumen use in Neolithic Iran (Gregg et al. 2007), subsistence practices and pottery use in Neolithic Jordan (Gregg et al. 2009), and evidence for the increased recovery of diagnostic organic compounds from 65 pottery fragments from nine Neolithic sites in the Middle East through the microwave-assisted liquid chromatography protocol (Gregg and Slater in press). These yields are greater than any previously reported from Neolithic sites in the Fertile Crescent (Shimoyama and Ichikawa 2000; Copley et al. 2005b; Evershed et al. 2008), and include 16 of those that had previously not produced measurable results through 'conventional' solvent extraction. These findings are presented in the context of the emerging debate concerning the efficacy of modern stable carbon isotope values in characterizing organic residues embedded in pottery fragments recovered from the earliest ceramic horizons in the Middle East and Europe (Spangenberg et al. 2006; Evershed et al. 2008; Gregg et al. 2009; Gregg and Slater in press).

Chapter 3
The use of 'conventional' solvent extraction techniques in the recovery of organic residues from archaeological potsherds from 20 Neolithic sites in the Middle East

3.1.1 Preface: contributions of individual authors to the multi-authored paper on which this chapter is based

The methods and findings discussed in this chapter are from a previously-published, multi-authored paper that appeared in a peer-reviewed volume entitled *Archaeological Chemistry: Analytical Techniques and Archaeological Interpretation*, published by the American Chemistry Society and Oxford University Press (Gregg et al. 2007). My collaborators were Dr. Benjamin Stern and Ms Rhea Brettell of the Department of Archaeological Sciences at the University of Bradford. Dr. Stern provided me with instruction on the recovery of organic residues from archaeological pottery using 'conventional' solvent extraction and alkaline hydrolysis techniques, and training in gas chromatography and mass spectrometry instrumental analytical methods. My extraction and analysis of residues surviving in archaeological pottery from the nine Neolithic sites is described below in sections 3.3 and 3.4. Dr. Stern provided me with guidance in the interpretation and categorization of molecular compounds.

Following my preliminary identification of molecular compounds surviving in pottery fragments from the sites of Ali Kosh and Chageh Sefid as those of bitumen, I subsequently obtained bitumen from a geological source nearby the archaeological sites, and 'bituminous earth' recovered from the Late Neolithic pastoral encampment at Tepe Tula'i in Khuzestan (Hole 1972) from the Iranian National Museum in Tehran. Using the same conventional solvent extraction methods and instrumental analytical techniques, Ms Brettell undertook GC-MS analysis on the modern bitumen and archaeological 'bituminous earth' samples working under the direction of Dr. Stern. Dr. Stern also made a small financial contribution towards the subsequent isotopic analysis of the bitumen by Iso-Analytical Limited from a grant provided by the Natural and Environmental Research Council of the United Kingdom.

I presented our findings at the Symposium on Archaeological Chemistry held at the National Meeting of the American Chemical Society, March 26-27, 2006 in Atlanta, Georgia. Following selection of our paper for inclusion in the edited volume by the symposium organizers, I drafted a paper for review by my colleagues, and subsequently submitted it for peer review and publication.

3.1.2 Introduction

In the fall of 2003, I began a preliminary examination of organic residues surviving in 80 pottery fragments from nine Neolithic settlements in the Middle East at the Department of Archaeological Sciences at the University of Bradford. These potsherds were recovered from a number of early ceramic horizons in the Fertile Crescent, including the sites of Abu Hureyra, Ali Kosh, Çayönü, Chageh Sefid, Furukabad, Kashkashok, Tepe Guran, Tepe Sarab, and Toll-e Bashi. Potsherds from Ali Kosh, Çayönü, Chageh Sefid, and Tepe Guran were recovered from horizons directly overlaying aceramic levels at these sites. Laboratory sample numbers, excavation recovery numbers, site publication references, and approximate radiocarbon dates can be found in Appendix A.1.1). The majority of potsherds were acquired from the collections of excavators, but I also recovered 12 pottery fragments specifically for organic residue analysis from excavations at Toll-e Bashi in southwestern Iran (Bernbeck et al. 2005; Gregg in press). Since the majority (80%) of pottery fragments were body sherds, possible correlations between pottery use and vessel form were not considered, and a detailed analysis of forming operations, surface treatments, and fabric inclusions was not undertaken.

3.2 'Conventional' solvent extraction

Working under the supervision of Dr. Benjamin Stern and Dr. Carl Heron at Bradford, I extracted residues from 80 pottery fragments following the 'conventional' solvent extraction method for archaeological pottery outlined by Stern et al. (2000). Potsherds were subsampled by grinding portions (0.1 g) into a fine powder using a high-speed modeling drill fitted with an abrasive tungsten bit. The lipid fractions were then obtained by repeated (X3) solvent extraction using dichloromethane: methanol (DCM/MeOH, 2:1, v/v) with ultrasonication to aid dissolution. Separation of the solid and soluble fractions was assisted by centrifuging at 2000 rpm for five minutes, with the solvent soluble fractions decanted and combined. The soluble fractions were evaporated to virtual dryness under a gentle stream of nitrogen gas and reactivated in 1 ml of DCM for analysis by gas chromatography (GC) and mass spectrometry (MS). Each sample was then derivatized with a single drop of BSTFA (bis-Trimethylsilyl-trifluoroacetamide) with 1% TMCS (trimethylsilyl) to improve gas chromatography peak resolution.

Extensive precautions were taken in this study to prevent contamination during the preparation of samples and the extraction and analysis of organic residues. Pottery fragments were ground into a fine powder under controlled conditions in a clean laboratory. Potsherds were handled with sterile rubber gloves and powder collected on sterile sheets of aluminum foil. The abrasive tungsten bit was rinsed successively (X3) with DCM between samples. Glassware was washed, combusted, and rinsed sequentially with MeOH, DCM and Hexane before use. Sample blanks were prepared and extracted following the same protocol as outlined above, and used to isolate any contaminants that may have been introduced during the extraction or analytical procedures. Plasticizers absorbed by the fragments stored in plastic bags were readily identified by their chromatographic

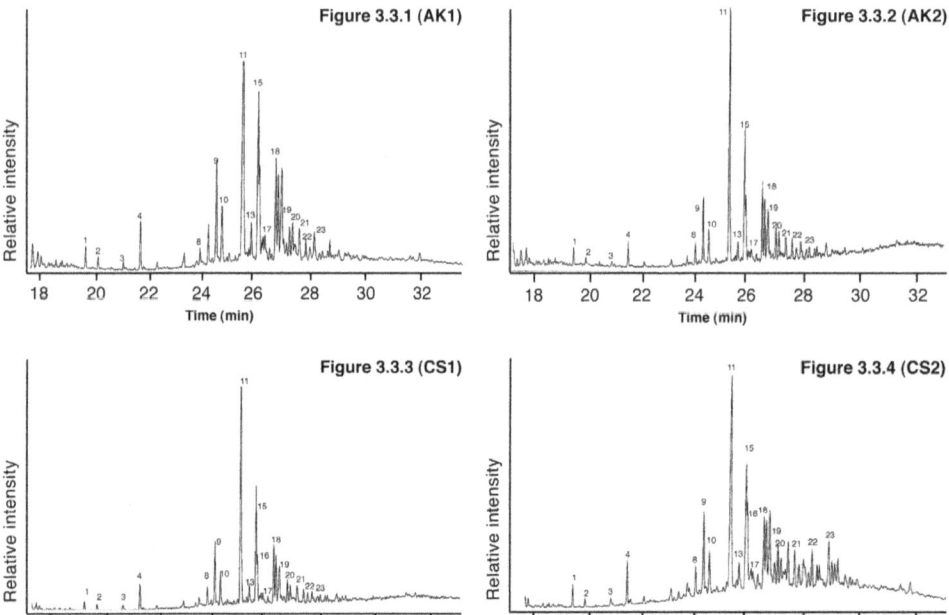

Figures 3.3.1 — 3.3.4 Selected ion chromatograms (m/z 191) of potsherd extracts from Ali Kosh and Chageh Sefid. These extracts exhibited abundances, elution orders, and molecular weights characteristic of petroleum. The key to terpane identification is shown in Table 3.3.1.

Peak number	Brief identification	Name/structure
1	23/3	C_{23} tricyclopolyprenane
2	24/3	C_{24} tricyclopolyprenane
3	25/3	C_{25} tricyclopolyprenane
4	24/4	C_{24} tetracyclic terpane
5	26/3	C_{26} tricyclopolyprenane
6	28/3	C_{28} tricyclopolyprenane
7	29/3	C_{29} tricyclopolyprenane
8	Ts	18α-22,29,30-trisnorneohopane
9	Tm	17α-22,29,30-trisnorhopane
10	28__H	17α,21β-29,30-dinorhopane
11	29__H	17α,21β-30-norhopane
12	30Me__H	2α-methyl-β-norhopane
13	29__H	17β,21α-30-norhopane
14	?	Possibly oleanane ($C_{30}H_{52}$)
15	30__H	17α,21β-hopane
16	31Me__H	2α-methyl-αβ-hopane
17	30__H	17β,21α-hopane (moretane)
18	31__HS+R	17α,21β-homohopane (22S) + (22R)
19	Gammacerane	$C_{30}H_{52}$
20	32__HS+R	17α,21β-homodishopane (22S) + (22R)
21	33__HS+R	17α,21β-trishomohopane (22S) + (22R)
22	34__HS+R	17α,21β-tetrakishomohopane (22S) + (22R)
23	35__HS+R	17α,21β-pentakishomohopane (22S) + (22R)
24	36__HS+R	17α,21β-sextakishomohopane (22S) + (22R)

Table 3.3.1
Key to chromatograms in Figures 3.3.1 - 3.3.4

elution orders and abundances, and confirmed through statistical matching of mass spectra of reference compounds in the ChemStation mass spectra database. The mass spectra of common organic contaminants can be found in Middleditch's *Analytical Artifacts* (1989).

3.3 *GC-MS analysis and preliminary molecular characterization of residues recovered through 'conventional' solvent extraction*

GC-MS analysis of total lipid extracts was conducted using a Hewlett Packard 5890 series II GC, fitted with a 15 m x 0.25 mm id, 0.1 mm film thickness OV1 phase fused silica column (MEGA) connected to a 5972 series mass selective detector. The splitless injector and interface were maintained at 300°C and 340°C respectively. The helium carrier gas was held at a constant inlet pressure of 1 psi. The GC oven was temperature programmed at 50°C for 2 minutes then increased by 10°C per minute to a maximum of 340°C, at which the temperature was held for 10 minutes. The column was directly inserted into the ion source where electron impact (70 eV) spectra were obtained.

Preliminary GC and GC-MS analysis revealed that only 5 of 80 potsherds demonstrated evidence for the survival of residues (Figures 3.3.1 – 3.3.4; 3.8.1). One pottery fragment from Çayönü (CU5; Figure 3.8.1) exhibited relative abundances of $C_{16:0}$ and $C_{18:0}$ fatty acids characteristic of degraded animal fats rather than plant lipids (Evershed et al. 1992; Heron & Evershed 1995), while two potsherds from Ali Kosh (AK1, AK2) and two from Chageh Sefid (CS1, CS2) exhibited abundances, elution orders, and molecular weights characteristic of petroleum (Figures 3.3.1 – 3.3.4) (Connan et al. 2004, Killop and Killop 2005; Gregg et al. 2007). The results from three samples (TS4, TS6, AH2) were equivocal, with lipid abundances falling below the threshold where molecular compounds could be securely characterized. The chromatograms of the Ali Kosh and Chageh Sefid samples revealed molecular and characteristic fragment ions of various lipid classes, including biomarkers of petroleum such as terpanes (*m/z* 191) and steranes (*m/z* 217) (Connan et al. 2004; Killops and Killops 2005).

3.4 *Further molecular and isotopic characterization of bitumen residues*

Following identification of various lipid classes indicative of petroleum in the four pottery fragments, I consequently obtained archaeological bitumen samples recovered from Ali Kosh, Chageh Sefid and the nearby site at Tepe Tula'i from the Iranian National museum in Tehran (Figure 3.4.1 left; Table 3.4.1). I also collected modern bitumen (Table 3.4.1) for comparative purposes from a seep at Chershme Ghir, (*spring of tar* in Farsi) where the foothills of the Zagros mountains meet the Mesopotamian plain, near Deh Luran in Khuzestan (N 32° 41' 26"; E 47° 19' 56"). Subsequent molecular and isotopic analysis (∂D and $\partial^{13}C$) of the archaeological materials and modern bitumen was undertaken at the University of Bradford and Iso-Analytical Limited, Cheshire in collaboration with Dr. Ben Stern and Ms Rhea Brettell (Gregg et al. 2007). The primary aim of our analysis was to confirm the excavators' contention that the interior surfaces of pottery fragments (Figure 3.4.1, right) recovered from the earliest ceramic horizons at Ali Kosh

Figure 3.4.1
Left, reed-impressed, bitumen-encrusted, mudbrick fragments (AK) from Ali Kosh; Right, pottery fragment (AK1) recovered from the Mohammad Jaffar phase at Ali Kosh, This pottery horizon has been AMS dated between 7300 and 7000 cal BC (Hole 2000).

and Chageh Sefid were coated with a thin layer of bitumen (Hole et al 1969; Hole 1976), and to identify the most likely geological source (Gregg et al. 2007).

3.5 Molecular characterization of archaeological residues and modern bitumen samples

Diagnostic molecular compounds were recovered from archaeological and modern bitumen samples using conventional solvent extraction protocol and instrumental analytical techniques outlined in sections 3.2 and 3.3. GC-MS analysis revealed that these compounds demonstrated an essential molecular similarity with terpane distribution patterns previously obtained from the archaeological potsherds (Figures 3.3.1 — 3.3.4), and showed parallels in the range and relative abundances of the diagnostic hopanes (examples are shown in Figure 3.5.1 — 3.5.3 and Table 3.5.1). The dominant families present were identified as $17\alpha(H),21\beta(H)$-hopanes, Ts ($18\alpha(H)$-22,29,30-trisnorneohopane) and Tm ($17\alpha(H)$-22,29,30-trisnorhopane) and tricyclopolyprenanes, with subordinate molecular classes being the methyl-$\alpha\beta$-hopanes, $17\beta(H),21\alpha(H)$-hopanes and hexahydrobenzohopanes. As a result, residues in potsherds and 'bituminous earth' collected during excavation can clearly be identified as bitumen, and confirm the earliest recorded presence of bitumen in pottery vessels in the Middle East ca 7100 cal BC (Gregg et al. 2007). The pottery fragments from Ali Kosh and Chageh Sefid were recovered from the earliest ceramic (Mohammad Jaffar) phase at the two sites with two new radiocarbon dates from Ali Kosh (Zeder and Hesse 2000; Hole 2000) placing this horizon between 7313 and 7040 cal BC (68% confidence; OxCal 2009). Fragments of bitumen lined baskets and matting were also recovered from two earlier aceramic phases at Ali Kosh and Chageh Sefid (Hole and Flannery 1967; Hole et al. 1969), with four radiocarbon dates (Zeder and Hesse 2000; Hole 2000) placing them between 7688 and 7000 cal BC (68% confidence; OxCal 2009).

	Find	Description	State	Color
Archaeological pottery samples	AK1	Pottery fragment with visible residue from Ali Kosh	Sherd	Dark brown
	AK2	Pottery fragment from Ali Kosh	Sherd	Orange brown
	CS1	Pottery fragment with visible residue from Chageh Sefid	Sherd	Dark brown
	CS2	Pottery fragment from Chageh Sefid	Sherd	Orange brown
Archaeological bitumen samples	AK	Bitumen recovered from Ali Kosh excavations	Earthy chunks	Brown Cream layers
	TT1	Bitumen recovered from Tepe Tula'i excavations	Earthy chunks	Brown Pink/cream layers
	TT2	Bitumen recovered from Tepe Tula'i excavations	Earthy chunks	Yellow-brown Cream inclusions
	TTD1.02	Bitumen recovered from Tepe Tula'i excavations	Earthy chunks	Grey/brown
Modern bitumen	CM	Bitumen from modern seep at Chershme Ghir	Viscous liquid	Black

Table 3.4.1 Archaeological pottery, and archaeological and modern bitumen samples.

Identification of bitumen sources through the use of GC-MS relies upon of the presence or absence of biomarker hopanes such as oleanane and gammacerane, and assessment of ratios of their relative abundance (Connan et al 2004; Killops and Killops 2005). Oleanane has been described by Jacques Connan (1999:40) as "a unique genuine chronostratigraphic biomarker" relating oil type to specific geological periods. The archaeological bitumen samples and the modern bitumen from Chershme Ghir all have minor chromatographic peaks in the expected location of oleanane, but this biomarker can only be tentatively identified through molecular criteria since the mass spectra do not show the required molecular ion and fragments. There is no clear indication of oleanane in any of the archaeological pottery fragments. These findings are somewhat unexpected, since oleanane has never been observed in bitumen from Iraq and Syria, and is generally abundant in sources from Iran, particularly those in Khuzestan and Fars provinces (Connan 1999). This lack of clearly identifiable oleanane may be due to the degraded nature of the samples or to instrumental analytical factors such as overlap of chromatographic peaks. However, gammacerane is present in all the residues obtained from

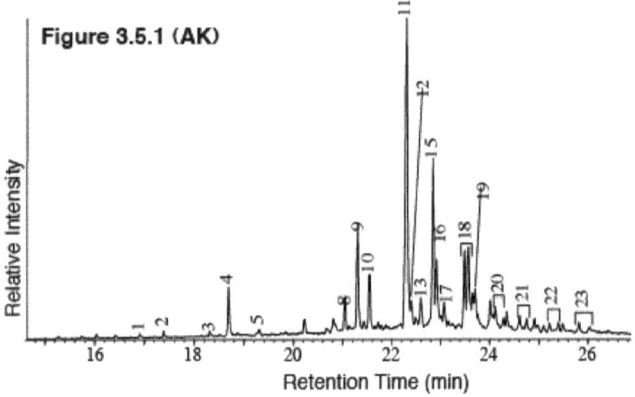

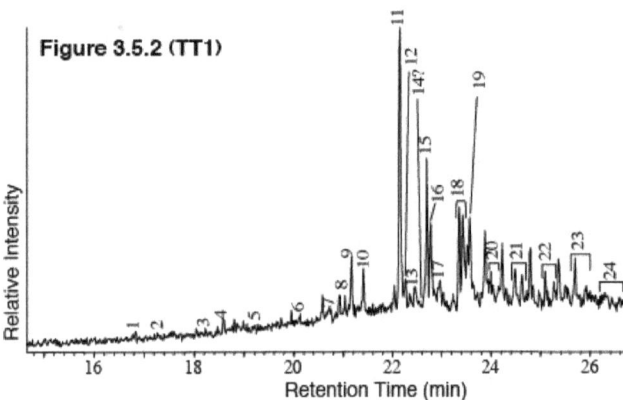

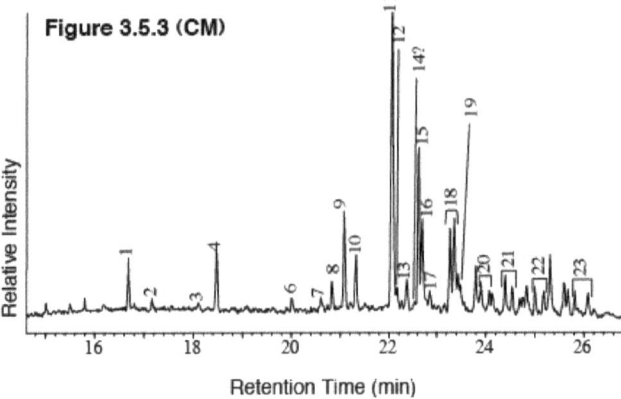

Figures 3.5.1 – 3.5.3
Partial ion chromatograms of terpanes (m/z 191) from archaeological bitumen samples (AK and TTI), and modern bitumen from the seep at Chershme Ghir (CM).

the archaeological pottery as well as the archaeological and modern bitumen samples (Figures 3.3.1-3.3.4; 3.5.1-3.5.3). The low abundance of gammacerane and the general pattern of the hopane abundance clearly relate all the archaeological samples to patterns observed in Iranian sources and distinguish them from bitumen from any of the Dead Sea sources or those at Jebel Bishri in northern Syria (Harrell et al. 2002; Haven et al.1989; Connan and Deschene 1998).

Because the biomarker fingerprints in all the archaeological samples display significant degradation with steranes showing particularly low abundance, it was not possible to use sterane-to-terpane ratios for source determination (Stern et al. 2007). However, the relationship between the terpanes themselves was of some utility in differentiating among bitumen sources.

Although the ratio of different terpanes to each other does not provide a secure basis for separation between samples, it does offer an indication of their maturity. The ratio of Tm to Ts terpanes increases with time (Stern et al. 2007). The ratio of Ts to Tm terpanes can also be compared to the ratio of gammacerane to $C_{30}\alpha\beta$ hopane, with ratios of less than 0.4 falling within the range of previously analyzed materials from Iranian oil seeps, most likely from the region in Khuzestan near Susa (Connan et al. 2004; Connan personal communication). Figure 3.5.4 compares the ratios of these compounds to one another using the GC-MS data obtained from potsherd extracts, and archaeological and modern bitumen. Numerical values of these diagnostic ratios are provided in Table 3.5.1. Ratios from one archaeological bitumen sample (TT1) and 2 potsherd extracts (AK1, CS2) are beyond the range of previously analyzed materials from Iranian oil seeps, but this may be due to the degraded nature of these samples.

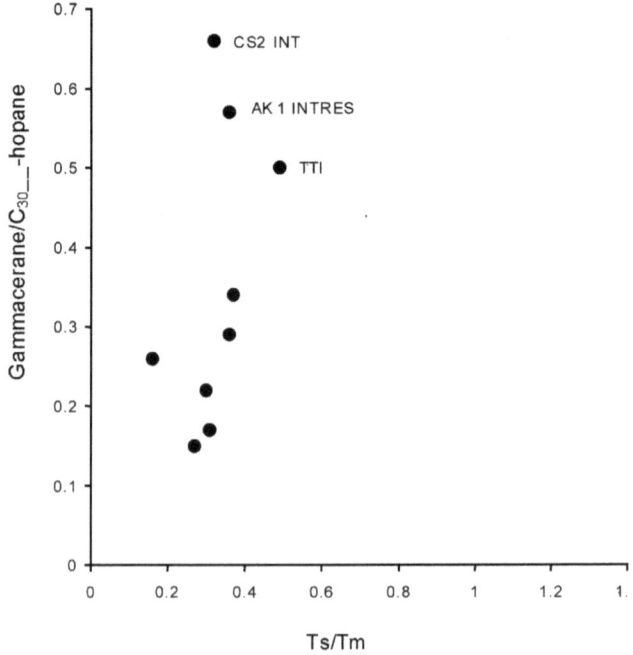

Figure 3.5.4
Comparison of ratios of Ts to Tm terpanes to the ratio of gammacerane-to-$C_{30}\alpha\beta$ hopane from potsherd extracts and archaeological and modern bitumen examined in the Gregg et al. 2007 study. Gammacerane-to-$C_{30}\alpha\beta$ hopane ratios of 0.4 or less are consistent with previously published observed values of materials from southwestern Iran (Stern et al. 2007).

Table 3.5.1
Numerical values of ratios of diagnostic Ts and Tm terpane lipid species represented in Fig. 3.5.

	Sample	GC RN/30αH	Ts/Tm
Archaeological pottery samples	AK1	0.57	0.36
	AK2	0.29	0.36
	CS1	0.15	0.27
	CS2	0.66	0.32
Archaeological bitumen samples	AK	0.22	0.30
	TTI	0.50	0.49
	TT2	0.26	0.16
	TTD1.02	0.34	0.37
Modern bitumen	CM	0.17	0.31

3.6 Further $\partial^{13}C$ and ∂D isotopic characterization of asphaltene fraction in bitumen residues

In order to identify the most likely geological source of the bitumen, further characterization of bulk isotopic analysis ($\partial^{13}C$ and ∂D) of the asphaltene fraction was undertaken. This fraction provides the most representative isotopic composition of the sample rather than the 'total extract' as used for GC-MS analysis (Connan et al 2004). The asphaltene was obtained by repeated (X3) washing of a portion of the 'total extract' in 5 ml of n-hexane with ultrasonication to aid dissolution. The 'total extract' had previously been obtained through the 'conventional' solvent extraction protocol outlined in section 3.2. Separation of the solid asphaltene fraction was assisted by centrifuging and careful decanting of the solvent. Any remaining solvent was then removed by placing the vial containing the asphaltene fraction on a warm hot-plate under a stream of nitrogen gas.

Bulk carbon isotopic values were obtained using continuous-flow isotope ratio mass spectrometry (IR-MS), with samples flash-combusted in a column containing chromium oxide (Cr_2O_3) and silvered cobalt (I) oxide held at a temperature of 1020°C. The resultant gases were then reduced to CO_2 in a column of elemental copper at 680°C and passed through a water trap of magnesium perchlorate before being separated in a GC column for introduction to a Finnigan delta plus XL mass analyzer. The reference CO_2 gas was standardized against the international standard IAEA600 (∂ -27.5 ± 0.2) and three methionine standards (∂ -26.6) were run as quality control check samples during batch analysis.

Hydrogen values were obtained by elemental analyzer-isotope ratio mass spectrometry (EA-IR-MS), the samples being released into a furnace set at 1080°C and thermally decomposed to H_2 and CO over glassy carbon. Any traces of water were then removed by a magnesium perchlorate trap and any CO_2 by a Carbosorb trap before the H_2 was resolved by a packed column gas chromatograph held at 35°C. The resultant chromatographic peak was then passed into the ion source of the IR-MS, ionized and accelerated, and gas species of different mass separated in a magnetic field. These were simultaneously measured on a Faraday cup universal collector array with masses 2 and 3 being monitored for deuterium.

Comparison of the bulk $\partial^{13}C$ and ∂D isotope ratios of the asphaltene fractions obtained from potsherd extracts and archaeological and modern bitumen clearly distinguishes these values from the published isotopic data on bituminous materials from the Dead Sea, Iraq, Lebanon and Syria (Stern et al. 2004). The $\partial^{13}C$ and ∂D isotope ratios of materials examined in this study (Figure 3.6.1) are all within the range of Iranian seeps from Khuzestan and Luristan (Stern et al. 2004), and those obtained from bituminous residues identified from the Achaemenid site at Susa (Connan & Deschene 1998). The bulk $\partial^{13}C$ and ∂D isotopic values for the asphaltene fraction of materials examined in this study are plotted in Figure 3.6.1. Numerical values of these isotopic ratios are provided in Table 3.6.1. The specific location of the seep or seeps used as the source of bitumen in the archaeological pottery from Ali Kosh and Chageh Sefid has yet to be identified (Gregg et al. 2007). The results from the nearest known modern seep, Chershme Ghir, or Jacques Connan's unpublished data from three other seeps within the immediate vicinity of the sites (Connan personal communication), do not adequately match the isotopic values obtained from the potsherds or archaeological bitumen (Table 3.6.1; Figure 3.6.1).

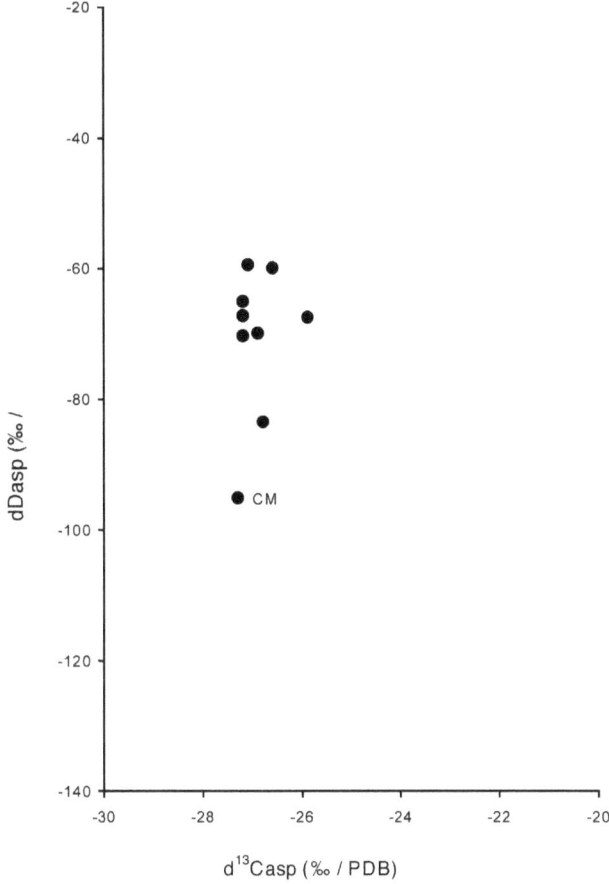

Figure 3.6.1
Plot of bulk $\partial^{13}C$ (‰ / PDB) v. ∂D (‰ / SMOW) isotopic values for the asphaltene fraction of materials examined in this study. All fall within the range of Iranian seeps from Khuzestan and Luristan (Stern et al. 2004). Results from the nearest known modern seep Chershme Ghir (CM), do not adequately match isotopic values obtained from potsherds or archaeological bitumen to confidently identify it as the bitumen source.

	Sample	$\delta^{13}C$	δD
Archaeological pottery samples	AK1	-27.2	-70
	AK2	-26.9	-70
	CS1	-25.9	-68
	CS2	-26.8	-83
Archaeological bitumen samples	AK	-27.2	-67
	TTI	-27.2	-65
	TT2	-26.6	-60
	TTD1.02	-27.1	-59
Modern bitumen	CM	-27.3	-95

Table 3.6.1
Numerical values of the bulk $\partial^{13}C$ and ∂D isotopic values for the asphaltene fraction of materials examined in this study and plotted in Figure 3.6.1.

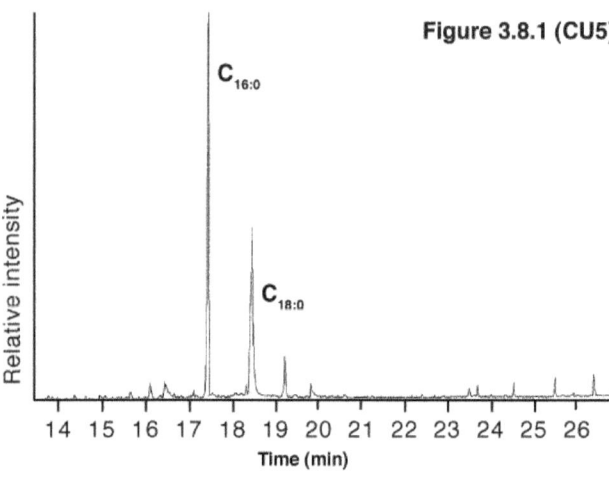

Figure 3.8.1 (CU5)

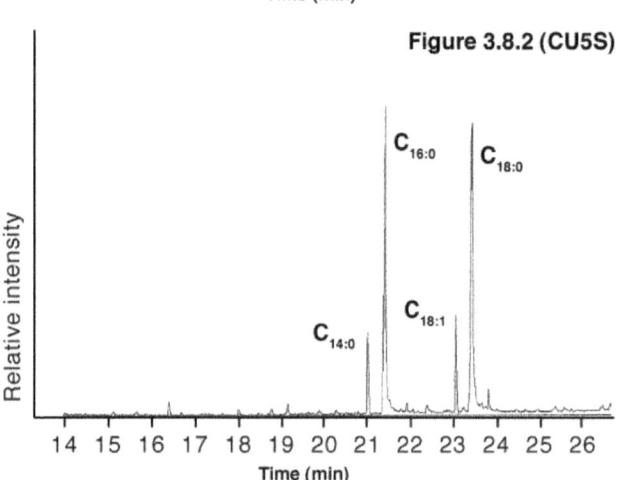

Figure 3.8.2 (CU5S)

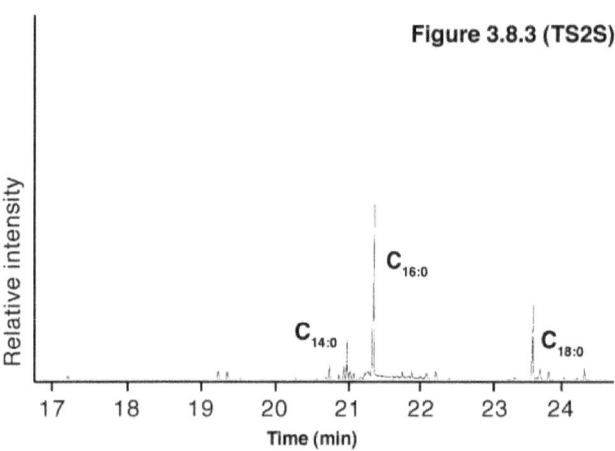

Figure 3.8.3 (TS2S)

Figures 3.8.1 – 3.8.3
Partial high-temperature chromatograms of potsherd extracts exhibiting abundances of free fatty acids through the use of 'conventional' solvent extraction (Figure 3.8.1, CU5) and through use of saponification extraction techniques (Figure 3.8.2, CU5S; Figure 3.8.3, TS2S).

The $\partial^{13}C$ value of the modern bitumen from Chershme Ghir (CM) is similar to values from the potsherd extracts and archaeological bitumen samples but its ∂D value is considerably lighter than those of the other materials. A comprehensive survey of bitumen sources in the region and further molecular and isotopic analysis would be required to fully address this issue. However, the results outlined above demonstrate that the bitumen from archaeological contexts at these important Neolithic sites shares many molecular and isotopic characteristics with regional modern sources in Khuzestan and Luristan.

3.7 *Further extraction of residues from four pottery fragments using saponification and BSTFA derivatization techniques*

Organic residues were again distilled from the three equivocal samples (TS2, TS6, AH2) and the one sample (CU5) that had yielded measurable abundance of fatty acids through the 'conventional' solvent method outlined in section 3.2. Increased fatty acid yields from archaeological potsherds had been observed by Stern et al. (2000) through use of a saponification / diazomethane derivatization protocol. Saponification is an alkaline hydrolysis process in which a base is used to induce a fatty-acid methyl ester to yield a carboxylic acid salt. An "S" was added to sample numbers to denote the use of saponification in the extraction of residues. Potsherds were subsampled by grinding portions (0.1 g) into a fine powder using a high-speed modeling drill fitted with an abrasive tungsten bit. The lipid fractions were obtained by adding 3ml of 0.5M methanolic NaOH to each sample and heating at 70°C for 3 hours in a sealed glass vial. After cooling, the supernatant was neutralized though the addition of a small quantity of HCl and tested with pH strips, and lipids were extracted with three aliquots of 3 ml hexane. The three aliquots were then combined, evaporated to virtual dryness under a gentle stream of nitrogen gas, and reactivated in 1ml of DCM in preparation for GC-MS analysis. On the advice of Dr. Stern, each sample was then derivatized with a single drop of BSTFA (bis-Trimethylsilyl-trifluoroacetamide) with 1% TMCS (trimethylsilyl) to improve gas chromatography peak resolution, rather than through the use of the diazomethane derivatization protocol used in Stern et al. (2000).

3.8 *GC-MS analysis and molecular characterization of residues recovered through saponification and BSTFA derivatization techniques*

GC-MS analysis was conducted as outlined above in section 3.3. However, the incremental increases in GC oven temperature were reprogrammed to facilitate greater peak separation of fatty acids surviving in the saponified potsherd extracts. Sample (CU5S) exhibited abundances of both saturated and unsaturated fatty acids (Figure 3.8.2), while this pottery fragment had yielded only $C_{16:0}$ and $C_{18:0}$ saturated fatty acids through 'conventional' solvent extraction (Figure 3.8.1). The saponified extract recovered from the Tepe Sarab potsherd (TS2S) also exhibited evidence for the survival of $C_{14:0}$ in addition to $C_{16:0}$ and $C_{18:0}$ saturated fatty acids (Figure 3.8.3).

3.9 *'Conventional' solvent extraction and GC analysis of 164 additional pottery fragments*

Following my preliminary examination of materials at Bradford, I attempted to extract residues from 164 additional pottery fragments from 11 Neolithic and Chalcolithic sites in the Fertile Crescent using the 'conventional' solvent protocol outlined above in the Department of Chemistry at the University of Toronto. Sample numbers, site publication references, and approximate radiocarbon dates can be found in Appendix A.1, Table A.1.2. For the sake of expediency, only GC analysis of potsherd extracts was undertaken, using a Perkin Elmer XL GC, fitted with a 15 m x 0.25 mm id, 0.1 mm film thickness OV1 phase-fused silica column (MEGA). The splitless injector and interface were maintained at 300°C and 340°C respectively. The helium carrier gas was held at a constant inlet pressure of 1 psi. The GC oven was temperature programmed at 50°C for 2 minutes then increased by 10°C per minute to a maximum of 340°C, and held there for 10 minutes. GC analysis revealed that none of these potsherd extracts exhibited measurable lipid abundances or elution orders characteristic of degraded plant oils or animal fats, nor the humped profiles characteristic of bitumen. As a result further mass spectroscopy of these potsherd extracts was not undertaken.

3.10 *Assessment of my preliminary results and the efficacy of extraction methods*

Slightly over 2% of the potsherds examined in this study produced measurable results through use of 'conventional' solvent extraction. Five of 244 pottery fragments yielded diagnostic compounds solely through 'conventional' solvent extraction, and only one of three samples that had previously produced equivocal results through solvent extraction exhibited measurable quantities of free fatty acids through use of the saponification / BSTFA derivatization method. Admittedly, only a very small number of pottery fragments (4) were saponified, and one of these (CU5S) did exhibit marked increases in the recovery of free fatty acids through use of this method. However, when I assessed my preliminary results and the efficacy of my extraction methods, I was also mindful of the recent findings of Copley et al. (2005e) in their examination of potsherd residues from late Neolithic Çatalhöyük. As I have previously noted, the 12% fatty acid yields obtained through saponification techniques in the Copley et al. study fell significantly below the 50-60% yields these researchers had 'routinely' obtained from Neolithic potsherds in Great Britain (Copley et al. 2005e). In hindsight, prolonged use of the 'conventional' solvent extraction protocol was a mistake, and greater lipid yields would likely have been realized through saponification and BSTFA derivitization.

However, in light of the poor recovery of diagnostic compounds during the preliminary stages of my study and the recently published findings from Çatalhöyük, I sought the advice of geochemist Dr. Greg Slater of the School of Geography and Earth Sciences at McMaster University. Slater suggested that increased fatty acid yields might be realized from Middle Eastern Neolithic potsherds through adaptation of a microwave-assisted liquid chromatography solvent protocol that had been developed for the isolation and concentration of free fatty acids in marine sediments. We agreed to collaborate on a pilot study examining residues from 10 pottery fragments from the late Neolithic site at al-Basatîn in northern Jordan using this protocol, and I subsequently received training in the systematic application of these liquid chromatography procedures. A detailed description this microwave-assisted extraction protocol and the instrumental analytical techniques employed in the molecular and isotopic characterization of organic residues recovered from al-Basatîn pottery fragments is presented in the following chapter.

Chapter 4
A new method for increasing fatty acid yields: microwave-assisted extraction of organic residues from archaeological pottery

4.1.1 Preface: Contributions of individual authors to the multi-authored and jointly-authored papers on which chapters 4 and 5 are based

The methods and findings discussed in this and the following two chapter are from multi-authored and jointly-authored papers that have appeared in the *Journal of Archaeological Science* (Gregg et al. 2009), or that have been accepted for publication in *Archaeometry* (Gregg and Slater in press). My collaborators on the multi-authored papers were Dr. Edward Banning and Dr. Kevin Gibbs of the Department of Archaeology at the University of Manchester, and Dr. Greg Slater of the School of Geography and Earth Sciences at McMaster University.

Dr. Banning introduced me to my research subject and oversaw the excavation of pottery fragments from the Late Neolithic site of al-Basatîn in northern Jordan examined in this study. Much of the archaeological contextual information used in the Gregg et al. (2009) paper draws on earlier work by Dr. Banning and his colleagues at the Late Neolithic site at Tabaqat al-Bûma (Banning et al. 1994; Banning et al. in press) as well as work at al-Basatîn (Banning et al. 2004; Banning et al. 2005). Dr. Banning made a financial contribution towards isotopic analysis of organic residues examined in this study from a grant provided by the Social Sciences and Humanities Research Council of Canada. Dr. Kevin Gibbs provided information on the pottery forms and clay fabric of vessels characteristic of the al-Basatîn assemblage, in addition to the drawings of pottery profiles used in the Gregg et al. (2009) paper.

Dr. Slater provided me with instruction on the use of the microwave extraction protocol outlined in this chapter and detailed in Appendix A.2, and I extracted fatty acids surviving in pottery fragments using this method. I subsequently collected modern reference fats for comparative purposes (section 5.4), and extracted fatty acids from the modern materials using the technique described in section 5.5. Dr. Slater's laboratory assistant Ms Jennie Kirby then ran instrumental molecular and isotopic analyses of archaeological and modern materials using the instrumental analytical methods described in sections 5.6 and 5.7. I then prepared plots of the $\partial^{13}C$ values of $C_{16:0}$ and $C_{18:0}$ fatty acids from the modern and archaeological samples for comparison with previously published ranges used in the categorization of potsherd extracts. Following review and discussion of these results with my colleagues, I wrote and circulated drafts of the multi-authored (Gregg et al. 2009) and jointly-authored (Gregg and Slater in press) papers.

4.1.2 Introduction

The microwave-assisted liquid chromatography solvent extraction protocol used in the pilot study of al-Basatîn potsherds was initially developed for the isolation, concentration, and transesterification of free fatty acids in marine sediments by Konrad Hughen and Timothy Eglinton of Woods Hole Oceanographic Institution. The non-fractionating nature of microwave-assisted extraction is well attested (Hayes 2002; Loupy 2002; Kappe and Stadler 2005), and this method has proven successful in recovering organic compounds from marine sediments for subsequent isotopic characterization of fatty acids (Hughen et al. 2004).

A total of twelve pottery fragments (Appendix A.1, Table A.1.3) were recovered specifically for organic residue analysis from the Late Neolithic site at al-Basatîn (WZ 135) in Wadi Ziqlab, northern Jordan, as part of an ongoing University of Toronto investigation of the late prehistory of the southern Levant (Banning et al. 2004; 2005; Gibbs et al. 2006; Kadowaki et al. 2008; Gregg et al. 2009). Many Neolithic artifacts were found during excavations in 2004 and 2006, including grinding stones, sickle elements, and almost 900 diagnostic pottery fragments. This pottery is handmade, crudely constructed and poorly fired, yet at times shows expressive surface treatment and similarity in form and decoration to assemblages of the Wadi Rabah culture in northern and western Israel (Garfinkel 1999a; Garfinkel and Matskevich 2002) and the project's earlier excavations at nearby Tabaqat al-Bûma (Banning et al. 1994; 2004; in press). The bulk of excavated faunal remains are those of sheep or goat, but domesticated cattle and pig are also important secondary livestock animals. Because of poor preservation of pig remains in the faunal assemblage, it was not possible to ascertain whether these were from wild boar or domesticated species.

Radiocarbon assays on visible charred organic residues on the interior surface of two pottery fragments (Figure 4.1.1) excavated in 2004 yielded dates of 5644-5538 cal BC (68% confidence, TO-12151, 6710 ± 70BP) and 5620-5483 cal BC (68% confidence, TO-12738, 6650 ± 40BP). However, these two potsherds (Figure 4.1.1 WZ04/RC1, WZ04/RC2) did not yield measurable quantities of diagnostic lipids through use of the 'conventional' solvent extraction protocol outlined in section 3.2 of the previous chapter.

The following procedures were consequently adopted for extraction of residues from 10 pottery fragments exhibiting evidence of charred remains found during the 2006 excavations. A more detailed step-by-step description of the microwave-assisted solvent extraction and liquid chromatography procedures can be found in Appendix A.2 for those wishing to employ this technique.

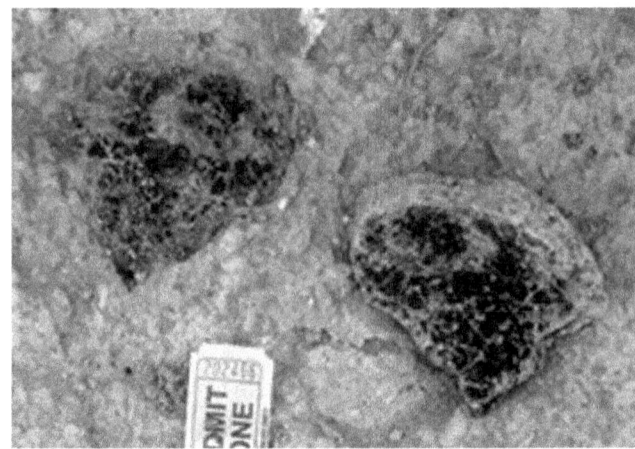

Figure 4.1.1
Two pottery fragments (WZ04/RC1, WZ04/RC2) with carbonized surface residues recovered specifically for chemical analysis from University of Toronto excavation of the Late Neolithic site at al-Basatîn in northern Jordan in 2004, and analyzed using 'conventional' solvent extraction methods.

4.2 Microwave extraction of lipids from archaeological pottery fragments

As the first samples to be tested with the microwave extraction protocol, 10 pottery fragments from al-Basatîn were subsampled by grinding portions of the charred remains adhering to interior surfaces and up to 2 mm of the ceramic matrix into a fine powder with a high-speed modeling drill fitted with an abrasive tungsten bit. The total organic fraction (TOF) surviving in 5 g of ceramic powder was extracted through application of 25 ml of dichloromethane and methanol organic solvents (DCM:MeOH, 90:10 v/v) in a microwave-accelerated reaction system (MARS). After microwave processing for 60 minutes at 100°C and 180 psi, solid and soluble fractions were separated by decanting through a pre-solvent-rinsed sterile micro-fiber filter. 5 ml of the TLF was archived, and the remaining soluble fraction was evaporated to virtual dryness under a gentle stream of nitrogen gas and reactivated in 1.5 ml of DCM in preparation for liquid chromatography separation.

4.3 Liquid chromatography separation of free fatty acids in potsherd extracts

In a multi-stage process, organic compounds potentially surviving in the soluble fraction were isolated from one another through sequential application of organic solvents of increasing polarity through fully activated SiO_2 and aminopropyl Pasteur pipette columns. To further the reader's understanding of this liquid chromatography protocol, the first stage is illustrated in Figure 4.3.1 and detailed below. Due to the similarity of subsequent stages, these procedures are only described, but not illustrated. In order to avoid contamination, glass materials were combusted and rinsed sequentially with methanol, DCM and hexane. Na_2SO_4, glass wool, and silica gel were also combusted before being used.

4.3.1 Silica gel columns

A 1.5ml charge from each sample was placed into a prepared Pasteur pipette column that had been plugged with a piece of pre-combusted glass wool, loaded with 4 cm of fully activated SiO_2, and rinsed with two bed volumes of hexane (Figure 4.3.1). The different organic fractions were eluted and collected, with 4ml of hexane yielding alkanes; 4ml of 1:1 toluene/hexane yielding polycyclic aromatic hydrocarbons; 4ml of 2% formic acid in DCM yielding fatty acids; and 4ml of 2% formic acid in MeOH yielding the most polar compounds. The fraction yielding free fatty acids was then evaporated to virtual dryness under a gentle stream of nitrogen gas and reanimated in 0.5ml DCM in preparation for further separation in aminopropyl columns.

4.3.2 Aminopropyl columns

A 0.5ml charge from each fraction yielding free fatty acids was then placed into a prepared Pasteur pipette column that had been plugged with a piece of pre-combusted glass wool, loaded with 3 cm of aminopropyl, and rinsed with two bed volumes of hexane. The original vial was rinsed twice with a small amount of DCM, and these rinses were transferred to the column as well. The different organic fractions were again eluted and collected, with 7 ml of 9:1 (v/v) DCM/Acetone yielding the less polar fraction; and 8 ml of 2% (v/v) formic acid in DCM yielding free fatty acids.

4.3.3 Transterification

The solvent in the fraction yielding free fatty acids was then evaporated completely under a gentle stream of nitrogen, and the fatty acids remaining in the vial were transesterified using a solution of 95:5 (v/v) MeOH/HCl as a catalyst to produce corresponding fatty acid methyl esters (FAMES). 10 ml of this solution was transferred to each vial containing fatty acids. The oxygen was purged from the headspace of each glass container under a gentle stream of nitrogen gas, capped quickly, and heated at 70°C for 12-15 hours. 20 ml of nano-pure water and 10 ml of hexane was then added to each vial and ultrasonicated for 5 minutes to aid in the partition of fatty acid methyl esters from the aqueous phase into hexane. The shift in isotope values due to addition of methyl carbon during transesterification of FAMES was corrected by the following mass balance equation:

$$\delta^{13}C_{measured} = f\, \delta^{13}C_{PLFA} + (1-f)\, \delta^{13}C_{CH3}$$

where $f = 16/17$ carbon atoms in the $C_{16:0}$ FAME; $f = 18/19$ carbon atoms in the $C_{18:0}$ FAME; and the $\delta^{13}C$ value of the methyl group = $-37.7‰$ (Hughen et al. 2004; Gregg et al. 2009; Gregg and Slater in press).

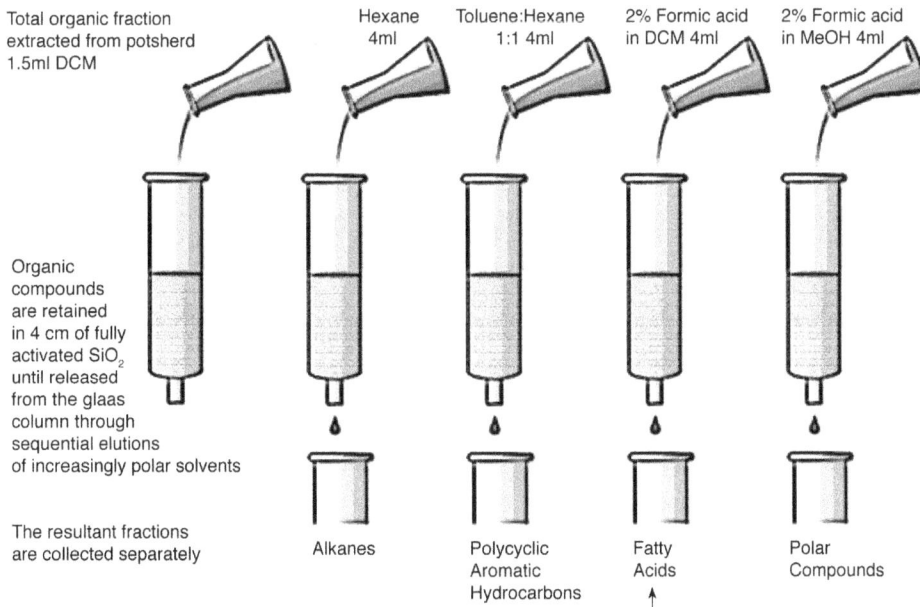

Figure 4.3.1
In the first stage of the liquid chromatography protocol, free fatty acids are separated from any other organic compounds that may survive in the potsherd extracts through sequential elutions of increasingly polar solvents in fully activated silica gel columns. The different organic fractions were eluted and collected as illustrated.

4.3.4 Na_2SO_4 Columns

The hexane and aqueous phases were allowed to separate completely after ultrasonication. Any water was removed from the hexane phase yielding FAMES by eluting the hexane through a prepared Pasteur pipette column loaded with 3 cm of anhydrous sodium sulphate. Partitioning of FAMES from the residual aqueous phase and removal of water was repeated twice. The hexane yielding FAMES was collected following each elution and combined.

4.3.5 Secondary liquid chromatography separation of FAMES from potsherd extracts

Each sample was then concentrated to a volume of 0.5 ml under a gentle stream of nitrogen gas, and transferred into a prepared Pasteur pipette column that had been plugged with a piece of pre-combusted glass wool, loaded with 2 cm of fully activated SiO_2, and rinsed with two bed volumes of hexane. The different organic fractions were again eluted and collected, with 4 ml of hexane yielding alkanes; 4ml of 5% ethyl acetate in hexane yielding FAMES; and 4 ml of MeOH yielding polar compounds. The fraction yielding FAMES was then solvent exchanged into 1 ml of hexane in preparation for analysis by gas chromatography and mass spectrometry (GC-MS).

4.4 Collection of modern animal fats for comparative purposes

In light of the conflicting ranges of $\delta^{13}C$ values of modern reference fats from northern and central Europe (Copley et al. 2003, 2005a-d; Spangenberg et al. 2006), I thought it prudent to compare the $\delta^{13}C$ values of $C_{16:0}$ and $C_{18:0}$ fatty acids of potsherd extracts from al-Basatîn to those of modern reference fats obtained from within the region. Modern adipose and dairy fats were obtained from ethnographically known, commercial, and government sources in Palestine, Israel and Jordan for comparison with organic residues recovered from potsherd extracts. Dairy fats from domesticated sheep (WD1), and adipose fats from domesticated goats (WC11, WC12) were provided by Bedouin herders living in Wadi Mujib in Jordan and Wadi Qilt in Palestine respectively. Adipose fats from wild boar (WC1, WC4, WC9, WC10) captured or killed in Wadi Qilt were provided by the Israel Nature and National Parks Protection Authority. Sheep adipose fat (MS1) was obtained from a commercial source in Israel. A fragment of a large pottery churn called a *dugran* was obtained from a small farming and herding community in central Anatolia (Table 5.4.1, KZ1micro; Appendix A.1.5). This churn had been used exclusively in the manufacture of raw butter *çig tereyagi*, yogurt *aryan* and curd cheese *cökelik* during the 1980s and 1990s (Ertug-Yaras 1997; Ertug 2008), and then discarded in a utility shed.

Because isotopic values of mammalian fats are greatly affected by the photosynthetic pathways of plants they consume (as described in Chapter 2, section 2.6; Morton and Schwarcz 2004; Pearson et al. 2007), adipose and dairy fats from modern cattle were not examined because of the widespread inclusion of non-native C_4 plants, such as corn, sorghum, and millet, in modern concentrated cattle feeding regimens in the Middle East. The ratio of C_3 and C_4 plants consumed by domesticated goats and sheep and wild boar in this study is uncertain, but Wadi Mujib, Wadi Qilt and Wadi Ziqlab all crosscut the modern Irano-Turanian phytogeographical region, an ecological niche known to sustain both C_3 and C_4 chenopods and temperate and tropical grasses (Shomer-Ilan et al. 1981; Vaks et al. 2006). A detailed reconstruction of the distribution of C_3 and C_4 plants in the Middle East during the early Holocene has yet to be undertaken, but the vegetation of both the Levant and central Anatolia included C_4 plants during the Neolithic period (Vaks et al 2006; Pearson et al 2007). The effects of C_3 and C_4 dietary input on the fractionation of carbon isotopes in fatty acid synthesis of animal fats, and implications for the categorization of organic residues are discussed further in chapters 5 and 6.

4.5 Extraction of free-fatty acids from modern reference fats

$C_{16:0}$ and $C_{18:0}$ saturated fatty acids were obtained from the modern reference materials described above following the extraction/methylation method of Ulberth and Henninger (1992). 5 mg of fat was mixed with 1 ml toluene and 3ml of 5% HCl in MeOH. The headspace of each vial containing the mixture was purged under a gentle stream of nitrogen gas and quickly capped. Samples were then heated to 70°C for 1 hour. Following cooling to room temperature, samples were neutralized through the addition of 5ml 6% NaOH/H$_2$O. 3 ml of toluene was added to each sample before vortexing. The methanolic and toluene fractions were then separated from one another by centrifuging, and the toluene fraction yielding fatty acids methyl esters decanted for instrumental analysis. In some samples, unsaturated C$_{18}$ fatty acids were found to be co-eluting too proximate to C$_{18:0}$ for sufficient resolution for isotopic analysis during GC-MS analysis. These unsaturated fatty acids were separated from the samples before GC-C-IRMS analysis through use of silver ion liquid chromatography (Morris 1966; Woodbury et al. 1995).

Organic residues were recovered from the modern pottery *dugran* used in the manufacture of yogurt using the microwave-assisted liquid chromatography protocol described above. Again, extensive precautions were taken to prevent contamination during the preparation of samples and the extraction and analysis of organic residues from the archaeological pottery and modern samples. Pottery fragments were ground into a fine powder under controlled conditions in a clean laboratory. Potsherds were handled with sterile rubber gloves and the fine ceramic powder was collected on sterile sheets of aluminum foil. The abrasive tungsten bit was rinsed successively (X3) with MeOH, DCM and hexane between samples. Glassware was washed, combusted, and rinsed sequentially with MeOH, DCM and hexane before use. The pressurized Teflon vessels used in microwave-assisted extraction were washed and then rinsed sequentially with MeOH, DCM and hexane successively (X3) before use. Procedural sample blanks were prepared and extracted following the same protocols.

4.6 GC-MS analysis
Organic residues extracted from the al-Basatîn potsherds and modern reference samples were examined using an Agilent 6890 GC equipped with a 5973 quadruple mass spectrophotometer in full scan mode. 1 μL of sample was introduced into the GC by splitless injection. The column used was a DB-XLB (J&W), 30 m x 0.320 mm with a 0.25 μm film thickness. The column was connected to a 1 m deactivated pre-column. Helium was the carrier gas. The temperature program was 50°C hold for 1 min, ramp to 130°C at 20 °C/min, ramp to 160°C at 4°C/min and finally ramp to 300°C at 8°C/min. C$_{16:0}$ and C$_{18:0}$ were quantified using external calibration. The molecular weights of C$_{16}$ and C$_{18}$ were compared to different concentration levels of calibration standards C$_{14}$ (methyl myristate) and C$_{20}$ (methyl arachidate), compounds with similar molecular weights and retention times to calculate the actual concentrations. Further concentration of the samples was required to determine if there was enough mass to analyze the samples by IRMS. The mass spectrophotometer was operated in the electron-ionization mode, scanning the m/z range 40-750. Acquisition and data analysis was performed using ChemStation 2.00 software.

4.7 GC-C-IRMS analysis
Saturated fatty acids by themselves are of limited diagnostic value in the molecular characterization of organic residues, and further compound-specific isotopic analysis was undertaken to characterize the δ^{13}C values of the animal fats the al-Basatîn vessels once contained. Samples were either diluted or concentrated in hexane for analysis by Gas Chromatography-Combustion-Isotope Ratio Mass Spectrophotometry (GC-C- IRMS). Gas chromatographic analysis was performed on an Agilent 6890 GC coupled to a Thermo-Finigan DeltaPlus XP isotope ratio mass spectrometer via a Conflo-III interface. The sample separation was performed on the same columns as for the GC/MS analysis, for ease of comparison and identification of components. Injection was achieved through a splitless injector at 325°C with an injection volume of 2 μL. The column was connected to a 1 meter deactivated pre-column. Helium was the carrier gas. The temperature program was 50°C hold for 1 min, ramp to 150°C at 10°C/min, ramp to 180°C at 1.5°C/min with a 20 minute hold, ramp to 280°C at 10°C/min and finally ramp to 320°C at 15°C/min with a 15 minute hold. Acquisition and data analysis were performed using ISODAT 2.03 software. Analytical accuracy was confirmed via isotopically characterized standards run before and after each set of samples. Accuracy and precision on standard analyses were better than 0.5 per mil (2 sigma) and precision on triplicate sample analysis was between 0.04 and 0.83 per mil (2 sigma). Mean ∂^{13}C and standard deviation values of C$_{16:0}$ to C$_{18:0}$ fatty acids recovered from potsherd extracts and modern reference fats are included in presentation of the results in Chapter 5, Table 5.3.1.

The δ^{13}C values of C$_{16:0}$ and C$_{18:0}$ fatty acids recovered from modern reference materials were not corrected for possible changes in stable carbon isotope ratios resulting from the release of fossil fuel carbon between the Neolithic and Chalcolithic periods and today. Based on a study of the isotopic composition of CO$_2$ trapped in Antarctic ice cores (Whalen 1994), Spangenberg et al. (2007) have recently corrected the δ^{13}C ratios of C$_{16:0}$ and C$_{18:0}$ fatty acids of modern reference fats by 1.6 ‰ to facilitate what they believe to be a more accurate comparison between their archaeological data from a Neolithic site in Switzerland and modern reference fats. This practice has yet to find widespread acceptance in archaeological sciences, with many researchers (Evershed et al. 1997; Dudd and Evershed 1998; Copley et al. 2003; 2005a,b; Craig et al. 2005; Craig et al 2007; Mukherjee et al. 2007; Evershed et al. 2008; Outram et al. 2009) relying on the earlier study of the isotopic composition of CO$_2$ in Antarctic ice cores by Friedli et al. (1986), and shifting the δ^{13}C ratios of fatty acids from modern reference fats toward more positive values by 1.2 ‰. The high-precision CO$_2$ and δ^{13}C ice-core record does not encompass the Neolithic and Chalcolithic periods in the Middle East (Trudinger et al. 1999), and there is currently no means of distinguishing long-term variability in the global carbon cycle from changes in the isotopic composition of stable carbon in CO$_2$ resulting from deforestation and agricultural growth (McCarroll & Loader 2004). McCarroll and Loader (2004: 789) caution against the use of such correction factors until the existing uncertainties concerning atmospheric CO$_2$ and δ^{13}C in the ice-core record are resolved. However, even if either of these two correction factors (1.2 ‰ or 1.6 ‰) were applied to the isotopic data obtained from modern reference fats examined in this study, it would not substantially alter the categorization of organic residues recovered from the archaeological pottery examined in this study.

Chapter 5
Results from use of microwave-assisted extraction techniques in recovery of free fatty acids from nine Neolithic sites in the Middle East

5.1 The archaeological pottery fragments
In my continued efforts to find direct evidence of the first uses of pottery vessels in the Middle East, I attempted to extract organic residues from 65 pottery fragments (Appendices A.1.3, A.1.4) from nine mid-to-late Neolithic sites in the Fertile Crescent using the microwave-assisted liquid chromatography protocol outlined in the previous chapter. This pottery had been recovered from a number of early pottery-bearing archaeological horizons in the Middle East, including those from the sites of al-Basatîn in Jordan, Abu Hureyra in Syria, Newe Yam in Israel, Çayönü in Turkey, and Hajji Firuz, Dalma Tepe, Tepe Sarab, Ali Kosh, and Toll-e Bashi in Iran (See map, Figure 1.2.1 and Table 1.2.1). Potsherds from the sites Çayönü and Ali Kosh come from contexts directly overlaying aceramic levels at these sites. Most potsherds were obtained from excavator or museum collections, but 17 pottery fragments were recovered specifically for organic residue analysis from the Late Neolithic sites at al-Basatîn (10) and Toll-e Bashi (7). 27 pottery fragments from Abu Hureyra (6), Çayönü (8), Ali Kosh (6), and Toll-e Bashi (7) that had previously produced no measurable results through 'conventional' organic solvent extraction in this study were re-examined using the microwave-assisted extraction protocol. Laboratory sample numbers, excavation recovery numbers, publication references, and approximate dates of the pottery-bearing horizons can be found in Appendices A.1.3 and A.1.4. Pottery fragments yielding organic residues are highlighted in these appendices in bold text. Potsherds that did not yield measurable abundances of lipids through conventional solvent extraction or saponification techniques, but that did subsequently yield results through use of the microwave-assisted liquid chromatography protocol, are highlighted with a light grey screen in Appendices A.1.1 and A.1.4.

5.2 GC-MS results from the al-Basatîn pilot study
GC-MS analysis of potsherd extracts revealed that 8 of 10 samples from al-Basatîn (Figures 5.2.1 - 5.2.8; Table 5.4.1) contained $C_{16:0}$ to $C_{18:0}$ saturated fatty acids with relative abundances consistent with those of degraded animal fats (Evershed et al. 1992; Heron and Evershed 1993; Copley et al. 2005e). Unsaturated $C_{18:1}$ and $C_{18:2}$ fatty acids were also recovered from one potsherd extract (WZ5 micro, Figure 5.2.2). None of the al-Basatîn potsherds from which residues were extracted using the microwave-assisted recovery technique exhibited evidence for the preservation of longer chain molecular compounds that could be matched to relative abundances, elution orders, and retention times of specific lipid classes from modern plant or animal species. Subsequent GC-MS analysis of the total organic fraction obtained through microwave-assisted solvent extraction did not reveal evidence for survival of any other lipid species. No evidence of contaminating fatty acids was observed in the procedural blanks.

The high recovery rate (80%) of saturated fatty acids from al-Basatîn potsherds may not have resulted solely from the efficacy of the microwave-assisted extraction protocol. Visible carbon surface residues on the interior surfaces of the pottery fragments likely protected lipids embedded in the ceramic matrix, and the relatively large amount (5g) of fine ceramic powder removed from each pottery fragment possibly contributed to the yields of $C_{16:0}$ and $C_{18:0}$ in this pilot study (Gregg et al. 2009). However, as will be discussed further in section 5.4, the recovery of fatty acids from samples that had not previously yielded measurable results through 'conventional' solvent extraction techniques demonstrates the value of this method even in less promising samples (Gregg and Slater in press).

5.3 GC-C-IRMS results of the al-Basatîn pilot study
The $\partial^{13}C$ values of $C_{16:0}$ and $C_{18:0}$ recovered from the modern reference materials and the 8 al-Basatîn potsherd extracts with fatty acid ratios consistent with degraded animal fats are plotted in Figure 5.3.1, and shown in the context of previously-published ranges of $\partial^{13}C$ values of modern reference fats from northern Europe. The $\partial^{13}C$ ratios of sheep butter fat and goat adipose fats from animals pastured in lands adjacent to the Jordan Valley are consistent with modern reference values used to categorize organic residues in Neolithic vessels from Great Britain (Evershed et al. 2002; Copley et al. 2003, 2005a,b; Mukherjee et al. 2007). However, the isotopic ratios of adipose fats of wild boar from Palestine, domesticated sheep from Israel, and dairy food residues from Turkey do not fall within the empirically-observed ranges of $\partial^{13}C$ values for pig fats, and ruminant adipose and dairy fats from northern Europe. The $\partial^{13}C$ values of $C_{16:0}$ and $C_{18:0}$ from wild boar adipose from Palestine are both significantly more negative than those of pig fats from northern Europe, while those of sheep adipose from Israel are significantly more positive, plotting near the observed range of domesticated pigs from Great Britain. The $\partial^{13}C$ value of $C_{18:0}$ of dairy residues recovered from a pottery vessel from the well documented ethnographic context in central Turkey (Ertug-Yaras 1997; Ertug 2008) is also significantly more positive than the previously-published values for dairy foods in northern Europe and that of butter fat obtained from Bedouin herders in Jordan. The $\partial^{13}C$ values of residues from this vessel not only plot above the $- 3.3 \, \Delta^{13}C$ line that has been used to differentiate dairy and adipose fats from ruminant animals, but also adjacent to the $0 \, \Delta^{13}C$ line distinguishing ruminant adipose fats from that of pigs in Great Britain.

None of the $\partial^{13}C$ ratios of potsherd extracts plot below the $\Delta^{13}C = -3.3$ line and as such would not be categorized as dairy foods on the basis of criteria used by Evershed et al. (2002), Copley et al. (2003, 2005a,b), Mukherjee et al. (2007),

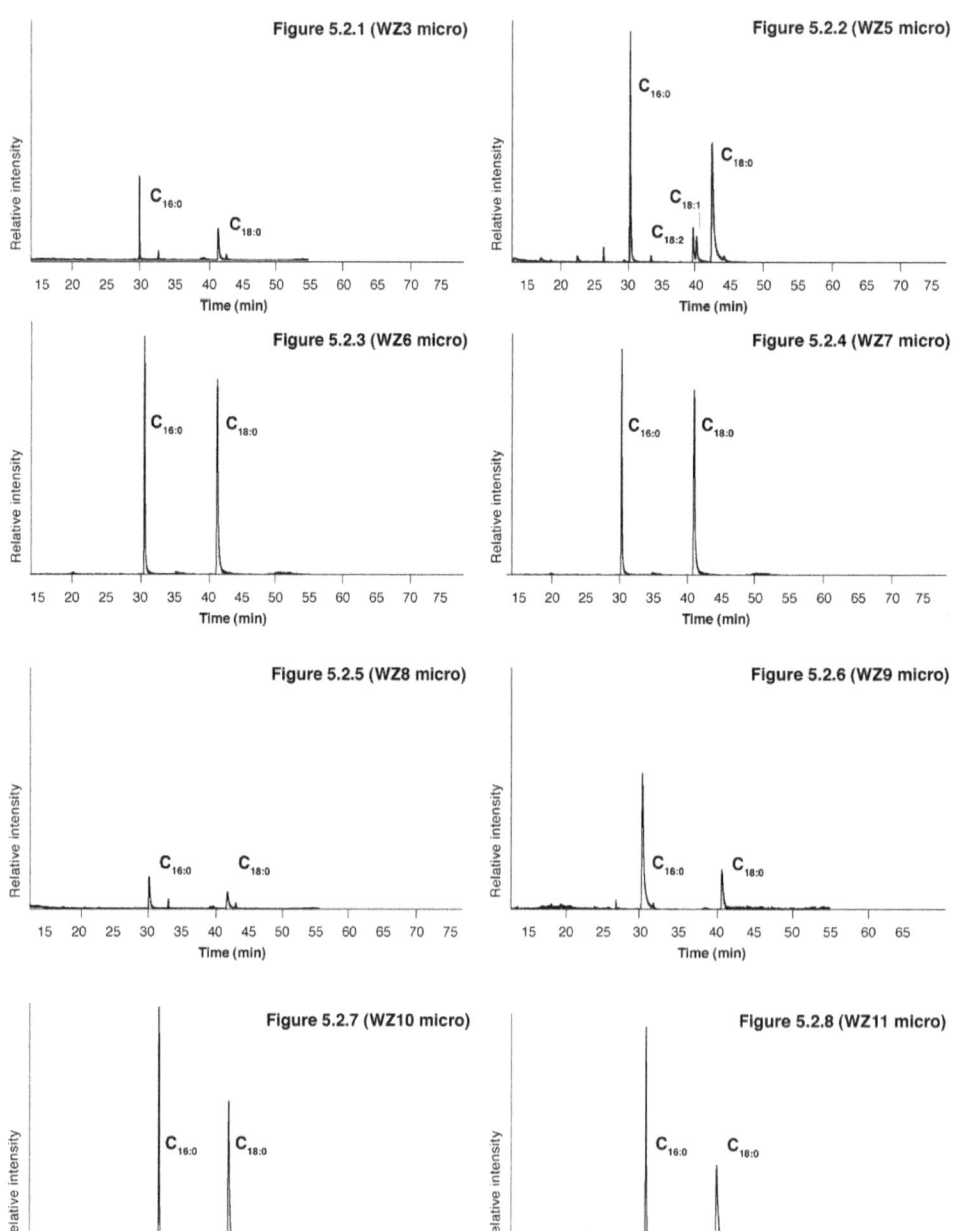

Figures 5.2.1 — 5.2.8 GC-MS analysis revealed that 8 of 10 al-Basatîn potsherd extracts recovered using the microwave-assisted liquid chromatography protocol contained $C_{16:0}$ and $C_{18:0}$ saturated fatty acids with abundances consistent with degraded animal fats.

Figure 5.2.2 Unsaturated $C_{18:1}$ and $C_{18:2}$ fatty acids were also recovered from one potsherd extract (WZ5 micro).

and Evershed et al. (2008). The $\partial^{13}C$ ratios of 5 potsherd extracts plot between the − 3.3 and 0 $\Delta^{13}C$ and appear consistent with modern values of goat adipose from the Jordan Valley. The $\partial^{13}C$ ratios values of 3 other potsherd extracts plot on or above the 0 $\Delta^{13}C$ line separating pig fats from ruminant adipose fats in northern Europe and appear consistent with the observed values of adipose fats of wild boar from Israel. However, because the $\partial^{13}C$ values of a number of al-Basatîn potsherd extracts also plot near the observed values of $C_{16:0}$ and $C_{18:0}$ fatty acids of dairy residues extracted from the pottery vessel from central Turkey (Gregg et al. 2009), the dairy origin of these residues cannot be ruled out. The implications of these results will be assessed further in section 5.6 in the context of the results from eight other Neolithic sites examined in this study, and the overlapping ranges of $\partial^{13}C$ values of adipose and dairy fats from sheep, goats, cattle, horses and pigs observed in Europe, the Middle East and central Asia (Figure 5.6.2).

Accuracy of these analyses was confirmed via isotopically characterized standards (hexadecane, m-terphenyl and octacosane) run before and after each set of samples. Accuracy and precision on standard analyses was better than 0.5 permil (1sigma) and precision on triplicate sample analysis was between 0.04 and 0.83 permil (1 sigma). Mean $\partial^{13}C$ and standard deviation values of $C_{16:0}$ to $C_{18:0}$ fatty acids recovered from potsherd extracts and modern reference fats are included in Table 5.3.1.

The differences in modern isotopic values between the Middle East and northern Europe remain even after the possible contribution of $\partial^{13}C$ from C_3 and C_4 plants to saturated fatty acids in animal fats is taken into account (Figure 5.3.2). Following Copley et al. (2005e, f) and Evershed et al. (2008), the differences in $\partial^{13}C$ values of $C_{16:0}$ and $C_{18:0}$ fatty acids are plotted against the values of $C_{18:0}$ alone [$\Delta^{13}C_{18:0 - 16:0}$ (‰) : $\partial^{13}C_{18:0}$ (‰)]. This proxy has been used by Copley et al. (2005e) and Evershed et al. (2008)

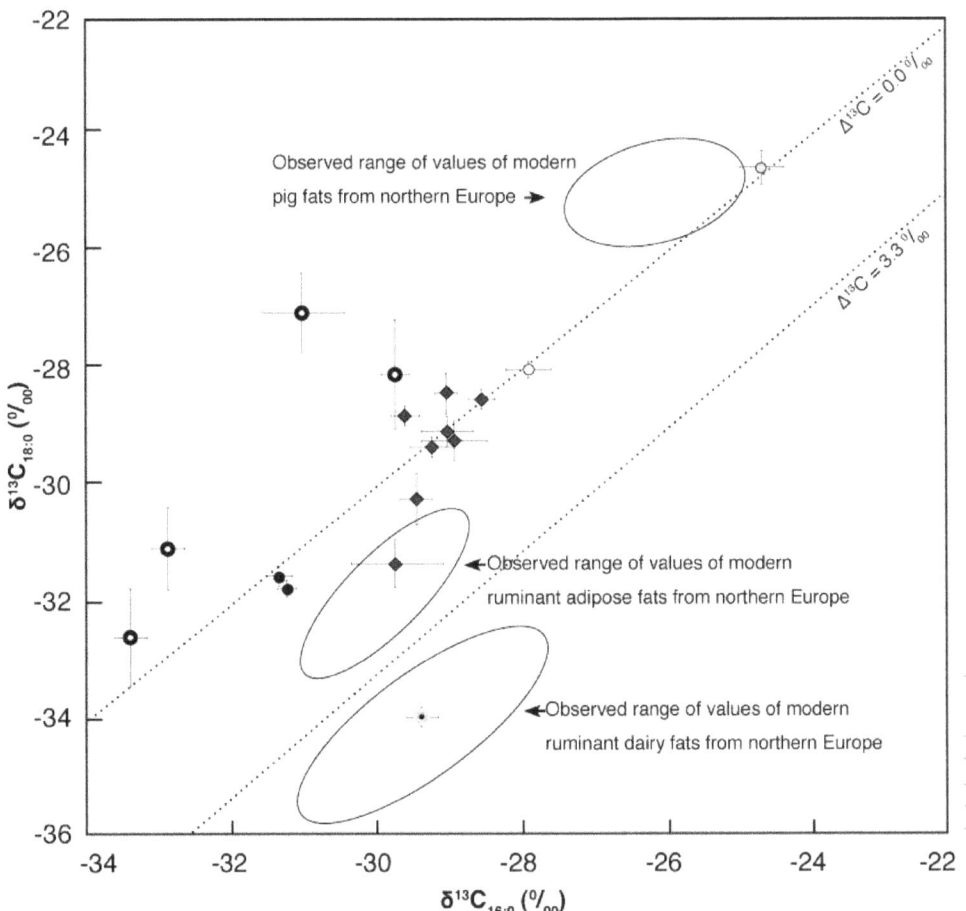

Figure 5.3.1
The $\partial^{13}C$ values of $C_{16:0}$ and $C_{18:0}$ fatty acids recovered from the al-Basatîn potsherds and modern reference fats. Data points and error bars are representative of the mean $\partial^{13}C$ and standard deviation values of triplicate GC-C-IRMS analyses. See Table 5.3.1 below for data.

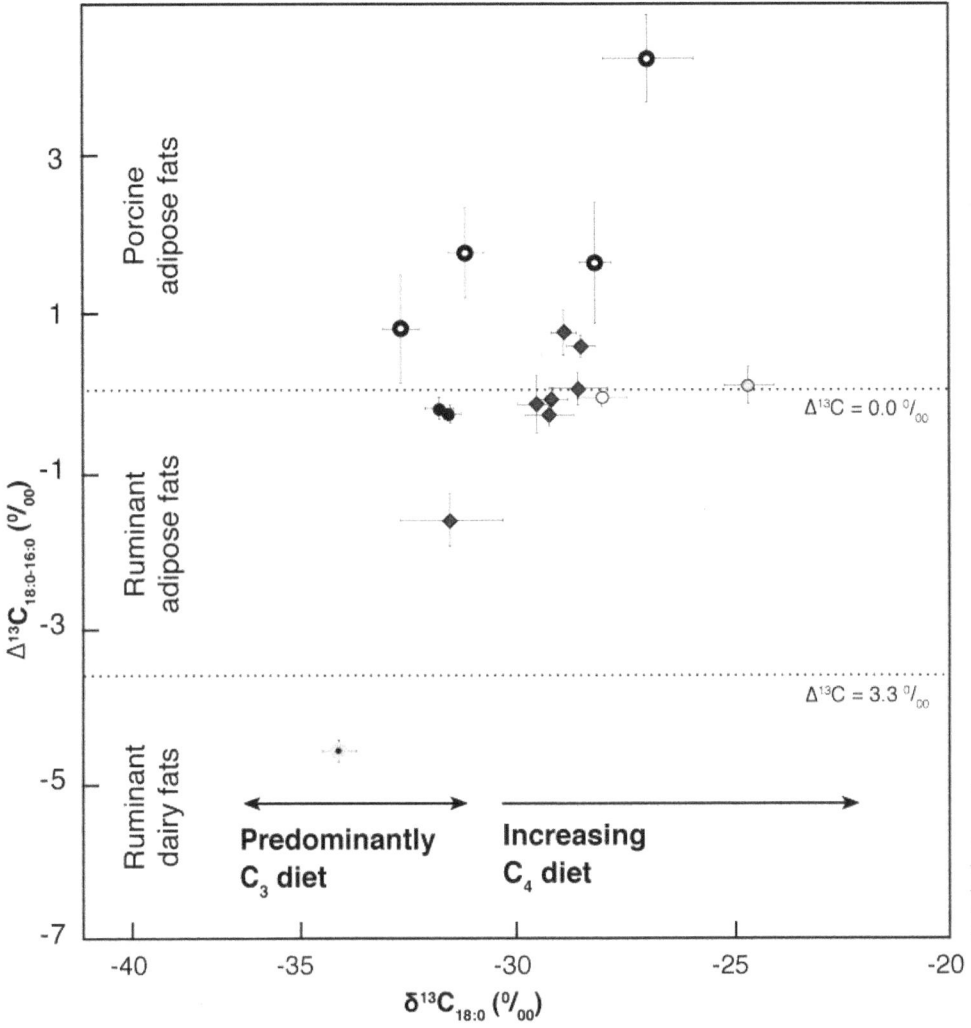

Figure 5.3.2
Differences in $\partial^{13}C$ values of $C_{16:0}$ and $C_{18:0}$ fatty acids plotted against the values of $C_{18:0}$ alone using the following mathematical proxy: $[\Delta^{13}C_{18:0 - 16:0}$ (‰) : $\partial^{13}C_{18:0}$ (‰)]. After applying this mathematical correction to our archaeological and modern reference data, the $\Delta^{13}C$ values of residues from a vessel used exclusively in the manufacturing of cheese, butter and yogurt and sheep adipose fats continue to plot outside the respective ranges associated with dairy fats and ruminant body fats (Gregg et al. 2009; Gregg and Slater in press).

Sample	$\partial^{13}C$ $C_{16:0}$	SD	$\partial^{13}C$ $C_{18:0}$	SD
WZ135/3 micro	-29.73	0.38	-31.41	0.70
WZ135/5micro	-29.41	0.11	-30.27	0.41
WZ135/6micro	-29.00	0.10	-28.46	0.28
WZ135/7micro	-29.58	0.19	-28.85	0.16
WZ135/8micro	-28.96	0.22	-29.16	0.41
WZ135/9micro	-28.92	0.30	-29.25	0.51
WZ135/10micro	-29.20	0.13	-29.37	0.33
WZ135/11micro	-28.53	0.13	-28.55	0.04
KZ1micro	-27.88	0.06	-28.01	0.20
WD1	-29.37	0.05	-34.05	0.19
WC1	-29.72	0.25	-28.12	0.77
WC3	-33.42	0.56	-32.62	0.39
WC4	-32.91	0.62	-31.13	0.34
WC10	-31.18	0.70	-26.94	1.03
WC11	-31.36	0.07	-31.60	0.10
WC12	-31.35	0.13	-31.62	0.10
MS1	-24.63	0.42	-24.59	0.29

Table 5.3.1
The precision on triplicate sample analyses of the al-Basatîn and modern reference samples was between 0.05 and 1.03 permil (1 sigma). The standard deviation of individual $C_{16:0}$ and $C_{18:0}$ fatty acids are shown as error bars on the mean $\partial^{13}C$ values plotted in Figure 5.3.1.

to demonstrate the relative contribution of primary carbon sources in animal diet to the $\partial^{13}C$ values of $C_{16:0}$ and $C_{18:0}$ fatty acids surviving in ancient potsherd extracts, and will be critically discussed in section 5.6. As can be seen in Figure 5.3.2, the efficacy of this proxy in assessing the extent of impact of different photosynthetic pathways on the fractionation of carbon isotopes during fatty acid synthesis is not substantiated by the modern data from the Middle East. Even after this mathematical correction is applied to the modern and archaeological data, the isotopic values of the residues from the vessel from central Turkey known to have been used exclusively in the manufacture of dairy foods, and sheep adipose fat from Israel, continue to plot outside the respective ranges of ruminant dairy and adipose fats previously observed in northern Europe (Gregg et al. 2009; Gregg and Slater in press).

5.4 Microwave extraction and GC-MS results of organic residues from 55 pottery fragments from eight additional Neolithic settlements

Based on the results of the al-Basatîn pilot study outlined above, organic residues were extracted from 55 additional pottery fragments from eight other Neolithic settlements in the Fertile Crescent dating between 7300 and 4700 cal BC (Appendix A.1.4; Table 1.2.1) using the microwave-assisted extraction protocols and instrumental analytical methods described in Chapter 4. GC-MS analysis of the 55 potsherd extracts again revealed high yields of $C_{16:0}$ and $C_{18:0}$ saturated fatty acids from archaeological pottery recovered from some of the earliest ceramic horizons in the Middle East (Table 5.4.1). The proportion of potsherds yielding fatty acids through use of this recovery method is greater than any previously reported from Neolithic and Chalcolithic sites in the Fertile Crescent (Shimoyama and Ichikawa 2000; Copley et al. 2005e; Gregg et al. 2007; Evershed et al. 2008). 26 of the 55 pottery fragments (47%) yielded measurable concentrations of free fatty acids. These include 16 of 27 potsherds (59%) that had previously yielded no fatty acids through 'conventional' solvent extraction (Appendix A.1.4). Recovery rates using the microwave-assisted solvent protocol ranged from 17% to 86%, and averaged 52% when the al-Basatîn fragments are included (Table 5.4.1).

17 of the 26 potsherd extracts yielding fatty acids exhibited relative abundances of $C_{16:0}$ and $C_{18:0}$ consistent with degraded animal fats (Table 5.4.1; Figures 5.4.1 – 5.4.17). Eight of these potsherd extracts also yielded other fatty acids ($C_{12:0}$, $C_{14:0}$, $C_{15:0}$, $C_{18:1}$, $C_{18:2}$; Figures 5.4.1–6, 10, 16). Implications of the presence of these lipid species for the categorization of organic residues based on the isotopic characterization of $C_{16:0}$ and $C_{18:0}$ fatty acids will be discussed further in section 5.6. Nine other pottery fragments in this group exhibited $C_{16:0}$ and $C_{18:0}$ fatty acid ratios consistent with degraded plant oils (Table 5.4.1; Figures 5.4.18 – 5.4.26). The ratio of $C_{16:0}$ and $C_{18:0}$ fatty acids observed in modern animal fats typically falls within the region of 1.0 to 2.0, while the observed ratios of these lipid species in modern vegetable oils is greater than 3.0 (Copley et al. 2005e). Example chromatograms exhibiting relative abundances of extant $C_{16:0}$ and $C_{18:0}$ fatty acids consistent with degraded plant oils and animal fats can be found in chapter 2 (Figures 2.5.1a,b).

Variations in chromatographic retention times of lipids recovered from potsherd extracts result from differences in the temperature programming of the Agilent 6890 GC. The temperature program initially used for al-Basatîn potsherd extracts and modern reference samples was as follows: 50°C hold for 1 min, ramp to 130°C at 20 °C/min, ramp to 160°C at 4°C/min and finally ramp to 300°C at 8°C/min. Temperature programming was modified to produce faster run times for the balance of the potsherd extracts from eight other Neolithic sites. For samples AK6 micro, CU5 micro, NY2micro, NY4micro, NY7micro, CU3micro, CU9 micro, CU11micro, CU14micro, CU15micro, HF5micro, TB5micro, TS1micro, TS1ROMmicro, and TS2micro the temperature programming was as follows: 50°C hold for 1 min, ramp to 150°C at 10 °C/min, ramp to 180°C at 1.5°C/min, hold for 20 min, ramp to 280°C at 10°C/min, and finally ramp to 320°C at 15°C/min, no hold. For samples AH1micro – AH6micro, DA1micro, HF3micro, HF4micro, TB2micro, and TB10micro the temperature programming was as follows: 40°C hold for 1 min, ramp to 130°C at 20 °C/min, ramp to 160°C at 4°C/min, hold for 20 min, ramp to 300°C at 8°C/min, and hold for 5 min. The presence of saturated and unsaturated fatty acids in all potsherd extracts yielding fatty acid ratios consistent with degraded animal fats was subsequently confirmed by GC-C-IRMS analysis using a single temperature program as described in section. These differences in temperature programming are designated by three numerical groupings in the GC Run column in Appendix A.4.1.

Site/dates potsherd yields	Sample	Fatty acids detected	Relative abundances $C_{16:0} / C_{18:0}$	Previously Extracted?	FA yields: µg/g $C_{16:0}$	$C_{18:0}$
Abu Hureyra 7000 - 6600 cal BC						
6 of 7 — 86%	AH1	$C_{12:0}$ $C_{14:0}$ $C_{15:0}$ $C_{16:0}$ $C_{18:0}$	animal ratios	Yes	0.50	0.45
	AH2	$C_{12:0}$ $C_{14:0}$ $C_{16:0}$ $C_{18:0}$	animal ratios	Yes	0.50	0.47
	AH3	$C_{12:0}$ $C_{14:0}$ $C_{16:0}$ $C_{18:0}$	animal ratios	Yes	0.67	0.58
	AH4	$C_{12:0}$ $C_{14:0}$ $C_{16:0}$ $C_{18:0}$	animal ratios	Yes	0.44	0.38
	AH5	$C_{12:0}$ $C_{14:0}$ $C_{16:0}$ $C_{18:0}$	animal ratios	Yes	1.36	1.09
	AH6	$C_{12:0}$ $C_{14:0}$ $C_{16:0}$ $C_{18:0}$	animal ratios	Yes	1.10	0.83
al-Basatin 5650 - 5400 cal BC						
8 of 10 — 80%	WZ1	$C_{16:0}$ $C_{18:0}$	animal ratios	No	0.25	0.14
	WZ3	$C_{16:0}$ $C_{18:0}$	animal ratios	No	0.48	0.68
	WZ5	$C_{16:0}$ $C_{18:0}$ $C_{18:1}$ $C_{18:2}$	animal ratios	No	0.61	0.75
	WZ6	$C_{16:0}$ $C_{18:0}$	animal ratios	No	1.63	1.67
	WZ7	$C_{16:0}$ $C_{18:0}$	animal ratios	No	0.18	0.16
	WZ8	$C_{16:0}$ $C_{18:0}$	animal ratios	No	0.86	0.79
	WZ9	$C_{16:0}$ $C_{18:0}$	animal ratios	No	0.23	0.29
	WZ10	$C_{16:0}$ $C_{18:0}$	animal ratios	No	0.35	0.37
	WZ11	$C_{16:0}$ $C_{18:0}$	animal ratios	No	0.25	0.14
Ali Kosh 7300 - 7000 cal BC						
1 of 6 — 17%	AK6	$C_{16:0}$ $C_{18:0}$	animal ratios	Yes	0.39	0.41
Çayonu 4900 cal BC						
6 of 8 — 75%	CU3	$C_{16:0}$ $C_{18:0}$	plant ratios	No	0.20	0.15
	CU5	$C_{16:0}$ $C_{18:0}$	animal ratios	Yes	3.23	3.82
	CU9	$C_{16:0}$ $C_{18:0}$	plant ratios	Yes	1.50	1.34
	CU11	$C_{16:0}$ $C_{18:0}$	plant ratios	Yes	0.36	0.21
	CU14	$C_{16:0}$ $C_{18:0}$	plant ratios	Yes	0.59	0.32
	CU15	$C_{16:0}$ $C_{18:0}$	plant ratios	Yes	8.60	7.20
Dalma Tepe 5000 - 4700 cal BC						
1 of 3 — 33%	DA1	$C_{16:0}$ $C_{18:0}$	animal ratios	No	4.25	3.07
Hajji Firuz 6150 - 5750 cal BC						
3 of 10 — 30%	HF3	$C_{16:0}$ $C_{18:0}$ $C_{18:1}$ $C_{18:2}$	animal ratios	No	0.60	0.53
	HF4	$C_{16:0}$ $C_{18:0}$	animal ratios	No	0.60	0.39
	HF5	$C_{16:0}$ $C_{18:0}$	plant ratios	No	0.29	0.15
Newe Yam 5500 - 5000 cal BC						
3 of 10 — 30%	NY2	$C_{16:0}$ $C_{18:0}$	animal ratios	No	3.42	3.42
	NY4	$C_{16:0}$ $C_{18:0}$	animal ratios	No	1.47	1.43
	NY7	$C_{16:0}$ $C_{18:0}$	animal ratios	No	0.44	0.44
Tepe Sarab 6800 - 6500 calBC						
3 of 4 — 75%	TS1	$C_{16:0}$ $C_{18:0}$	animal ratios	Yes	0.82	0.87
	TS2	$C_{16:0}$ $C_{18:0}$	plant ratios	No	2.25	0.99
	TSROM1	$C_{16:0}$ $C_{18:0}$	plant ratios	No	1.09	1.29
					0.82	0.87
Toll-e Bashi 6000 - 5750 cal BC						
3 of 7 — 42%	TB2	$C_{16:0}$ $C_{18:0}$	animal ratios	Yes	1.01	1.01
	TB4	$C_{16:0}$ $C_{18:0}$	plant ratios	Yes	1.28	0.93
	TB10	$C_{16:0}$ $C_{18:0}$ $C_{18:1}$ $C_{18:2}$	animal ratios	Yes	10.71	7.86

Table 5.4.1 Samples yielding measurable abundances of fatty acids using the microwave-assisted liquid protocol described in chapter 4.

5.5 GC-C-IRMS characterization of residues from potsherds from eight additional Neolithic sites

Isotopic analysis was conducted on the 17 ancient potsherd extracts exhibiting abundances of free fatty acids consistent with degraded animal fats (as shown in Figures 5.4.1 — 5.4.17). The low abundance of $C_{18:0}$ relative to $C_{16:0}$ in the nine potsherd extracts with fatty acids ratios proximate to or greater than 3.0 (as shown in Figures 5.4.18 — 5.4.26) very strongly suggests they are of plant origin (Copley et al 2005e), and no further isotopic analyses were undertaken on them. It is possible to distinguish the $\partial^{13}C$ values of C_3 and C_4 plant oils from one another (Rossell 1998). However, there is currently no archaeobotanical evidence that C_4 plants took on an important role in the agricultural economy of the Middle East until corn, sorghum, and millet were introduced into the region in much later periods, and isotopic criteria alone cannot be confidently used to differentiate organic compounds from C_3 plants such as wheat, barley, lentils, and olives.

Isotopic analysis of the 17 potsherd extracts yielding fatty acid ratios consistent with degraded animal fats revealed stable carbon isotopic compositions similar to those observed in the al-Basatîn pilot study. The $\partial^{13}C$ values of $C_{16:0}$ and $C_{18:0}$ fatty acids again plot between, or near, the observed values of goat adipose fats obtained in Palestine, wild boar fats obtained in Israel, and dairy residues recovered from the modern pottery vessel from Turkey (Figure 5.5.1). None of

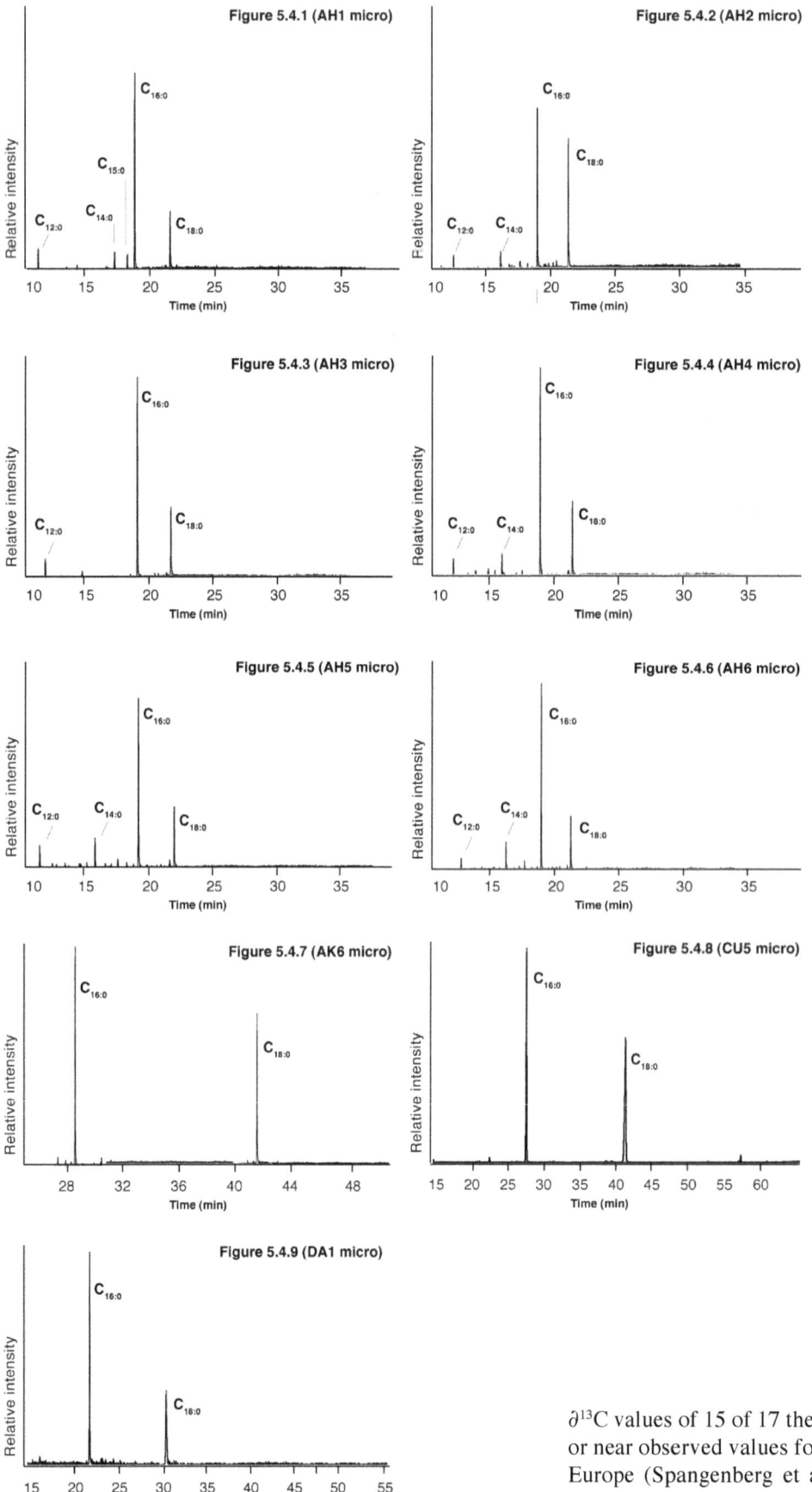

Figures 5.4.1 – 5.4.9 High-temperature chromatograms of potsherd extracts yielding fatty acid abundances consistent with degraded animal fats.

the $\partial^{13}C$ ratios of potsherd extracts plot below the $\Delta^{13}C = -3.3$ line and as such would not be categorized as dairy foods on the basis of criteria used by Evershed et al. (2002), Copley et al. (2003, 2005a-e), Mukherjee et al. (2007), and Evershed et al. (2008). However, because the $\partial^{13}C$ values of 15 of 17 the potsherd extracts plot between or near observed values for modern dairy foods in central Europe (Spangenberg et al. 2006) and the Middle East (Gregg et al. 2009), dairy origin of the residues from a number of these pottery fragments again cannot be ruled out. Categorization of the ancient residues from the eight Neolithic sites and those of the al- Basatîn pilot study is addressed in the next section (5.6), and the archaeological implications of these findings in determining the first uses pottery in the Middle East will be discussed in the following chapter.

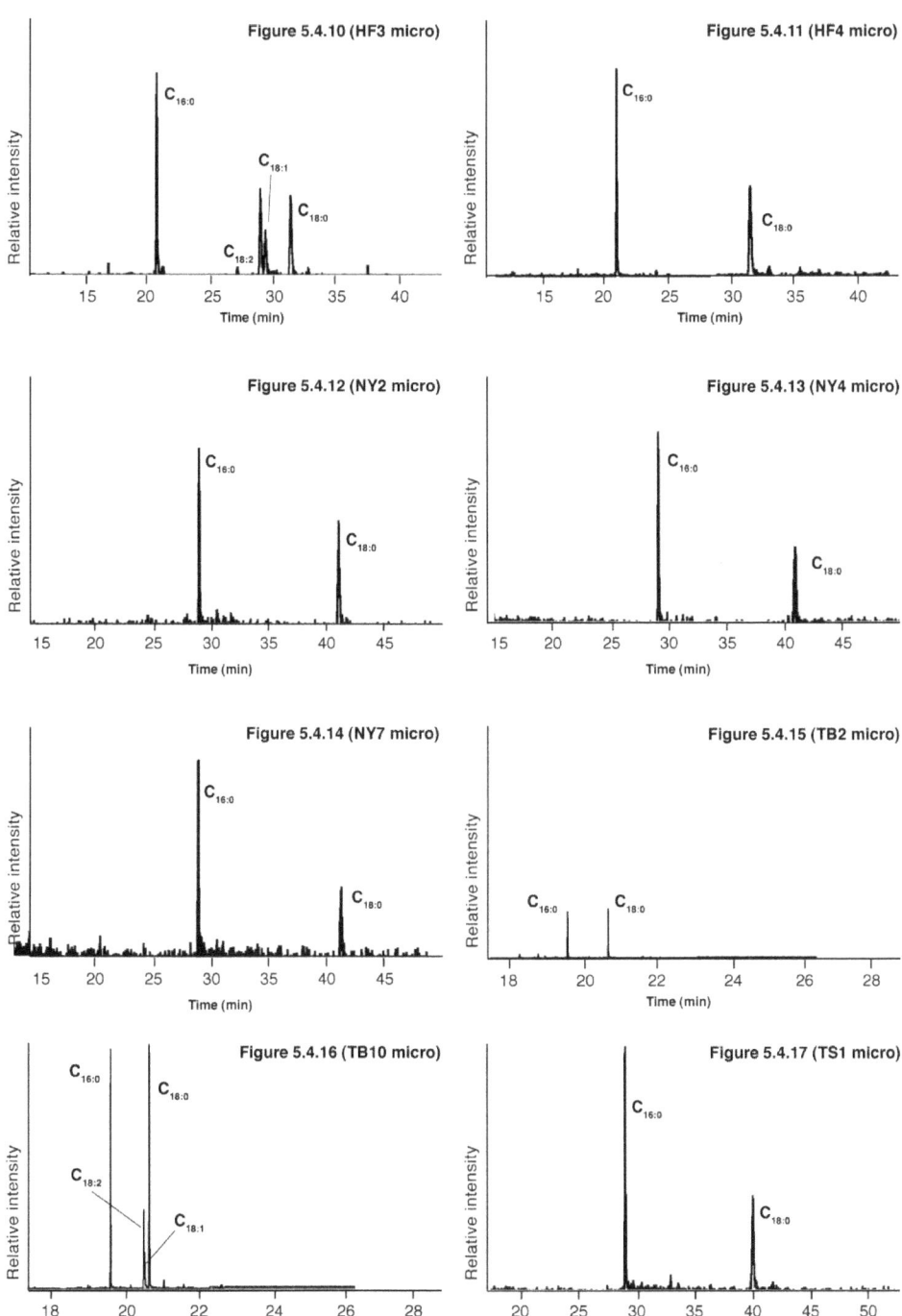

Figures 5.4.10 — 5.4.17 High-temperature chromatograms of potsherd extracts yielding fatty acid abundances consistent with degraded animal fats.

Accuracy of these analyses was again confirmed via isotopically characterized standards (hexadecane, m-terphenyl and octacosane) run before and after each set of samples. Accuracy and precision on standard analyses was better than 0.5 permil (1 sigma) and precision on triplicate sample analysis was between 0.01 and 0.83 permil (1 sigma). Mean $\partial^{13}C$ and standard deviation values of $C_{16:0}$ to $C_{18:0}$ fatty acids recovered from potsherd extracts and modern reference fats are included in Table 5.5.1.

The possible contribution of $\partial^{13}C$ from C_3 and C_4 plants to saturated fatty acids in animal fats was again taken into account (Figure 5.5.2). Using the mathematical outlined in section 5.3.2, the $\Delta^{13}C$ values of only one sample (AH5micro) shifted below the $\Delta^{13}C = 0.0\ ^0/_{00}$ line used to distinguish ruminant adipose and pig fats. As mentioned previously in section 5.3, efficacy of this proxy is not substantiated by isotopic analysis of modern reference fats from the Middle East, and its use in the categorization of fatty acids surviving in potsherd extracts is critically discussed in section 5.6.

5.6 Assessment of the diagnostic resolution of stable carbon isotopes in identifying ancient animal fats in potsherds from the earliest ceramic horizons in the Middle East

In our recent paper on subsistence practices and pottery use in Neolithic Jordan (Gregg et al. 2009), my colleagues and I noted that there is a greater diversity in the fractionation of carbon isotopes associated with the synthesis of $C_{16:0}$ and $C_{18:0}$ fatty acids in ruminant and non-ruminant animals fats

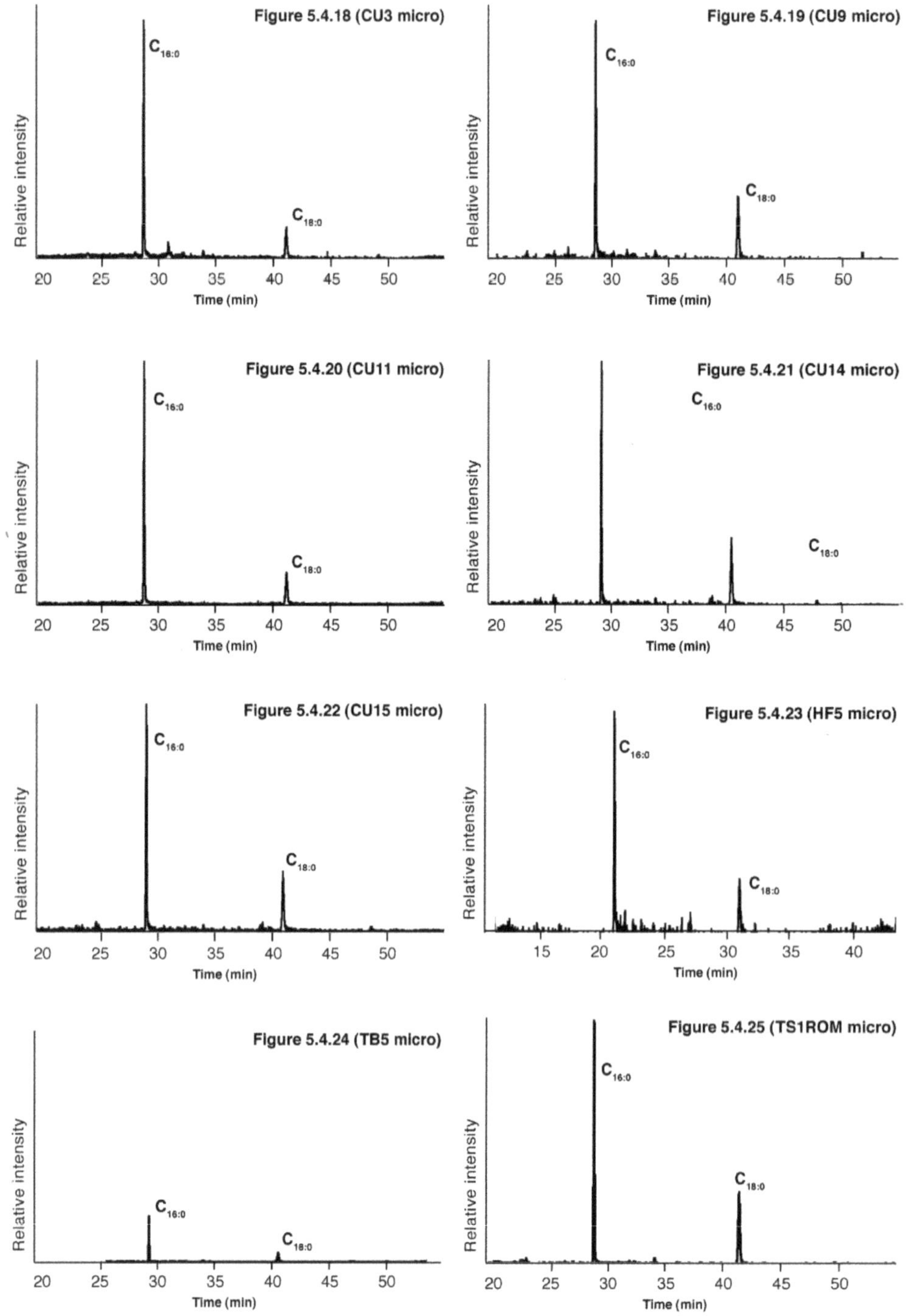

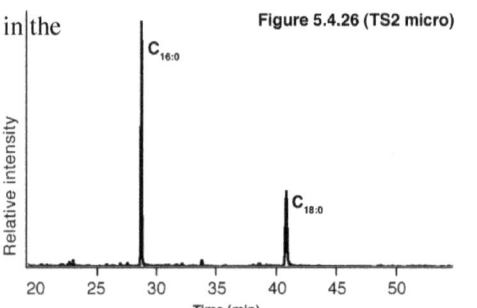

Figures 5.4.18 – 5.4.26 High temperature chromatograms of nine potsherd extracts yielding fatty acid abundances consistent with degraded plant oils.

Middle East than the ranges of $\partial^{13}C$ values previously used to categorize potsherd extracts northern Europe (Copley et al. 2003, 2005a-e, Mukherjee et al. (2007). Great variability has also been observed in the stable carbon isotope composition of saturated fatty acids from ruminant and non-ruminant animals from central Europe exclusively fed a diet of C_3 forage grasses (Spangenberg et al. 2006), and more recently in modern fats from Kazakhstan, including adipose and milk fats from ruminants, horses, and pigs fed on "natural steppe vegetation" (Outram et al. 2009:1334). As can be seen in Figure 5.6.1, in many instances the previously observed ranges from northern Europe are unable to unambiguously distinguish between the $\partial^{13}C$ values of non-ruminant and ruminant adipose fats and dairy fats from ruminant animals.

Our analysis of modern reference fats from the Middle East supports the observation that $C_{16:0}$ and $C_{18:0}$ fatty acids plotting below the $\Delta^{13}C = -3.3$ line are consistent with modern dairy fat from the region, as argued by Copley et al. (2005e) and Evershed et al. (2008). Nevertheless, our results also demonstrate that residues obtained from a pottery vessel used exclusively in the manufacture of dairy foods can also plot above this line. The possible use of sheep stomach or an animal udder as a starter for cheese or yogurt (Ertug-Yaras 1997: 346, 352) may explain the more positive $\partial^{13}C$ values

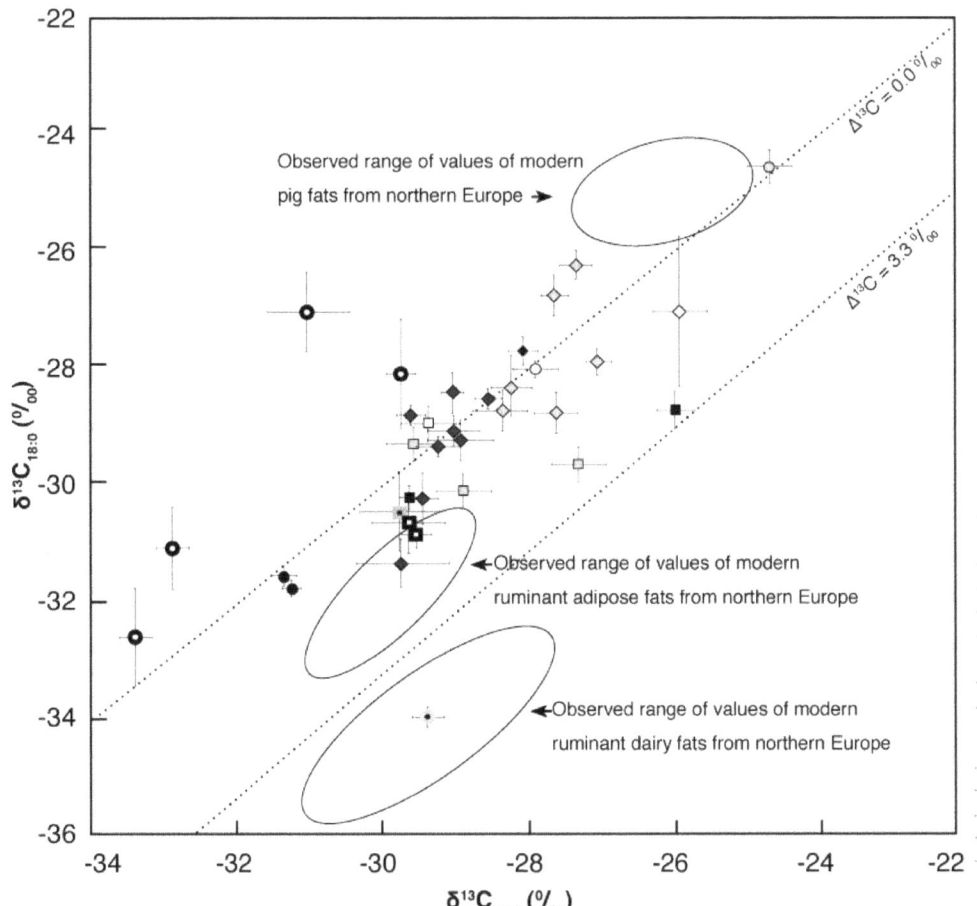

Figure 5.5.1
Isotopic analysis of the 17 potsherd extracts exhibiting abundances of free fatty acids consistent with degraded animal fats (Figure 5.4.1 – 5.4.17) revealed $\partial^{13}C$ values of $C_{16:0}$ and $C_{18:0}$ fatty acids consistent with those of the al-Basatîn pilot study. Data points and error bars are representative of the mean $\partial^{13}C$ and standard deviation

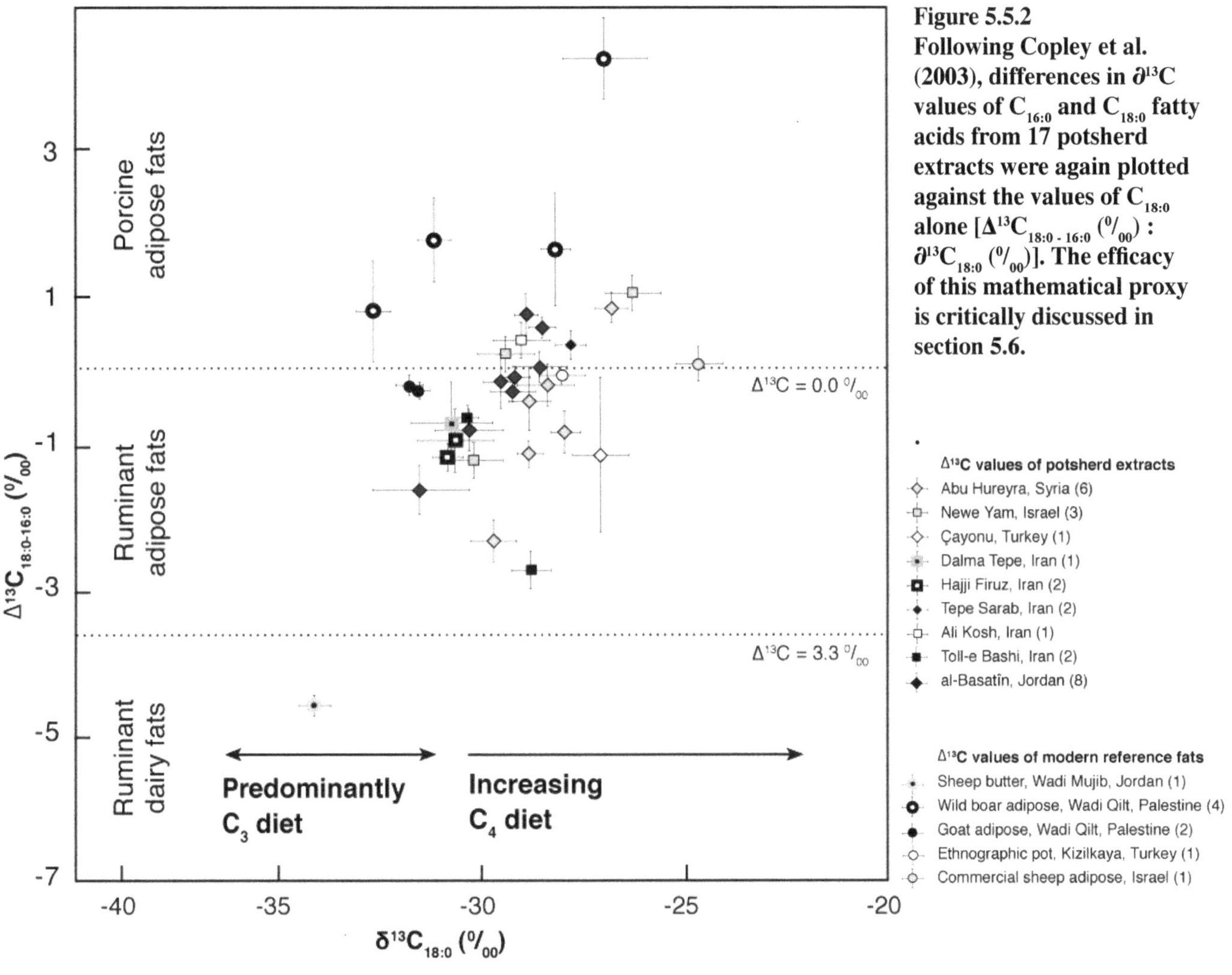

Figure 5.5.2
Following Copley et al. (2003), differences in $\partial^{13}C$ values of $C_{16:0}$ and $C_{18:0}$ fatty acids from 17 potsherd extracts were again plotted against the values of $C_{18:0}$ alone $[\Delta^{13}C_{18:0-16:0}\ (‰) : \partial^{13}C_{18:0}\ (‰)]$. The efficacy of this mathematical proxy is critically discussed in section 5.6.

Sample	$C_{16:0}$ $\partial^{13}C$	SD	$C_{18:0}$ $\partial^{13}C$	SD
AH1	-27.28	0.12	-29.65	0.15
AH2	-27.60	0.08	-26.78	0.05
AH3	-28.19	0.17	-28.35	0.29
AH4	-28.32	0.23	-28.76	0.37
AH5	-27.57	0.11	-28.77	0.22
AH5	-27.02	0.19	-27.93	0.22
AK6	-29.34	0.26	-28.95	0.10
CU5	-25.87	0.31	-27.08	0.25
DA1	-29.65	0.79	-30.53	0.46
HF1	-29.56	0.01	-30.80	0.06
HF4	-29.64	0.28	-30.62	0.24
MS1	-24.63	0.42	-24.59	0.29
NY2	-27.28	0.27	-26.24	0.24
NY4	-28.85	0.83	-30.11	0.34
NY7	-29.54	0.46	-29.34	0.11
TB2	-25.93	0.13	-28.73	0.17
TB10	-29.60	0.07	-30.28	0.10
TS1	-28.03	0.10	-27.74	0.26

Table 5.5.1
The precision on triplicate sample analyses of was between 0.02 and 1.20 permil (1 sigma). The standard deviation of individual $C_{16:0}$ and $C_{18:0}$ fatty acids are shown as error bars on the mean $\partial^{13}C$ values plotted in Figure 5.5.1.

of $C_{18:0}$ obtained from residues surviving in this vessel than that of sheep butter from the Jordan Valley, but the implication of this observation is that samples plotting even adjacent to the $\Delta^{13}C = 0$ line may also be the result of dairying activity.

Spangenberg et al. (2006) have also reported $\partial^{13}C$ values for both raw milk and processed dairy foods plotting above the $\Delta^{13}C = -3.3$ line, and values for pig fats falling within the range of values previously observed for body fats of ruminant animals and values for ruminant body fats plotting within the range previously observed for pig fats. Spangenberg et al. attribute this inconsistency to the high ratio of glucose carbon from mother's milk in the diet of young ruminant animals (Vernon 1981; Spangenberg et al. 2006), and have shown that the overlap in $\partial^{13}C$ values can result not only in the synthesis of fatty acids in the animals themselves, but also from the fractionation of stable carbon isotopes during the preparation of foods for human consumption. In addition to a high degree of variability in isotopic values of whole milk from the different milk-producing species, Spangenberg et al. (2006) have also reported more positive $\partial^{13}C$ values for goat, cow, and sheep cheese than raw milk from the same species resulting from increased temperatures during manufacturing, fermentation, and bacterial degradation during storage.

Isotopic values overlapping the previously published ranges have also been reported in the recent study examining prehistoric horse harnessing and milking practices in Kazakhstan. Although the authors have not directly addressed the issue of the ability of the previously published ranges to distinguish ruminant adipose and dairy fats in this study, Outram et al. (2009) have observed isotopic values for modern ruminant dairy fats plotting above the $\Delta^{13}C = -3.3$ line, and $\partial^{13}C$ values of both equine milk and adipose fats fall squarely within the range of previously published values for body fats of ruminant animals in Great Britain (Figure 5.6.1). Richard Evershed and his colleagues have argued that uncertainties in categorizing extant residues based on $^{12}C / ^{13}C$ composition of potsherd extracts can be mitigated through use of a mathematical proxy ostensibly removing the influence of C_3 and C_4 plants on the $\partial^{13}C$ values of fatty acids (Copley et al. 2003, 2005a,b; Mukherjee et al. 2007; Evershed et al. 2008), but it is worth noting that this proxy is not employed in the Outram et al. (2009) study to account for the inconsistencies in the observed $\partial^{13}C$ values of ruminant dairy fats.

This mathematical proxy is intended to account for differences in the ^{13}C values of fatty acids and carbohydrates in plants that animals consume by plotting the differences in the ^{13}C values of $C_{16:0}$ and $C_{18:0}$ fatty acids against the ^{13}C values of $C_{18:0}$ alone $[\Delta^{13}C_{18:0-16:0} (‰) : \partial^{13}C_{18:0} (‰)]$ to produce numeric values that more directly reflect the biochemical and physiological origins of animal fats recovered from archaeological pottery (Copley et al 2003; Evershed et al. 2008). Although use of this proxy is predicated on the assumptions that the depletion of ^{13}C associated with the synthesis of lipids is limited primarily to the building block carbonyl carbon atom acetyl coenzyme A (CoA) and that this depletion is the same in all organisms (DeNiro and Epstein 1977: 262-263), a wide range of ^{13}C depletions (between 5 - 10 ‰ relative to the carbon source) have been observed in the same lipids from different species during in vitro experimentation, and may indicate varying contributions of at least two sources of acetyl-CoA associated with different metabolic pathways (Hayes 2001: 266).

Much of the variability in the isotopic composition of fatty acids in modern animal fats that can be seen in Figure 5.6.1 is undoubtedly related to the different photosynthetic pathways of plants consumed by animals in these regions (DeNiro and Epstein 1978; Morton and Schwartz 2004; Pearson et al. 2007). However, a comprehensive survey of the $^{12}C / ^{13}C$ isotopic composition of fatty acids in C_3 and C_4 plants from different ecological systems has yet to be undertaken (Dungait et al. 2008), and the efficacy of mathematical proxy outlined above is not substantiated by direct comparison of $\partial^{13}C$ values of $C_{16:0}$ and $C_{18:0}$ fatty acids from animals known to have consumed a range of plants with different photosynthetic pathways. As I have previously noted, even after applying this mathematical proxy to the archaeological and modern reference data examined in this study, the $\Delta^{13}C$ values of residues from a vessel known to have been used exclusively in the manufacturing of cheese, butter, and yogurt by pastoralists in central Turkey and sheep adipose fats from Israel continue to plot outside the respective ranges associated with dairy fats and ruminant body fats (Gregg et al. 2009; Gregg and Slater in press).

The modern data presented in Figure 5.6.1 demonstrate that the previously reported ranges of isotopic values of animal fats must be applied with caution in categorizing organic residues from archaeological sites in the Middle East (Gregg et al. 2009), but the complexity of categorizing organic residues recovered from archaeological pottery fragments based solely on $^{12}C / ^{13}C$ composition of extant $C_{16:0}$ and $C_{18:0}$ fatty acids can perhaps better be seen in Figure 5.6.2.

As I have pointed out previously, none of the $\partial^{13}C$ ratios of potsherd extracts plot below the $\Delta^{13}C = -3.3$ line and as such would not be categorized as dairy foods on the basis of criteria used by Evershed et al. (2002), Copley et al. (2003, 2005a,b), Mukherjee et al. (2007), and Evershed et al. (2008). However, as can be seen Figure 5.6.2, the ^{13}C ratios of 11 potsherd extracts examined in this study

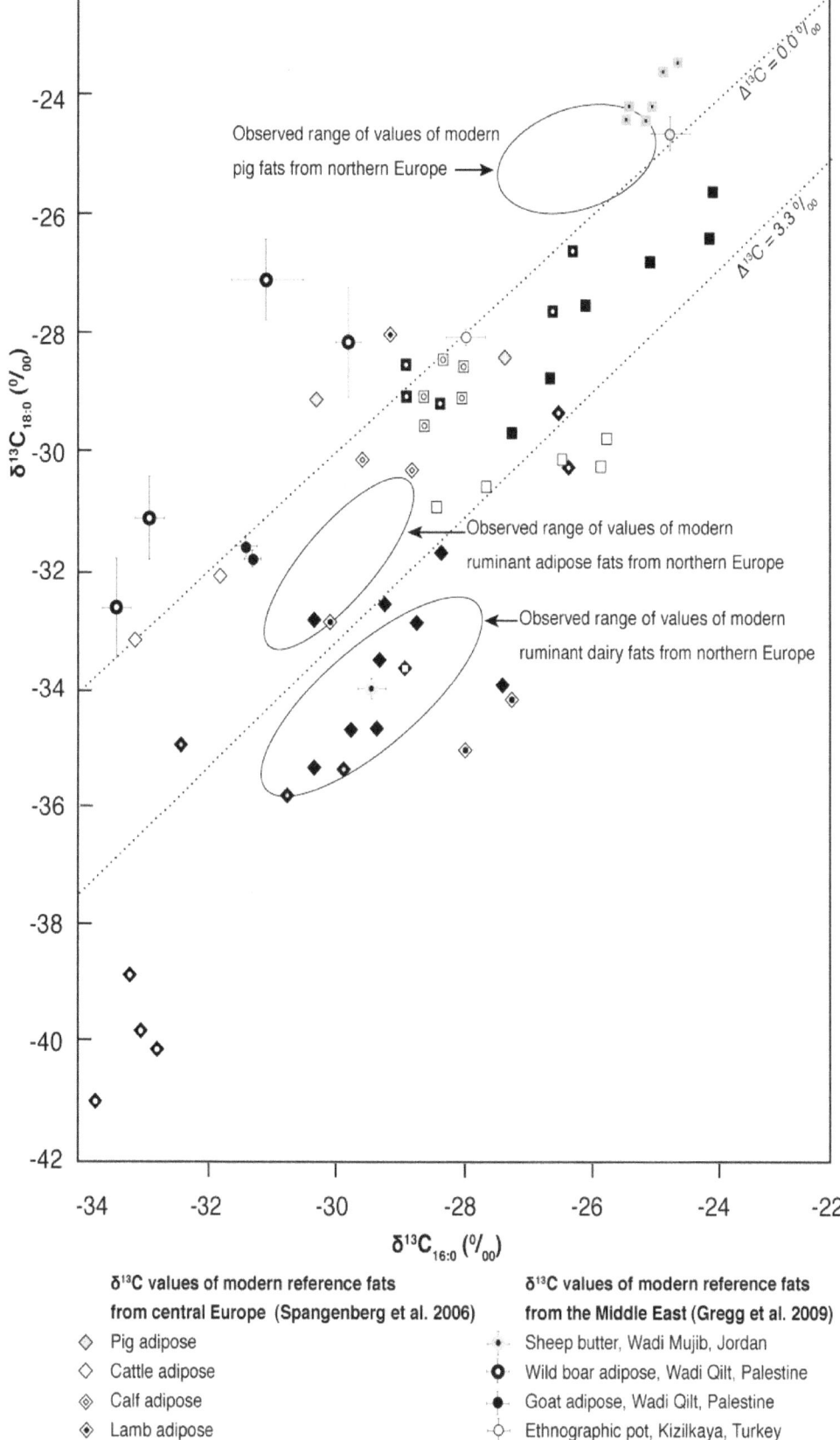

Figure 5.6.1
The observed $\partial^{13}C$ values of $C_{16:0}$ and $C_{18:0}$ fatty acids from modern reference fats from animals central Europe, the Middle East and central Asia are shown in context of the previously-published ranges of values used to categorize organic residues in archaeological pottery from early ceramic horizons in Great Britain (Copley et al. 2003, 2005a-e, Mukherjee et al. (2007). These values for animal fats from central Europe, the Middle East and central Asia were reported respectively by Spangenberg et al. (2006), Gregg et al. (2009) and Outram et al. (2009)

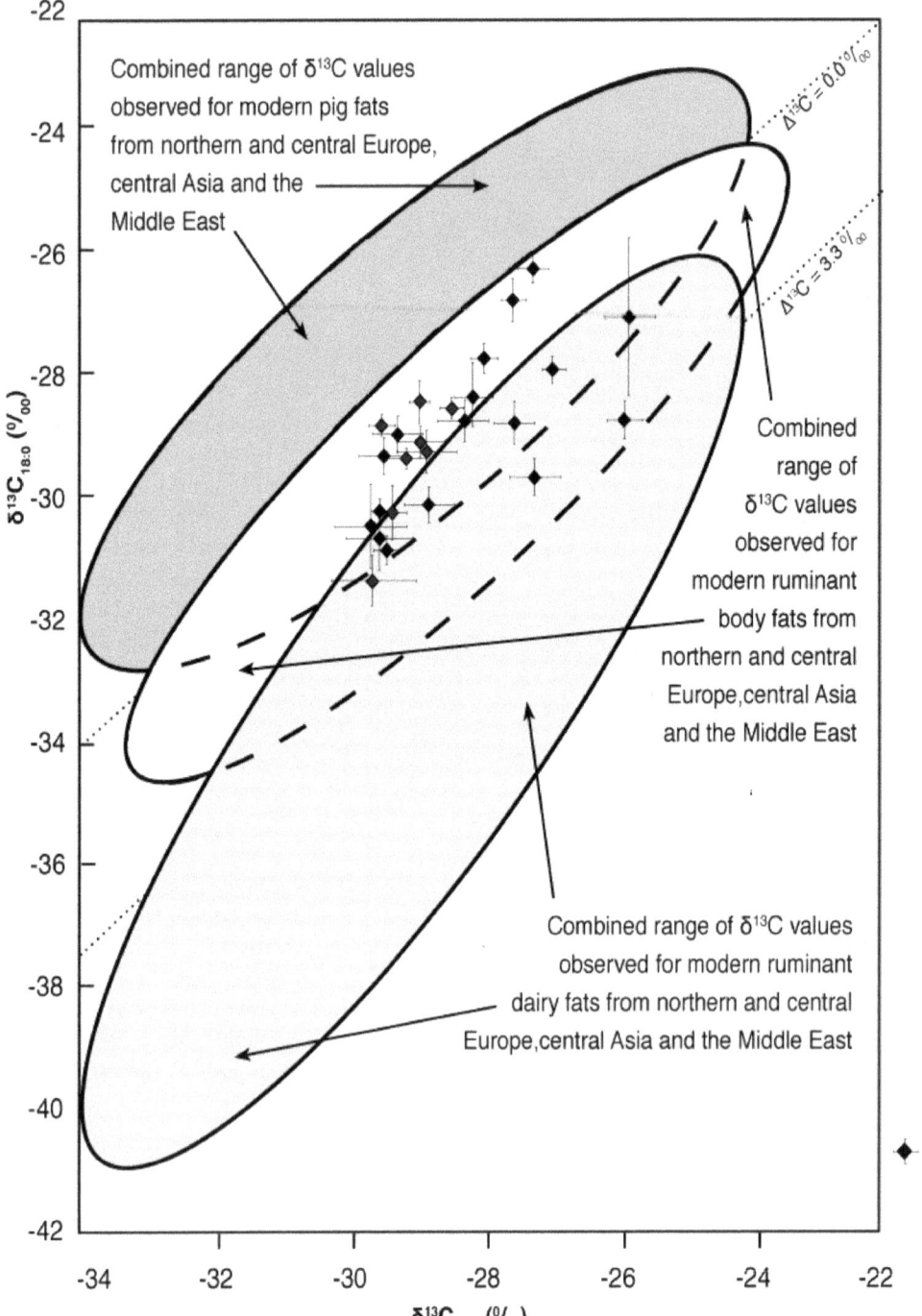

Figure 5.6.2
The observed $\partial^{13}C$ values of fatty acids recovered from 25 potsherds from nine Middle Eastern Neolithic settlements are shown in the context of combined ranges of isotopic values observed for ruminant adipose, ruminant dairy fats and pig fats from northern and central Europe, central Asia and the Middle East. Data points and error bars are representative of the mean $\partial^{13}C$ and standard deviation values of triplicate GC-C-IRMS analyses.

plot near or between the values that have been observed for $C_{16:0}$ and $C_{18:0}$ fatty acids of modern dairy residues from central Turkey, central Europe, and central Asia. Although dairy origin of these 11 potsherd extracts cannot be ruled out, the isotopic values of all 25 are consistent with the $\partial^{13}C$ values observed for modern ruminant adipose and pig fats.

The likelihood that at least some of the residues examined in this study may be of dairy origin is further supported by the preservation of short-chain saturated fatty acids in six potsherd extracts from the site of Abu Hureyra (Figures 5.4.1 – 6). Dodecanoic $C_{12:0}$ fatty acids are found in most milk fats (Evershed et al. 2001; Christie 2008; Signorelli et al. 2008), but only rarely in the adipose tissues of ruminant and non-ruminant animals (Banskalieva et al. 2000; Evershed et al. 2001). However, the presence of $C_{15:0}$ pentadecanoic fatty acid in one of the Abu Hureyra samples (AH1) could result from either the preservation of bacterial flora in ruminant milk, or through dietary uptake of this lipid species by a young suckling animal and subsequent fatty acid synthesis in ruminant adipose fat (Brevik et al. 2005).

When taken together, the archaeological, molecular, and isotopic evidence recovered from the charred remains in the al-Basatîn pottery fragments suggests that ceramic vessels were most likely used for cooking of meats or extraction of marrow from both ruminant and non-ruminant animals. The close proximity of many of the al-Basatîn $\partial^{13}C$ values to one another suggests multiple use of vessels and the possibility of the mixture of pork and ruminant adipose in antiquity but, because the charred remains adhering to the potsherds could not be separated from the fine ceramic powder prior to lipid extraction and analysis, I was unable to determine whether vessels were used multiple times or in a single cooking or processing episode. In the following chapter, I discuss the archaeological implications of these findings in the context of the diagnostic potential and limitations of organic residues in providing direct evidence of the first uses of pottery vessels in the Middle East.

Chapter 6
Diagnostic potential and limitations of different analytical methods in identifying the earliest uses of pottery in the ancient Middle East

6.1 Overview

Molecular and isotopic characterization of organic residues can provide direct evidence of economic activities, subsistence practices, and trade in specific commodities that may have only previously been able to be tenuously inferred from the physical or stylistic attributes of prehistoric pottery vessels. But organic residue analysis is no 'silver bullet' in the high-tech arsenal of methodologies on which archaeologists and archaeometrists may now draw. In this chapter, I discuss the diagnostic potential and limitations of the methodological approaches outlined in the previous chapters, and the implications of the use of these methods in answering long-standing archaeological research questions. I begin by summarizing the major factors affecting the preservation of organic residues in archaeological pottery, and the likelihood for survival of compounds that can be confidently linked to one or more of the different substances that pottery vessels may once have contained. Although bitumen and tree resins can survive burial for prolonged periods, because fatty acids from animal fats and vegetable oils are the most common organic compounds likely to be recovered from early pottery fragments (Heron and Evershed 1995; Evershed et al. 2001; Pollard et al. 2007), my evaluation focuses on the efficacy of different extraction methods and the molecular and isotopic analytical techniques used in the recovery and identification of fatty acids. In view of the results presented in the previous chapter, I outline the environmental, physiological, and anthropogenic factors that need to be more carefully considered in the characterization of isotopic values of animal fats in archaeological pottery, and propose a series of measures that will allow us to more confidently categorize organic residues from early ceramic horizons in the Middle East.

6.2 Likelihood for survival and identification of different substances in archaeological pottery

The possibility of gaining new insights into long-standing archaeological questions through chemical analysis of organic residues imbedded in archaeological pottery is governed not only by the diagnostic potential of the materials being examined, but also by the limitations of current recovery protocols and instrumental analytical techniques. The survival of all organic matter is influenced by variations in temperature and precipitation (Pollard et al. 2007). However, it is the differences in the physical characteristics of organic compounds themselves, and the physical, chemical, and biological processes associated with individual depositional environments that result in the preferential preservation of animal fats, vegetable oils, waxes, bitumen, and plant resins rather than other organic substances (Eglinton and Logan 1991; Pollard et al. 2007). Geoffrey Eglinton and Graham Logan (1991:323) note that "few integrated studies have been carried out to discover how different compounds have behaved within the same organism from the same environment", but Robert White's *Principles and Practice of Soil Science* (2006) is a useful guide to the physical and chemical process involved in biodegradation of organic compounds under different soil and climatic conditions.

Colonizing insects, arthropods, annelids, fungi, and bacteria can all affect the survival of buried organic matter (White 2006), but microbial degradation is accelerated in most depositional environments through increases in temperature, moisture, and hydrolysis resulting from the acidic or alkaline conditions of the soil (Enwhistle et al. 2000; White 2006). Among the major factors governing the molecular survival of compounds imbedded in the ceramic matrix of archaeological potsherds are the intermolecular forces holding the atoms of the compound together (McMurray 2004). Highly polar substances, such as sugars and starches, very rarely survive in archaeological pottery because of the asymmetrical distribution of electrons in the molecular bonds holding carbon atoms in the compound together (Pollard et al. 2007). These bonds are easily dissolved in water, also a highly polar substance (McMurray 2004). Although isotopic analyses of long-chain carbon compounds surviving in Mississippian potsherds have been used to substantiate the cooking of maize in pottery vessels between 1000 and 1100 cal AD (Reber et al. 2004b), there is no evidence for survival of sugars or starches in archaeological pottery for more prolonged periods, other than microscopic starch grains imbedded in potsherds recovered from continuously desiccated deposits at the 18th dynasty Egyptian capital at Amarna circa 1500 BC (Samuel 1996). Despite the apparent initial success in the identification of biomarkers associated with the fermentation of sugars and starches in wine and beer (Michel et al. 1992, 1993; McGovern et al. 1996; McGovern et al. 1997), the potential for 'false positive' results has been subsequently pointed out by a number of researchers (Hornsey 2003; Boulton & Heron 2000; Pollard et al. 2007; Stern et al. 2008; Evershed 2008), casting doubt not only on the analytical methods used in these early studies, but also on those employing a biomarker approach to sugar and starch remains with more sophisticated instrumental techniques (Guasch-Jané et al. 2004, 2006).

Polar amino acids make up the bulk of plant and animal proteins, but these highly diagnostic compounds are also not likely to survive for long periods in most depositional contexts (Eglinton and Logan 1991). Non-polar amino acids anchoring proteins to membranes and fats have electron distributions that more strongly bond peptides to the adjacent tissues, and are consequently less affected by hydrolysis in alkaline or acidic soils, or subject to oxidation and microbial degradation during burial (White 2006). Nevertheless, even non-polar amino acids have only rarely been identified as surviving in archaeological pottery (Craig et al. 2000; Sollazo et al. 2008), as has also been the case with ancient DNA. Because the external sugar-phosphate backbones of DNA molecules are made up of polar ribose sugars and phosphates, they are highly susceptible to biodegradation processes. The internal nitrogenous bases (adenine, guanine, thymine, and cytosine) making up genetic replication sequences in DNA, however, are non-polar and hydrophobic, and therefore more likely to survive (Hughes 2008). Maria Hansson and Brendan Foley (2008) have recently extracted fragmentary strands of olive, oregano, and *Pistachea lentiscus* DNA from scrapings of the interior surfaces of two amphorae from a 2400 year-old shipwreck off the Greek island of Chios using polymerase amplification techniques and existing criteria established for authenticating ancient DNA (Cooper and Poinar 2000; Paabo et al., 2004). The low water solubility of olive oil suspected to have been contained in these vessels and the relatively anaerobic conditions of the deep-water location from which they were recovered would both have inhibited oxidation and decomposition, aiding preservation (Hansson and Foley 2008).

Classes of lipids that share electrons between atoms symmetrically, such as non-polar saturated fatty acids in animal fats and vegetable oils and longer carbon chain compounds in bitumen, waxes, and tree resins, are often the only substances to survive microbial degradation during burial for prolonged periods of time (Eglinton and Logan 1991; Heron et al. 1994; Heron & Evershed 1995; Connan 1999; Christie 2008; Stern et al. 2008). The most common compounds to survive in pottery from early ceramic horizons are the most non-polar and hydrophobic lipid classes in animal fats and vegetable oils — $C_{16:0}$ and $C_{18:0}$ saturated fatty acids (Evershed et al. 1992; Evershed et al. 2001; Christie 2008). Other diagnostic lipids, such as shorter carbon chain fatty acids and triacyglycerides have been much more rarely observed in early pottery horizons (Heron and Evershed 1995; Evershed et al. 2001), with the notable exceptions of potsherds recovered from permanently waterlogged and thus relatively anaerobic and protective archaeological environments (Spangenberg et al. 2006; Mirabaud et al. 2007; Stern et al. 2008). Because sugars, starches, proteins, and DNA are unlikely to be preserved in pottery recovered from many if not most archaeological contexts, the vast majority of researchers examining organic residues from early ceramic horizons today are using extraction protocols and instrumental techniques developed for molecular and isotopic characterization of animal fats, vegetable oils, waxes, bitumen, and plant resins (Pollard et al. 2007).

6.3 *Efficacy of different extraction methods*
A detailed evaluation of the extraction methods used in the recovery of organic compounds from archaeological pottery from the earliest ceramic horizons in either the Middle East or Europe has yet to be undertaken. As I have pointed out in section 2.5, in their comparison of five protocols that have been used in the recovery of lipids from archaeological pottery, Stern et al. (2000) have observed high yields of fatty acids through the use of saponification and diazomethane derivitization while 'conventional' solvent extraction and diazomethane derivitization resulted in more highly resolved triacylglycerol distributions than all other methods. However, regional preservation conditions also appear to play a large part in recovery rates of organic residues from early archaeological pottery. Saponification of potsherd extracts and diazomethane derivitization of fatty acid methyl esters have 'routinely' delivered 50 – 60% recovery rates of fatty acids from early pottery horizons in Great Britain (Evershed et al. 2002; Copley et al. 2005e), but in their recent examination of organic residues in pottery fragments from 23 early agricultural settlements in southeastern Europe and the Middle East, Evershed et al. (2008) were able to recover fatty acids from only 11.5% of the more than 2200 potsherds they examined using these extraction techniques. Since no additional diagnostic compounds were recovered from the samples and isotopic criteria alone cannot be confidently used to differentiate C_3 vegetable oils from one another, only 8% of the 2200 potsherds yielded $C_{16:0}$ and $C_{18:0}$ ratios consistent with animal fats in the Evershed et al. (2008) study and were able to be further characterized based on their stable carbon composition.

As I have noted in section 3.10, slightly over 2% of the potsherds examined in my doctoral research produced measurable results through use of 'conventional' solvent extraction and BSTFA derivatization. Five of 244 pottery fragments yielded diagnostic compounds solely through 'conventional' solvent extraction, and only one of three samples that had previously produced equivocal results through solvent extraction exhibited measurable quantities of free fatty acids through use of the saponification / BSTFA derivatization method. Admittedly, only a very small number of pottery fragments (4) were saponified, and one of these (CU5S) did exhibit marked increases in the recovery of free fatty acids through use of this method. But the use of the microwave-assisted solvent protocol outlined in chapter 4 is far more promising in the recovery of fatty acids than any of the five methods compared by Stern et al. (2000) or the saponification and diazomethane derivitazation techniques used by Evershed et al. (2008). Through use of this extraction protocol, I was able to recover $C_{16:0}$ and $C_{18:0}$ fatty acids from 52% of potsherds, including 16 of 27 potsherds (59%) that had previously yielded no fatty acids through 'conventional' solvent extraction and BSTFA derivitazation. 34 of the 65 potsherds yielded fatty acids, with 25 (38%) exhibiting relative abundances of $C_{16:0}$ and $C_{18:0}$ consistent with degraded animal fats. These yields of saturated fatty acids from archaeological pottery from the early ceramic horizons in the Middle East are unprecedented (Gregg and Slater in press).

6.4 *Environmental, physiological, and anthropogenic factors affecting the composition of stable carbon isotopes in early pottery vessels*
Many well-conceived and well-documented studies inform our understanding of the environmental and physiological processes involved in the division of carbon isotopes into relative amounts of ^{12}C and ^{13}C during the synthesis of fatty acids in plants and animals (DeNiro and Epstein 1977, 1978; Hayes et al. 1990; Hayes 1993; Evershed et al. 1999; Mottram et al. 1999; Morton and Schwarz 2004; Spangenberg et al. 2006). However, a comprehensive investigation of the

interrelationship between these processes and those factors resulting in the further division of relative amounts of ^{12}C and ^{13}C during the subsequent processing and preparation of plant and animal foods for human consumption has yet to be undertaken. Malainey et al. (1999) have shown that ratios of saturated to unsaturated fatty acids of a wide range of plant and animal foods are greatly affected by cooking in pottery vessels, with saturated fatty acids levels generally increasing and unsaturated fatty acids decreasing as a result of thermal degradation and oxidation. Changes of up to $\pm 3^0/_{00}$ in the bulk $\partial^{13}C$ values of both C_3 and C_4 plants resulting from boiling or roasting have also been observed by DeNiro and Hastorf (1985). Spangenberg et al. (2006) have demonstrated that $\partial^{13}C$ values of fatty acids in raw milk can be either depleted or enriched depending on cooking temperature and variations in the molecular composition of milk fats from different ruminant species. In a series of experimental studies, Warinner and Tuross (2009) have more recently found that the $\partial^{13}C$ values of bone collagen of pigs were systematically enriched as a result of consuming maize prepared through alkaline cooking methods. But no study has thus far compared all of the possible factors affecting the multiple fractionations of carbon isotopes in the wide range of animal fats and plant oils that may survive in archaeological pottery. Nor has there been an evaluation of the assumption that the isotopic values of fatty acids from modern uncooked animal fats and whole milk are the same as those in cooked fats and dairy byproducts, a supposition that underlies the methodological and interpretive framework of many previous studies (Evershed and Dudd 1998; Evershed et al., 2002; Copley et al. 2003, 2005a-e; Craig et al. 2005, 2007; Mukherjee et al., 2007; Evershed et al. 2008; Outram et al. 2009). As a result, there remains great potential for the reporting of false positive results in the categorization of both dairy residues and adipose fats in archaeological pottery, and for serious misunderstandings and misidentification of the early uses of pottery vessels.

6.5 Recommended measures for more confident categorization of organic residues from early ceramic horizons in the Middle East

As I have demonstrated in chapter 5, the discrete ranges of isotopic values previously used to characterize potsherd extracts in northern Europe (Dudd and Evershed 1998; Evershed et. al 2002; Copley et al. 2003, 2005a-d) must be used with great caution in categorizing remnant animal fats surviving in early pottery vessels from the Middle East. In many instances, these previously published ranges cannot distinguish between the overlapping and contradictory isotopic values that have been observed for modern dairy fats and ruminant adipose and pig fats in the Middle East and central Europe (Spangenberg et al. 2006; Gregg et al. 2009; Gregg and Slater in press). As a result of these findings, new criteria for the isotopic characterization of fatty acids in potsherd extracts need to be established.

Because stable carbon isotope values would be expected to differ if animals consumed plants with different photosynthetic pathways (Richards et al. 2003; Pearson et al. 2007), I propose comparing the $\partial^{13}C$ ratios of bone collagen from ancient faunal remains to those of the $\partial^{13}C$ values of individual fatty acids in pottery fragments recovered from the same archaeological context. Such a comparison would provide an independent measure of quantities of C_3 and C_4 plants in animal diet, and remove the uncertainties currently associated with the mathematical proxy ostensibly demonstrating the relative contribution of primary carbon sources to the $\partial^{13}C$ values of $C_{16:0}$ and $C_{18:0}$ fatty acids surviving in ancient potsherd extracts (Copley et al. 2003; 2005e, f; Evershed et al. 2008; Gregg et al. 2009). Moreover, because highly diverse range of isotopic values for both adipose and dairy fats could result from differences in herd management strategies, any assessment of the isotopic values of organic residues of animal fats in pottery from the Middle East needs to be accompanied by a detailed appraisal of the faunal assemblage from the same archaeological horizon from which the pottery was recovered. Individual herds of animals feeding exclusively on C_3 grasses close to archaeological sites are likely to have very different $\partial^{13}C$ values than coeval transhumant herds consuming a larger proportion of C_4 plants from a broad geographic area (Pearson et al. 2007). Spangenberg et al. (2006) have also shown that there is a high degree of variability between the $\partial^{13}C$ values of adipose fats of suckling ruminant animals and those of adults of the same species, both exclusively being fed C_3 plants. The cooking of meat or the rending of marrow from young ruminant animals is likely to result in the same range of $\partial^{13}C$ values of $C_{16:0}$ and $C_{18:0}$ as those of domesticated pig or wild boar, so the confident categorization of organic residues using isotopic criteria alone necessitates comparison with the $\partial^{13}C$ ratios of bone collagen of both juvenile and adult ruminant animals.

Since our current understanding of the effects of cooking on the depletion or enrichment of $\partial^{13}C$ in different fatty acids is also somewhat limited (DeNiro and Hastorf 1985; Spangenberg et al. 2006; Warinner and Tuross 2009), I recommend that further experimental studies, such as that conducted by Spangenberg et al. (2006) and Warinner and Tuross (2009) be carried out on a wider range of animal and plant foods to more fully address the consequences of heating of different foods to different temperatures, alone and in combination, on the fractionation of stable carbon isotopes. Our understanding of the anthropogenic factors affecting the isotopic composition of remnant fatty acids surviving in pottery vessels could also benefit from an experimental study attempting to determine the temperatures at which different foods were likely cooked in antiquity.

Reconstruction of all the factors that may have affected the fractionation of stable carbon isotopes in organic residues from early pottery vessels will certainly be a daunting task. However, such an undertaking is essential in order to develop new analytical criteria capable of differentiating between the $\partial^{13}C$ values of ancient dairy residues and those of carcass fats of sheep, goats, cows and pigs in early pottery vessels.

Chapter 7
Summary of research findings and suggestions for archaeologists considering the use of organic residue analysis

7.1 Summary of research findings

In my doctoral research, I have attempted to obtain direct evidence of the use of early pottery vessels in the Middle East from pottery fragments recovered from 22 early agricultural and pastoral settlements. I have been successful in recovering organic residues from 38 of 280 pottery fragments from 10 Neolithic settlements in the Fertile Crescent (Appendices A.1.1 - A.1.4; Gregg et al. 2007; Gregg in press; Gregg et al. 2009; Gregg and Slater in press). My preliminary examination of 244 of these pottery fragments using 'conventional' solvent extraction techniques yielded evidence for the survival of diagnostic organic compounds in only five potsherds, or 2% of the materials I examined. However, I was able to identify molecular compounds characteristic of bitumen in four of these fragments recovered from the earliest pottery-bearing horizons in southwestern Iran at the sites of Ali Kosh and Chageh Sefid. Subsequent analyses of the stable carbon and hydrogen isotopic composition ($\partial^{13}C$ and ∂D) of the asphaltene fraction of residues from these fragments revealed the geological source of the bitumen lies within the Deh Luran region of Khuzestan, and confirmed the earliest recorded presence of bitumen in pottery vessels in the Middle East (Gregg et al. 2007). A single potsherd from Çayönü in central Anatolia yielded saturated fatty acids with relative abundances consistent with degraded animal fats through use of the 'conventional' solvent extraction method, and increased yields of $C_{16:0}$ and $C_{18:0}$ fatty-acids from this potsherd were achieved through saponification and diazomethane derivatization techniques.

The poor recovery of organic compounds using 'conventional' solvent extraction and saponification techniques during the preliminary stages of my doctoral research led me to seek the advice of geochemist Dr. Greg Slater of the School of Geography and Earth Sciences at McMaster University. Dr. Slater suggested that increased lipid yields might be realized through use of a microwave-assisted liquid chromatography protocol described in chapter 4. Together we undertook a pilot study (Gregg et al. 2009) using these microwave-assisted recovery techniques to extract lipids from 10 pottery fragments that had been specifically excavated for residue analysis from the late Neolithic site at al-Basatîn in northern Jordan. GC-MS analysis of potsherd extracts revealed that 8 of 10 al-Basatîn pottery fragments (80%) yielded measurable concentrations of free fatty acids using this recovery method, with all extracts exhibiting relative abundances of $C_{16:0}$ and $C_{18:0}$ consistent with degraded animal fats (Table 5.4.1; Figures 5.2.1- 5.2.8). Based on the results of the al-Basatîn pilot study, organic residues were subsequently extracted from 55 additional pottery fragments from eight other Neolithic settlements in the Fertile Crescent using the microwave-assisted extraction protocol (Table 5.4.1). GC-MS analysis of the 55 potsherd extracts again revealed high yields of saturated fatty acids (Figures 5.4.1-5.4.26), with 26 of 55 pottery fragments (47%) yielding measurable concentrations of $C_{16:0}$ and $C_{18:0}$ fatty acids, including 16 of 27 potsherds (59%) that had previously yielded no fatty acids through 'conventional' solvent extraction. Recovery rates using the microwave-assisted solvent protocol ranged from 17% to 86%, and averaged 52% when the al-Basatîn fragments are included (Table 5.4.1). 17 of the 26 potsherds from the eight additional Neolithic settlements yielded fatty acids exhibiting relative abundances of $C_{16:0}$ and $C_{18:0}$ consistent with degraded animal fats (Figures 5.4.1- 5.4.17) while nine other pottery fragments in this group exhibited $C_{16:0}$ and $C_{18:0}$ fatty acid ratios consistent with degraded plant oils (Figures 5.4.18 - 5.4.26). The proportion of potsherds yielding fatty acids through microwave-assisted extraction is greater than any previously reported from the earliest pottery-bearing horizons in the Middle East (Shimoyama and Ichikawa 2000; Copley et al. 2005e; Gregg et al. 2007; Evershed et al. 2008), and suggest that potential use of this protocol may have broad implications for the recovery of diagnostic compounds from archaeological pottery from other time periods and other regions of the world.

Our subsequent isotopic analyses of residues from the 25 potsherds yielding fatty acids consistent with degraded animal fats revealed $\partial^{13}C$ ratios consistent with those of adipose fats of ruminant and non-ruminant animals pastured on lands adjacent to the Jordan Valley (Gregg et al. 2009; Gregg and Slater in press). However, our comparison of isotopic values of modern adipose and dairy fats obtained in Israel, Palestine, Jordan, and Turkey with those previously used to categorize potsherd extracts (Evershed et al. 2002; Copley et al. 2003, 2005a, b; Mukherjee et al. 2007) also established that the ranges of isotopic values from the Middle East differ substantially from those in northern Europe, and demonstrated that the previously reported ranges from northern Europe must be applied with caution in the categorization of organic residues from archaeological sites in the Middle East (Gregg et al. 2009; Gregg and Slater in press).

7.2 Molecular and isotopic evidence of early pottery use in the Middle East

In this study, I have found no conclusive proof to substantiate my working hypothesis that the invention or early adoption of pottery by mobile pastoralists facilitated the widespread acceptance of a new means of subsistence throughout the Middle East based on the herding of sheep and goats and the manufacture of dairy foods during the early Holocene. The molecular and isotopic evidence obtained from pottery fragments from ten Neolithic settlements in the Fertile Crescent demonstrates that early pottery containers were used for a number of purposes. The absorption of organic compounds into the clay fabric of a pottery container can result through different uses of a vessel, whether it be cooking, serving, transportation, or storage (Evershed 1993; Heron and Evershed 1995). In most instances, confident determination of vessel use from organic residues in pottery fragments requires further confirmation from the archaeological context in which they were found, or additional inferential evidence from physical or stylistic attributes of the pottery vessel.

Although I had limited success in identifying residues during the preliminary stages of my doctoral research (Gregg et al. 2007), the first use of a microwave-assisted liquid chromatography protocol in the recovery of organic compounds from archaeological pottery resulted in unprecedented yields of $C_{16:0}$ and $C_{18:0}$ fatty acids from pottery fragments from early ceramic horizons in the Middle East (Gregg et al. 2009; ; Gregg and Slater in press). Twenty-five of the 65 pottery fragments from which residues were extracted using this method exhibited relative abundances of $C_{16:0}$ and $C_{18:0}$ fatty acids consistent with degraded animal fats. Nine (9) others exhibited relative abundances of $C_{16:0}$ and $C_{18:0}$ fatty acids consistent with degraded plant oils. As I have previously pointed out, subsequent isotopic analysis of residues from 25 potsherds yielding fatty acids consistent with degraded animal fats revealed $\partial^{13}C$ ratios most consistent with those of adipose fats of ruminant and non-ruminant animals pastured on lands adjacent to the Jordan Valley (Gregg et al. 2009; Gregg and Slater in press). However, comparison of isotopic values of modern adipose and dairy fats from the Middle East with those previously used to categorize potsherd extracts (Evershed et al. 2002; Copley et al. 2003, 2005a,b; Mukherjee et al. 2007) and those that have been observed in central Europe (Spangenberg et al. 2006) has shown that the collection and processing of milk for human consumption in pottery vessels cannot be ruled out at the sites of Abu Hureyra, al-Basatîn, Ali Kosh, Çayönü, Dalma Tepe, Hajji Firuz, Tepe Sarab and Toll-e Bashi (Gregg et al. 2009; Gregg and Slater in press). A single pottery fragment from the earliest pottery horizon in southwestern Iran from the site of Ali Kosh also exhibited molecular and isotopic ratios consistent with animal fats (Gregg and Slater in press). Nevertheless, the use of pottery in cooking or serving of meats or the rending of marrow and storage of grease at these sites appears to be the most common use for vessels. This likelihood is most apparent from the archaeological, molecular and isotopic evidence recovered from the charred remains adhering to the interior surfaces of the eight pottery fragments from al-Basatîn suggesting that pottery vessels were used for cooking of meats or extraction of marrow from both ruminant and non-ruminant animals during the Late Neolithic period in the southern Levant.

Thin layers of a dark resinous substance adhering to the interior surfaces of two pottery fragments from the same horizon at Ali Kosh and two potsherds from the nearby site at Chageh Sefid were identified as bitumen (Gregg et al. 2007), indicating that at least some pottery vessels at these sites were used for purposes other than cooking. The resinous layers could have been applied as a sealant, or coated on the interior surfaces of the pottery container during transport of bitumen from geological sources known to be within short distances of the sites. The bitumen adhering to the interior surfaces would have precluded further use of the vessel for cooking by either stone boiling or direct placement on the coals of a fire, due the volatile and noxious nature of petrocarbon compounds that would be released into a liquid at temperatures between 85° and 100° C (Killops and Killops 2005).

The presence of plant oils in nine pottery fragments from the sites of Çayönü, Hajji Firuz, Tepe Sarab, and Toll-e Bashi most likely resulted from either the sustained boiling of cereal grains or pulses in a porridge or gruel, or from the rending or subsequent storage of oils from oil-rich seeds known from the Taurus and Zagros mountain regions, such as shepherd's-purse, *Capsella boursa pastoris* (Helbaek 1964). However, as has been noted in section 5.5, no compound-specific isotopic analysis was undertaken on these nine potsherd extracts, due to the inability of stable carbon isotopes alone to differentiate between organic compounds from the major C_3 plants that were domesticated in the region, such as wheat, barley, lentils, and olives. Although there is currently no evidence that any C_4 plants played an important role in the subsistence economy of the Proto-Neolithic or Neolithic cultures in the Middle East, it may be possible to further characterize these plant oils in the future if they were derived from plants such as C_4 chenopods.

7.3 *Suggestions for archaeologists considering the use of organic residue analysis*

Chemical analysis of absorbed organic residues in archaeological pottery is becoming an increasingly useful tool in identifying economic activities and subsistence practices associated with different prehistoric cultural traditions in both the Old and the New Worlds. However, due to variable rates of degradation of individual molecular components in organic compounds, and uncertainties as to whether some 'biomarkers' are unique indicators of individual substances, the isolation and categorization of the commodities imbedded in the fabric of a pottery vessel is not a straightforward task. In addition to constraints placed on the identification of residues by the chemical processes involved in biodegradation of different substances, the low-level generalizations that can be made from the observation and classification of molecular or isotopic compositions of organic matter in pottery fragments must be evaluated in the context of the complementary or contradictory lines of evidence that inform our understanding of the archaeological problem we are hoping to clarify. We must be confident that the molecular or isotopic biomarkers recovered from archaeological pottery are unique to a specific organism or physiological process before we use it as evidence of a specific human activity. We must also ensure our interpretation of this evidence considers all the possible uses of a pottery vessel that can be associated with that specific substance. Molecular or isotopic evidence of a substance in a pottery container or fragment is confirmation of its existence, not necessarily of the specific or exclusive use of the vessel.

I recommend that any archaeologists looking to answer long-standing (or even brand new) research questions through analysis of organic residues familiarize themselves with the basic tenets of analytical chemistry in archaeology. In addition to detailed descriptions of the major instrumental analytical techniques used in organic residue analysis, an overview of basic chemistry for archaeologists can be found in Pollard et al. (2007). Chapters in this volume include sections on subatomic particles and isotopes, molecular structures and bonding, the electromagnetic spectrum, sample preparation, and quality assurance procedures; all are useful subjects for those hoping to interpret molecular and isotopic data recovered from archaeological pottery.

In recent years, research councils in the United Kingdom have invested heavily in archaeological science (Oppenheim 1997; Norris and Oppenheim 2003; Killick and Goldberg 2009), which has led to the development of interdisciplinary expertise and the purchase of dedicated instrumentation by departments of archaeology at a number of universities in Great Britain. However, due to the structure of anthropology departments in North America, the same levels of funding for dedicated archaeological science programs and facilities has not been forthcoming at as large a proportion of academic institutions (Trigger 1989; DeAtley and Bishop 1991; Gosden 1999; Killick and Goldberg 2009). With some notable exceptions, the financial and human resources necessary for the molecular and isotopic characterization of organic residues in archaeological pottery are unlikely to be allocated to anthropology departments in the United States and Canada within the foreseeable future. Institutions having strong archaeological science mandates and capabilities are much more spread out in North America, making it more difficult for the research centres to be in such close collaboration with as large a number of researchers as in the United Kingdom. Given the distances involved, American and especially Canadian archaeologists are much less likely to become directly involved in analysis of organic residues, and are often reliant on collaborators from the physical or biological sciences with laboratory facilities, instrumentation, and analytical proficiency necessary for the identification of organic residues. Research councils in France, Germany, Italy, and Japan have also recently made large investments in archaeological science, but archaeometrists and archaeologists in these countries have yet to develop innovative applications of organic chemistry to archaeological materials or been awarded research training grants to anywhere near the same degree as in Great Britain (Killick and Goldberg 2009).

Thirty years ago, Bruce Trigger (1988:7) noted that archaeologists are also "generally poorly equipped to criticize the techniques used by other sciences", and rarely subjected the conclusions and interpretations of physicists and chemists to the rigorous review they might otherwise demand of their own work or that of their colleagues. The flow of information between disciplines has often been unidirectional (Trigger 2006), with archaeometrists choosing to investigate research problems based on an avocational interest in archaeology, or on the availability of instrumentation and knowledge of specific analytical techniques (DeAtley and Bishop 1991; Heron and Pollard 2008). Because investigations are frequently undertaken within a multidisciplinary rather than interdisciplinary framework, there is often no genuine sharing of ideas and research objectives (DeAtley and Bishop 1991; Yoffee and Sherratt 1993; Pollard and Heron 2008).

Although it might not be practicable for most archaeologists to extract residues and conduct analysis themselves, it is essential that they develop a degree of confidence in assessing the methods used in acquisition of molecular and isotopic data, and a sound understanding of how the chemical processes involved in the recovery and measurement of organic residues affect the accuracy, precision, and ultimately the interpretation of chemical data. This level of awareness can be readily gained through participation in short-term courses in biomolecular archaeology now offered by several archaeology departments at universities in Great Britain and elsewhere. While only in the early stages of development, research institutions associated with the Worldwide Universities Network are planning a series of interdisciplinary specialist workshops and a video seminar series on lipid and isotopic analysis, with participation by the University of Wisconsin - Madison, the University of California — San Diego, and the University of Illinois at Urbana - Champaign (Collins 2008).

For most archaeologists in North America, potential collaboration with researchers in the physical or biological sciences will be based largely on the ability of the analytical instrumentation to accurately measure the substance the archaeologist wants to identify, the interest of the scientist in the project, and the availability of funds. After having identified the archaeological problem to be clarified through chemical analysis of organic residues (and before approaching a potential collaborator), I recommend that the archaeologist:

1. become as familiar as possible with the current state of knowledge on the subject;
2. assess the likelihood for survival of organic compounds that he or she is hoping to identify;
3. determine whether there might be any other avenues (such as zoological; typological; use-wear; or charring) that should be investigated in order to produce complementary lines of evidence.

I would suggest that the scientist then be engaged in a series of discussions concerning the development of a research strategy that includes the following points:

1. setting of research objectives and agreement on the theoretical framework for interpretation.
2. selection of materials to be analyzed. Is the question about the use of pottery in general, or a particular type of vessel? Are the data likely to be produced going to be adequate to ascribe exclusive use of a substance to an individual type of vessel? What inferences about economic practices, subsistence, or trade can be made from non-diagnostic pottery fragments in a ceramic assemblage? If a particular substance is found, what implications might be inferred from the ubiquity of vessels?
3. selection of recovery protocol and analytical method. Is the extraction method likely to yield diagnostic molecular compounds? Will further isotopic analysis likely be required following molecular characterization?
4. selection of modern reference materials for comparison with ancient residues. What environmental,

physiological, or anthropogenic factors need to be considered in the categorization of residues?

What plants and animals were in the vicinity of the archaeological site when it was occupied?

What species were subsequently introduced into the region? What effect might modern plant foods have on the characterization of the isotopic values of animal's fats?

5. What individual or joint sources of funding are available for such a project?
6. How the results will be disseminated?

7.4 Conclusion

Difficulties in the identification of organic residues from the earliest pottery horizons in the Middle East result not only from the poor preservation of animal fats and plant oils (Evershed et al. 2008; Gregg et al. 2009; Gregg and Slater in press), but also from misconceptions among both archaeologists and archaeometrists about the adequacy of analytical criteria to address specific archaeological problems. It is clear that overlapping and contradictory ranges of isotopic values have been observed for dairy foods and adipose fats of ruminant and non-ruminant animals from Europe, the Middle East and Central Asia (Dudd and Evershed 1998; Evershed et al. 2002; Copley et al. 2003, 2005a-e; Spangenberg et al. 2006; Mukherjee et al. 2007; Outram et al. 2009; Gregg et al. 2009; Gregg and Slater in press). In many instances, these overlapping ranges currently prevent us from unambiguously categorizing organic residues of degraded animal fats in early pottery vessels. The measures I have recommended in section 6.5 (and that I am planning to use in future studies) will facilitate greater certainty in the identification of organic residues in pottery fragments from early ceramic horizons in the Middle East. However, as I have noted in chapter 6, organic residue analysis is no 'silver bullet' for determining the function(s) of early pottery vessels. In addition to reconstructing all the possible diagenetic and physiological factors affecting the molecular and isotopic composition of organic residues that may survive in early pottery vessels, it is essential for researchers to not only establish an independent measure of the proportion of C_3 and C_4 plants in animal diet for the region and time period they are examining, but to also conduct a series of experiments focused on discovering the consequences of cooking different plant and animal foods on the preservation of different molecular compounds and the fractionation of stable carbon isotopes. Such studies will provide a comprehensive set of archaeological 'biomarkers' of different foods, prepared alone and in combination, that can then be used as evidence of past human activity.

Many of the leading scientists undertaking organic residue analyses on archaeological pottery today are "archaeologically literate", and believe that by "joining forces" with "scientifically empathetic archaeologists" they will produce "optimal results" (Evershed 2008:911). However, as has been clearly demonstrated through my doctoral research, archaeologists cannot rely on their colleagues in the physical or biological sciences to be aware of all the possible physiological, environmental, and anthropogenic factors affecting molecular and isotopic composition of residues that may or may not survive in early pottery vessels. In addition to close collaboration with archaeometrists in the setting of research objectives and the selection of recovery protocols and analytical techniques, archaeologists themselves must also have a high degree of familiarity with the methods used in the acquisition and analysis of molecular and isotopic data in order to be able to critically evaluate the adequacy of the analytical criteria being used to address the archaeological questions they hope to answer.

Bibliography

Abdi, K., 2003, The Early Development of Pastoralism in the Central Zagros Mountains, *Journal of World Prehistory*, 17/4: 395-448.

Alizadeh, A., 1988, Socio-Economic Complexity in Southwestern Iran During the Fifth and Fourth Millennia BC: The Evidence from Tall-e Bakun A., *Iran*, Journal of the British Institute of Persian Studies, 26:17-34.

Akkermans, P.M.M.G., 1991, New Radiocarbon dates for the Later Neolithic of northern Syria, *Paléorient*, 17:121-5.

Amiran, R., 1965, The Beginnings of Pottery-Making in the Near East, *Ceramics and Man*, ed. F.R. Matson, Wenner-Gren Foundation, Aldine, Chicago, 240-247.

Amiran, R., 1969, *Ancient Pottery in the Holy Land from its Beginnings in the Neolithic period to the end of the Iron Age*, Ramat Gan, Jerusalem.

Amoroso, E.C., Jewell, P.A., 1963, The exploitation of the milk-ejection reflex by primitive peoples, in *Man and Cattle*, edited by A.E. Mourant and F.E. Zeuner, Occasional papers of the Royal Anthropological Institute, 18:222-234.

Arnold, D.E., 1985, *Ceramic theory and cultural process*, Cambridge University Press, Cambridge.

Atalay, S., 2005, Domesticating Clay: The Role of Clay Balls, Mini Balls and Geometric Objects in Daily Life at Çatalhöyük, *Changing Materialities at Çatalhöyük*: Reports from the 1995-99 Seasons, McDonald Institute for Archaeological Research, Cambridge, 139-168.

Atalay, S., Hastorf, C.A., 2006, Food, meals, and daily activities: food habitus at Neolithic Çatalhöyük, *American Antiquity*, 71:22, 283-319.

Aurenche, O.,Galet, P., Régagnon-Caroline, E., Evin,J., 2001, Proto-Neolithic and Neolithic cultures in the Middle East, The birth of agriculture, livestock raising, and ceramics: A calibrated C-14 chronology 12,500-5500 calBC, *Radiocarbon*, 43:1191-1194.

Bacon, F., 1620, *Novum organum, Instauratio magna, Multi petrasibunt & augebitur scientia*, J. Billium, London.

Baker, H.B., 1938, Uniformitarianism and inductive logic, *Pan-American Geologist*, 161065.

Banning, E.B., 1997, Excavations at Tubna, Wadi Ziqlab, Jordan. *Échos du Monde Classique / Classical Views* 41(1) : 75-80.

Banning, E.B., 1998, The Neolithic Period: Triumphs of Architecture, Agriculture, and Art, *Near Eastern Archaeology*, 61/4:188-237.

Banning, E.B., 2000, *The Archaeologist's Laboratory: the Analysis of Archaeological Data*, Kluwer Academic/Plenum Publishers, New York.

Banning, E.B., 2003, Housing Neolithic Farmers, *Near Eastern Archaeology*, 66/1/2:4-21.

Banning, E.B., 2007, Wadi Rabah and Related Assemblages in the Southern Levant: Interpreting the Radiocarbon Evidence, *Paléorient*, 33/1: 77-101.

Banning, E.B., Rahimi, D., Siggers, J., 1994, The Late Neolithic of the southern Levant: Hiatus, settlement shift or observer bias? the perspective from Wadi Ziqlab. *Paléorient* 20: 151-64.

Banning, E. B., Blackham, M., Lasby. D., 1998, Excavations at WZ 121, a Chalcolithic site at Tubna in Wadi Ziqlab, *Annual of the Department of Antiquities of Jordan* 41: 141-159.

Banning, E. B., Gibbs, K., Gregg, M.W., Kadowaki, S., Maher, L., 2004, Excavations at a Late Neolithic site in Wadi Ziqlab, northern Jordan, *Antiquity*, 78:302. http://www.antiquity.ac.uk.ProjGall/projindex.html.

Banning, E. B., Gibbs, K., Kadowaki, S., 2005, Excavations at Late Neolithic al- Basatîn, in Wadi Ziqlab, northern Jordan, *Annual of the Department of Antiquities of Jordan* 49: 229-243.

Banning, E. B., Gibbs, K., Kadowaki, S., 2005, The Late Neolithic at al-Basatîn in Wadi Ziqlab, northern Jordan, *Antiquity*, 80(310).

Banning, E. B., Gibbs, K., and Kadowaki, S., in press, Changes in ceramics and other material culture at Late Neolithic Tabaqat al-Bûma, in Wadi Ziqlab, northern Jordan, *Culture, Chronology, and the Chalcolithic: Theory and Transition*, eds. J. Lovell and Y. Rowan, Council for British Research in the Levant, London.

Banskalieva,V., Sahlu, T., Goetsch, A. L., 2000, Fatty acid composition of goat muscles and fat depots: a review, *Small Ruminant Research*, 37/3: 255-268.

Brevik, A., Veierød, M. B., Drevon, C.A., Andersen, L.F., 2005, Evaluation of the odd fatty acids 15:0 and 17:0 in serum and adipose tissue as markers of intake of milk and dairy fats, *European Journal of Clinical Nutrition*, 59, 1417–1422.

Bar-Gal, G., Ducos, P., Horwitz, L.2003, The Application of Ancient DNA Analysis to Identify Neolithic Caprinae: A Case Study from the Site of Hatoula, Israel, *International Journal of Osteoarchaeology*, 13: 120-131.

Bar-Matthews M., Ayalon, A., Kaufman, A., 1999, The Eastern Mediterranean paleoclimate as a reflection of regional events: Soreq cave, Israel, *Earth and Planetary Science Letters*, 166/1-2: 85-95.

Bar-Oz, G., Munro, N.D., 2007, Gazelle bone marrow yields and Epipalaeolithic carcass exploitation strategies in the southern Levant, *Journal of Archaeological Science,* 34/6: 946-956.

Bar-Yosef, O., 1985, A cave in the desert: Nahal Hemar: 9,000-year-old-finds, Israel Museum, Jerusalem.

Bar-Yosef, O., 1995, Earliest Food Producers — Pre Pottery Neolithic (8000-5500), *The Archaeology of society in the Holy Land*, edited by Thomas Levy, Leicester University Press, London, 190 - 204.

Bar-Yosef, O., 1998, The Natufian Culture in the Levant, Threshold to the Origins of Agriculture, *Evolutionary Anthropology*, 6/5:159 – 177.

Bar-Yosef, O., 2002, The raw or the cooked: Aspects of early human evolution, *Antiquity*, 76/293: 605-607.

Bar-Yosef, O., 2003, The Natufian Culture and the Early Neolithic: Social and Economic Trends in Southwest Asia, in *Examining the farming/language hypothesis*, edited by P. Bellwood & C. Renfrew, McDonald Institute, Cambridge, 113-126.

Bar-Yosef, O., Valla, F., 1990, The Natufian Culture and the Origin of the Neolithic in the Levant, *Current*

Anthropology 31(4):433-436

Bar-Yosef, O., Khazanov, A., 1992, *Pastoralism in the Levant: Archaeological Materials in Anthropological Perspectives*, Prehistory Press, Madison. 1-9.

Bar-Yosef, O., Belfer-Cohen, A., 2002, Facing environmental crisis. Societal and cultural changes at the transition from the Younger Dryas to the Holocene in the Levant, *The Dawn of Farming in the Near East*, Studies in Early Near Eastern Production, Subsistence and Environment 6, R.T.J. Cappers and S. Bottema eds., Ex oriente, Berlin, 55-66.

Bellwood, P.S., 2005, *First farmers : the origins of agricultural societies*, Blackwell, Malden, MA.

Bender, D.A. 2005, *A Dictionary of Food and Nutrition*, Oxford University Press, Oxford.

Bernbeck, R., in press, The Neolithic Pottery, *Excavations at Toll-e Bashi, Fars Province, southwestern Iran: a preliminary report*, edited by Susan Pollock and Reinhard Bernbeck, German Archaeological Institute, Berlin.

Bernbeck, R., Pollock, S., Abdi, K., 2003, Reconsidering the Neolithic at Toll-e Bashi, Iran, *Near Eastern Archaeology*, 66/1-2: 76-78.

Bernbeck, R., Abdi, K., Gregg, M.W., 2006, A note on the Neolithic of the Qara Aghaj valley, Fars province, *Archaeological Reports* 4, Iranian Center for Archaeological Research, Tehran 27-36.

Bernbeck, R., Gregg, M.W., in press, Burnt Clay Fragments, *Excavations at Toll-e Bashi, Fars Province, southwestern Iran: a preliminary report*, edited by Susan Pollock and Reinhard Bernbeck, German Archaeological Institute, Berlin.

Bernbeck, R., Pollock, S., Abdi, K., in press, The Stratigraphy, *Excavations at Toll-e Bashi, Fars Province, southwestern Iran: a preliminary report*, edited by Susan Pollock and Reinhard Bernbeck, German Archaeological Institute, Berlin.

Berthelot, M., 1906, Liquides provenant d'un flacon trouvé pres de Reims, *Archéologie et Histoire des Sciences*, Mémoires de l'Académie des Sciences de Paris, tome 49: 128-129.

Biehl, P., 2009, personal communication following a seminar entitled: *Rethinking the Transition Between the Neolithic and Chalcolithic in Çatalhöyük, Turkey*, Monday, January 19, 2009, Archaeology Centre, University of Toronto.

Bieniek, A., 2002, Archaeobotanical analysis of some early Neolithic settlements in the Kujawy region, central Poland, with potential plant gathering activities emphasized, *Vegetation History and Arcaheobotany*, 11/1-2: 33-40.

Binford, L.R., 1962, Archaeology as Anthropology, *American Antiquity*, 28:217-25.

Binford, L.R., 1967, Response to K.C. Chang, Major Aspects of the Interrelationship of Archaeology and Ethnology, *Current Anthropology*, 8/3: 234.

Bogucki, P.I., 1984, Ceramic Sieves of the Linear Pottery Culture and their economic implications, *Oxford Journal of Archaeology*, 3/1:15-30.

Bökönyi, S., 1977, *The animal remains of four sites in the Kermanshah Valley*, BAR Supplementary Series 34, Oxford.

Bottema, S., 1986, A late Quaternary Pollen Diagram from Lake Urmia (Northwestern Iran), *Review of Palaeobotany and Palynology*, 47/3-4: 241-248.

Boulton, N., Heron, C., 2000, Chemical detection of ancient wine, in Murray M.A., Viticulture and wine production, *Ancient Egyptian Materials and Technology*, Nicholson, P.T., Shaw, I. (Eds.), Cambridge University Press, Cambridge, 599-603.

Bourdieu, P., 1977, *Outline of a Theory of Practice*, Cambridge University Press, Cambridge.

Braidwood, R.J., 1952, From Cave to Village, *Scientific American*, October, 62-66.

Braidwood, R., 1960, Preliminary Investigations Concerning the Origins of Food-Production in Iranian Kurdistan, *British Association for the Advancement of Science*, 17:214-218.

Braidwood, R.J., 1961, The Iranian Prehistoric Project, *Iranica Antiqua*, 1:3-7.

Braidwood, R.J., 1962, The earliest Village Communities in Southwestern Asia Reconsidered, *Atti del VI Congresso Internazionale Delle Scienze Preistoriche e Protostoriche*, ed. G.C. Sansoni, Union Internazionale Delle Scienze Preistoriche e Protostoriche, Rome.

Braidwood, R.J., Sauer, R., Helbaek, H., Mangelsdorf, P.C., Cutler, H.C., Coon, C.S., Linton,R., Steward, J., Oppenheim A.L., 1953, Did Man Once Live by Beer Alone? *American Anthropologist*, 55/4: 515-526.

Braidwood, R., Howe, B., Reed, C., 1960, *Prehistoric investigations in Iraqi Kurdistan*, University of Chicago Press, Chicago.

Braidwood, R., Howe, B., Reed, C., 1961, The Iranian Prehistoric Project, *Science*, Vol. 133: 2008-2010.

Braun, D.P., 1983, Pots as Tools, in *Archaeological Hammers and Theories*, ed. J.A. Moore and A.S. Keene, Academic Press, New York.

Breasted, J., 1914, *Outlines of European History*, Longmans, Chicago.

Brevik, A., Veierød, M. B., Drevon, C.A., Andersen, L.F., 2005, Evaluation of the odd fatty acids 15:0 and 17:0 in serum and adipose tissue as markers of intake of milk and dairy fats, *European Journal of Clinical Nutrition*, 59, 1417–1422.

Brongniart, A., 1844, *Traité des arts céramiques ou des poteries considérées dans leur histoire, leur pratique et leur théorie*, A. Mathias, Paris.

Brown, J.A., ,1989, The beginnings of pottery as an economic process, *What's New? A closer look at the process of innovation*, edited by Sander van der Leeuw and Robin Torrence, Unwin Hyman, London, 203-224.

Byers, F.M., Schelling, G.T., 1988, Lipids in Ruminant Nutrition, *The Ruminant Animal: Digestive Physiology and Nutrition*, edited by D.C. Church, Prentice Hall, Inglewood Cliffs, N.J.

Çambel, H., 1981, Chronologie et organisation de l'éspace à Çayönü, *Préhistore du Levant: Chronologie et organisation de l'éspace depuis les origines jusqu'au VIe millenaire*, Colloque International du CNRS, Paris, 531-553.

Campbell, S., 2007, Rethinking Halaf Chronologies, *Paléorient*, 33/1:103-135.

Caneva, I., 1988, The History of a Middle Nile Environment: A suggested cultural model, in El Geili:

The History of a Middle Nile Environment 7000 BC – AD 1500, BAR, Oxford, 359-377.

Cauvin, J., 2000, *The Birth of the Gods and the Origins of Agriculture*, translated by Trevor Watkins, Cambridge University Press, Cambridge.

Cavalieri, D., McGovern, P.E., Hartl, D.L., Mortimer, R., Polsinelli, M., 2003, Evidence for *S. cerevisiae*, fermentation in ancient wine, *Journal of Molecular Evolution*, 57/1: S226-S232.

Cessford, C., 2001, A new dating sequence for Catalhoyuk, *Antiquity*, 75/290:717-725.

Chapman, J., 2000, Fragmentation in Archaeology: People, Places, and Broken Objects in the Prehistory of Southeastern Europe, Routledge, London.

Charters, S., Evershed, R.P., Goad, L.J., Leyden, A., Blinkhorn, P.W., Denham, V., 1993, Quantification and distribution of lipids in archaeological ceramics, *Archaeometry*, 35:211-223.

Charters, S., Evershed, R.P., Quye, A., 1997, Simulation experiments for determining the use of ancient pottery vessels: The behavior of epicuticular leaf wax during boiling of a leafy vegetable, *Journal of Archaeological Science*, 24/1: 1-7.

Childe, V.G., 1928, *The Most Ancient East: The Oriental Prelude to European Prehistory,* Kegan Paul, London.

Childe, V.G., 1936, *Man Makes Himself*, Watts, London.

Christie, W., 2008, Medium-chain fatty acids, *The Lipid Library*, online electronic resource, accessed October 24, 2008 at: http://www.lipidlibrary.co.uk/Lipids/fa_sat/index.htm.

Clark, J.D., 1989, An Early Khartoum Settlement on the White Nile, in *Late prehistory of the Nile Basin and the Sahara*, edited by L. Krzyaniak and M. Kobusiewicz, Pozna Archaeological Museum, Pozna, 387 - 410.

Collins, M., 2008, *New Directions in Ancient Biomolecules*, A virtual seminar series from the Worldwide Universities Network, accessed online on November 16, 2008 at: http://www.wun.ac.uk/view.php?id=57; http://www.wun.ac.uk/bioarch/index.html

Connan, J., 1999, Use and trade of bitumen in antiquity and prehistory: molecular archaeology reveals secrets of past civilizations, *Philosophical Transactions of the Royal Society of London* Series B – Biological Sciences, 354/1379: 46.

Connan, J., Nieuwenhuysetm O.P., Van As, A., Jacobs, L., 2004, Bitumen in Early Ceramic Art: Bitumen-painted ceramics from Late Neolithic Sabi Abyad (Syria), *Archaeometry,* 46, pp 115-124.

Coolidge, J. W., 2005, *Southern Turkmenistan in the Neolithic: a petrographic case study*, BAR Publishing, Oxford.

Coon, C.S., 1951a, Excavations at Hotu Cave, Iran, 1951a, A Preliminary Report, *Proceedings of the American Philosophical Society*, 96/3: 2231-249.

Coon, C.S., 1951b, *Cave Explorations in Iran 1949*, University of Pennsylvania Museum, Philadelphia.

Cooper, A., Poinar, H.N., 2000, Ancient DNA: Do it right or not at ALL, *Science*, 289/5482: 1139-1139.

Copley, M.S., Bertan, R., Dudd, S.N., Docherty, G., Mukherjee, A.J., Straker, V., Payne, S., Evershed, R.P., 2003, Direct chemical evidence for widespread dairying in prehistoric Britain, *Proceeding of the National Academy of Sciences*, vol. 100/4: 1524-1529.

Copley, M.S., Jim, S., Jones, V., Evershed, R.P., 2004, Short and long-term foraging and foddering strategies of domesticated animals from Qasr Ibrim, Egypt, *Journal of Archaeological Science*, 31/9:1273-1286.

Copley, M.S., Berstan, R., Dudd, S.N., Aillaud, S., Mukherjee, A.J., Straker, V., Payne, S., Evershed, R.P., 2005a, Processing of milk products in pottery vessels through British prehistory, *Antiquity*, 79/306: 895-908.

Copley, M.S., Berstan, R., Dudd, S.N., Straker, V., Payne, S., Evershed, R.P., 2005b, Dairying in antiquity. I. Evidence from absorbed lipid residues dating to the British Iron Age, *Journal of Archaeological Science*, 32/4: 485-503.

Copley, M.S., Berstan, R., Straker, V., Payne, S., Evershed, R.P., 2005c, Dairying in antiquity. II. Evidence from absorbed lipid residues dating to the British Bronze Age, *Journal of Archaeological Science*, 32/4: 505-521.

Copley, M.S., Berstan, R., Dudd, S.N., Straker, V., Payne, S., Evershed, R.P., 2005d, Dairying in antiquity. III. Evidence from absorbed lipid residues dating to the British Neolithic, *Journal of Archaeological Science*, 32/4: 523-546.

Copley. M.S., Clark, K., Evershed, R.P., 2005e, Organic-r residue Analysis of Pottery Vessels and Clay Balls, *Changing Materialities at Çatalhöyük*: Reports from the 1995-99 Seasons, McDonald Institute for Archaeological Research, Cambridge, 169-174.

Copley, M.S., Bland, H.A., Rose, P., Horton, M., Evershed, R.P., 2005f, Gas chromatographic, mass spectrometric, and stable carbon isotopic investigations of organic residues of plant oils and animal fats employed as illuminants in archaeological lamps from Egypt, *Analyst*, 130: 860-871.

Cordell, L.S., 1984, *Prehistory of the Southwest,* Academic Press, Orlando.

Coughenour, R. A., 1976, Preliminary Report on the Exploration and Excavation of Mugharat el Wardeh and Abu Thawwab *Annual of the Department of Antiquities of Jordan,* Amman, 21: 71-78.

Craig, O.E., Collins, M.J., 2000, An improved method for immunological detection of mineral bound protein using hydrofluoric acid and direct capture, *Journal of Immunological Methods*, 236: 89-97.

Craig, O.E., Collins, M.J., 2002, The removal of protein from mineral surfaces: Implications for residue analysis of archaeological materials, *Journal of Archaeological Science* 29, 1077-1082.

Craig, O. E., Mulville, J., Parker-Pearson, M., Gelsthorpe, K., Sokol, R., Stacey, R., Collins, M., 2000, Detecting Milk Proteins in Ancient Pots, in *Nature*, 408: 312-312.

Craig O.E., Chapman J., Heron C., Willis, L.H., Bartosiewicz, L., Taylor, G., Whittle, A., Collins, M., 2005, Did the first farmers of central and eastern Europe produce dairy foods? , *Antiquity*, 79/306 : 882-894.

Craig, O. E., Forster, M., Andersen, S. H., Koch, E., Crombe, P., Milner, N. J., Stern, B., Bailey, G. N., Heron, C. P, 2007, Molecular and isotopic demonstration of the processing of aquatic products in northern European prehistoric pottery, *Archaeometry*, 49:135-152.

Crane, H.R., Griffin, J.B., 1972, University of Michigan Radiocarbon Dates XIV, *Radiocarbon*, 14, 155-194.

Curwen, E.C., 1938, Early Agriculture in Denmark, *Antiquity*, 12:135-153.

Custer, J.F., Ilgenfritz, J., Doms, K.R., 1998, A cautionary note on the use of Chemstrips for detection of blood residues on prehistoric tools, *Journal of Archaeological Science*, 15: 343-345.

Daintith, J., 2008, A *Dictionary of Chemistry*, Oxford University Press, Oxford Reference Online, Oxford University Press. University of Toronto Libraries. 31 August 2008, http://www.oxfordreference.com.myaccess.library.utoronto.ca/views/ENTRY.html?subview=Main&entry=t81.e1907.

Dalman, G., 1938, *Arbeit and Sitte in Palastina*. Druck und verlag von C. Bertelsmann in Gütersloh.

Darwin, C., 1859, *On the origin of species by means of natural selection, or, The preservation of favored races in the struggle for life*, J. Murray, London.

Davis, S., 1982, *Some evidence of the Origin of Wool and Milk Production in the Near East based upon the sequence of Faunal Assemblages from Western Iran*, Paper delivered at the Fourth International Conference on Archaeozoology, London.

Davis, S., 1984, The advent of milk and wool production in western Iran: some speculations, in *Animals and Archaeology* III, edited by Juliet Clutton-Brock and Caroline Grigson, BAR 202, Oxford, p. 265-278.

Dietler, M., 1996, Feasts and Commensal Politics in the Political Economy, *Food and the Status Quest: An Interdisciplinary Perspective*, edited by Polly Wiessner and Wulf Schiefenhövel, Berghahn Books, Providence, RI.

Dekoning, P.M., Smith, A.B., 1985, Gas-liquid Chromatography of fatty-acids in food residues found in the southwestern cape, South Africa, *Archaeometry*, 27:231-236.

Dean, J.S., 1978, Independent Dating in Arhaeological Analysis, *Advances in ArchaeologicalMethod and Theory*, 1: 223-225.

DeAtley, S.P., Bishop, R.L., 1991, Toward an Integrated I Interface for Archaeology and Archaeometry, The *Ceramic Legacy of Anna O. Shepard,* University of Colorado Press, Denver.

DeNiro, M.J., Epstein, S., 1977, Mechanism of Carbon Isotope Fractionation Associated with Lipid Synthesis, *Science*, 197:261-263

DeNiro, M.J., Epstein, S., 1978, Influence of diet on the distribution of carbon isotopes in animals, *Geochimica Cosomochimica Acta*, 42:495-506.

Dolukhanov, P., Shukurov, A, Gronenborn, D., 2005, The chronology of neolithic dispersal in Central and Eastern Europe, *Journal of Archaeological Science*, 32/10: 1441-1458.

Downs, E.F., Lowenstein, J.M., 1995, Identification of Archaeological Blood Proteins: A Cautionary Tale, *J Journal of Archaeological Science*, 22: 11-16.

Driver, H.E., Massey, W.C., 1957, Comparative Studies of North American Indians, *Transactions of the American Philosophical Society*, New Series, 47/2:165-456.

Ducos, P., 1993, Proto-élevage et élevage au Levant sud au VIIe Millénaire b.c.: les Données de la Damascène, *Paléorient*, 19 (1): 153-173.

Dudd, S.N., Regert, M., Evershed, R.P., 1998, Assessing microbial lipid contributions during laboratory \ degradations of fats and oils and pure triacylglycerols absorbed in ceramic potsherds, *Organic Geochemistry*, 20 (5-7):1345-1354.

Dudd, S.N., Evershed, R.P., 1998, Direct demonstration of milk as an element of archaeological economies, *Science* 282:1478-1481.

Dudd, S.N., Evershed, R.P., Gibson, A.,1999, Evidence for varying patterns of exploitation of animal products in different prehistoric pottery traditions based on lipids in surface and absorbed residues, *Journal of Archaeological Science*, 26: 1473 –1482.

Dungait, J.A.J., Docherty, G., Straker, V., Evershed, R.P., Interspecific variation in bulk tissue, fatty acid and monosaccharide $\Box^{13}C$ values from a mesotrophic grassland plant community, 2008, *Phytochemistry*, 69:2041-2051.

Dyson, R.H., 1965, Problems in the Relative Chronology of Iran, 6000-2000 BC, *Chronologies in Old World Archaeology*, ed. R.W. Ehrich, University of Chicago Press, Chicago, 215-255.

Dyson, R.H., 1991, Ceramics I. The Neolithic Period through the Bronze Age in Northeastern and North-Central Persia, *Encyclopaedia Iranica* 5 (3): 266-275.

Ebeling, W., 1986, Handbook of Indian Foods and Fibers in Arid America, University of California Press, Berkeley.

Eglinton, G., Logan, G.A., 1991, Molecular Preservation, *Philosophical Transactions of the Royal Society, London*, B. 315-327.

Englund, R.K., 1995, Late Uruk Cattle and Dairy Products in Domestic Animals of Mesopotamia II, *Bulletin on Sumerian Agriculture*, Cambridge, p 33-47.

Entwhistle, J.,Abrahams, P., Dodgshon, R., 2000, The Geoarchaeological Significance and Spatial Variability of a Range of Physical and Chemical Soil Properties from a Former Habitation Site, Isle of Skye, *Journal of Archaeological Science*, 27, 287-303.

Ericson, J.E., Read, D.W., Burke, C., 1971, Research Design: The relationship between the primary functions and physical properties of ceramic vessels and their implications for ceramic distributions on an archaeological site. *Anthropology UCLA* III(2): 84-95

Ertug, F., 2008, personal communication with Michael Gregg concerning the use of an ethnographically-known pottery vessel used in manufacturing cheese, butter and yogurt by goat and sheep herders in central Turkey.

Ertug-Yaras, F., 1997, *An ethnoarchaeological study of subsistence and plant gathering in Central Anatolia*, unpublished Ph.D. thesis, Department of Anthropology, Washington University, St. Louis.

Evershed, R.P., 1993, Biomolecular archaeology and lipids, *World Archaeology*, vol. 25/1:74-93.

Evershed, R.P., 1994, Gas chromatography of lipids; Mass spectrometry of lipids in *Lipid Analysis: A Practical Approach* , edited by R.J Hamilton & S. Hamilton, Oxford University Press, Oxford, pp. 113 - 152; 263-306.

Evershed, R.P., 2008, Organic Residue Analysis in Archaeology, The Archaeological Biomarker Revolution, *Archaeometry*, 50/6:895-924.

Evershed, R.P., Heron, C., Goad, J., 1990, Analysis of Organic Residues of Archaeological Origin by High-temperature Gas Chromatography - Mass Spectrometry, *Analyst*, 115: 1339-42.

Evershed, R.P., Heron, C., Charters, S., Goad, L.J., 1992a, The survival of food residues: new methods of analysis, interpretation, application, *Proceedings of the British Academy*, 77:187-208.

Evershed, R.P., Heron, C., Charters, C., Goad, J.1992b, Chemical analysis of organic residues in ancient pottery: methodological guidelines and applications, in *Organic Residues in Archaeology: Their Identification Analysis*, edited by R. White and H. Page, UKIC Archaeology Section, London, p. 11-25.

Evershed, R.P., Dudd, S.N., Lockheart, M.J., Jim, S., 2001, Lipids in Archaeology, *Handbook of Archaeological Sciences*, edited by D.R. Brothwell & A.M. Pollard, John Wiley & Sons, London, 331-349.

Evershed, R.P., Dudd, S.N., Copley, M.S., Mukherjee, A., 2002, Identification of animal fats via compound specific $\partial^{13}C$ values of individual fatty acids: assessments of results for reference fats and lipid extracts of archaeological pottery vessels, *Documenta Praehistorica*, XXIX: 73-96.

Evershed, R.P., Mottram, H.R., Dudd, S.N., Charters, S., Stott, A.W., Lawrence, G.J., Gibson, A.M., Conner, A., Blinkhorn, P., Reeves, V., 1997, New criteria for the identification of animal fats in archaeological pottery, *Naturwissenschaften*, 84:402-406.

Evershed, R. P., Payne, S., Sherratt, A. G., Copley, M. S., Coolidge, J., Urem-Kotsu, D., Kotsakis, K., Özdogan, M., Özdogan, A. E., Nieuwenhuyse, O., Akkermans, P. M. M. G., Bailey, D., Andeescu, R.-R., Campbell, S., Farid, S., Hodder, I., Yalman, N., Özbagaran, M., Bıçakcı, E., Garfinkel, Y., Levy, T., and Burton, M. M., 2008, Earliest date for milk use in the Near East and southeastern Europe linked to cattle herding. *Nature*. Advance online publication: 6 August 2008 doi:10.1038/nature07180; http://www.nature.com/nature/journal/vaop/ncurrent/fig_tab/nature07180_ft.html

Evershed, R.P., Tuross, N., 1996, Proteinaceous Material from Potsherds and Associated Soils, *Journal of Archaeological Science*, 23: 429-436.

Fairbairn A., Asouti, E., Near, J., Martinoli, D., 2005, Macrobotanical investigation of the north, south and KOPAL area excavations at Çatalhöyük East. In: I. Hodder, Editor, *Inhabiting Çatalhöyük: Reports from the 1995-99 Seasons,* McDonald Institute for Archaeological Research/British Institute of Archaeology at Ankara, Cambridge, London (2005), pp. 137–202.

Fall, P.L., Falconer, S.E., Lines, L., 2002, Agricultural intensification and the secondary products revolution along the Jordan Rift, *Ecology*, 30/4:445-482.

Fauer, G., 1986, *Principles of Isotope Geology*, John Wiley and Sons, New York.

Fenn, J.B., Mann, M., Meng, C.K.,Wong, S.F., 1990, Electrospray ionization — principles and practice, *Mass Spectrometry Reviews,* 9:37-70.

Finlayson, B., Kuijt, I., Arpin, T., Chesson, M., Dennis. S., Goodale, N., Kadowaki, S., Maher, L., Smith, S. Schurr, M., McKay, J., 2003, Dhra', Excavation Project, 2002 Interim Report. *Levant*, 35: 1-38.

Forbes, R.J., 1936, Note on a lump of asphalt from Ur, *Journal of the Institute of Petroleum Technology*, XXII: 180.

Frankfort, H., 1927, *Studies in Early Pottery of the Near East*, Occasional Papers No. 8, Royal Anthropological Institute, London.

Frankfort, H., 1955, *Stratified Cylinder Seals from the Diyala Region*, Oriental Institute Publications, Vol. LXXII, University of Chicago Press, Chicago.

Friedli, H., Lötscher, H., Oeschger, H., Siegenthaler, U., Stauffer, B., 1986, Ice core record of the $^{13}C/^{12}C$ ratio of CO_2 in the past two centuries, *Nature*, 324:237-238.

Fukai, S., Horiuchi, K., and Matsutani, T., 1973, *Marv Dasht III: The Excavations at Tall-i Mushki*, 1965, Institute ot Oriental Culture, Tokyo.

Fuller, D.Q., 2006, Agricultural origins and frontiers in South Asia: A working synthesis, *Journal of World Prehistory*, 20/1: 1-86.

Galili E., Sharvit J., and Nagar A., 1998, Neve-Yam - underwater survey, *Excavations and Surveys in Israel*, 18: 54-56, (English edition of *Hadashot Arkheologiyot*, 1996 106: 35-36).

Galili, E., 2004, *Submerged Settlements of the Ninth to Seventh Millenium BP off the Carmel Coast*, unpublished PhD thesis, Tel Aviv University.

Garfinkel, Y., 1997, Excavations and surveys - Sha'ar-ha-Golan, 1997, *Israel Exploration Journal*, 47/3-4: 271-273.

Garfinkel, Y., 1999a, *Qedem 39: Neolithic and Chalcolithic Pottery*, Institute of Archaeology, Hebrew University of Jerusalem.

Garfinkel, Y., 1999b, Radiometric Dates from Eighth Millennium B.P. Israel, *Bulletin of the American Schools of Oriental Research*, 315, 1-13.

Garfinkel, Y., Miller, M., 2001 *Sh'ar Hagolan: Neolithic Art in Context*, Oxbow, Oxford.

Garstang, J., Garstang, J.B.E. 1940, *The story of Jericho*, Hodder & Stoughton, London.

Gayton, A. H., 1948, Yokuts and Western Mono Ethnography, II, Northern Foothills Yokuts and Western Mono Ethnography, *University of California Anthropological Records* 10: 143-301.

Gebel, H.G., 1988, Late Epipalaeolithic-Aceramic Neolithic sites in the Petra area, *The Prehistory of Jordan: The State of Research in 1986*, British Archaeological Reports, Oxford.

Gernaey, A.M., Waite, E.R., Collins, M.J., Craig, O.E., 2001, Survival and Interpretation of Archaeological Proteins, in *Handbook of Archaeological Sciences*, edited by D.R. Brothwell and A.M. Pollard, John Wiley & Sons, London, p. 323-329.

Gibbs, K., Kadowaki, S., Banning, E. B., 2006, The Late Neolithic at al-Basatîn, Wadi Ziqlab, northern Jordan, *Antiquity*, 80(310), http://www.antiquity.ac.uk.ProjGall/gibbs/index.html.

Gilead, I., 1994, The History of the Chalcolithic Settlement in the Nahal Beer Sheva Area: the Radiocarbon Aspect, *Bulletin of the American Schools of Oriental Research*, 296:1-13.

Gilead, I., Fabian, P., 2001, Nevatim: a site of the Chalcolithic period in the Northern Negev. *In Settlement, Civilization and Culture*, Proceedings of the Conference in Memory of David Alon. Edited by A.M.Maeir and E. Baruch, pp. 67-86. Ramat Gan: Bar Ilan University.

Gilead, I., Rosen, S., Fabian, P., Rothenberg, B., 1992, New Archaeo-Metallurgical Evidence for the Beginnings of Metallurgy in the Southern Levant. Excavations at Tell Abu Matar, Beersheba (Israel) 1990/1, *TAMS Newsletter*, 18:11-14.

Gillet, E., Gillet, C., 1983, Jebel Abu Thawwab, Jordan, *Levant*, Journal of the British School of Archaeology in Jerusalem, 15: 187-191.

Gokturk, E.H., Hillegonds, D.J., Lipschutz, M.E., Hodder, I., 2002, Accelerator mass spectrometry dating at Catalhoyuk, *Radiochimica Acta*, 90/7:407-410.

Goodyear, A.C., 1988, On the Study of Technological Change, *Current Anthropology*, 29/2: 320-323.

Gopher, A., Gophna, R., 1993, Cultures of the Eighth and Seventh Millennia BP. in the Southern Levant, *Journal of World History*, 7/3: 297-353.

Gopher, A., 1995, Early Pottery-bearing groups in Israel — the Pottery Neolithic Period, *The Archaeology of society in the Holy Land*, edited by Thomas Levy, Leicester University Press, London, 205 – 225.

Goring-Morris, N., Horwitz, L.K., 2007. Funerals and feasts during the Pre-Pottery Neolithic B of the Near East, *Antiquity* 81/314.

Gosden, C., 1999, *Anthropology and Archaeology: A Changing Perspective*, Routledge, New York.

Gostner P., Vigel E.E., 2002, Report of radiological-forensic findings on the Iceman, *Journal of Archaeological Science*, 29/3: 323-326.

Gould, S. J., 1965, Is uniformitarianism necessary? *American Journal of Science*, 263: 223 - 228.

Gregg, M.W., 2003, Biomolecular Research into the Origins of Dairy Foods in Southwest Asia, *Neolithics*, 1/03:33.

Gregg, M.W., in press, Organic Residue Analysis, *Excavations at Toll-e Bashi, Fars Province, southwestern Iran: a preliminary report*, edited by Susan Pollock and Reinhard Bernbeck, German Archaeological Institute, Berlin.

Gregg, M.W., Stern, B., Brettell R., 2007, Bitumen in Neolithic Iran: Biomolecular and Isotopic Evidence, *Archaeological Chemistry: Analytical Methods and Interpretation*, ed. Michael Glascock, American Chemical Society, Oxford University Press, 137-151.

Gregg, M.W., Banning, E.B., Gibbs, K., Slater, G.F., 2009, Subsistence practices and pottery use in Neolithic Jordan: molecular and isotopic evidence, *Journal of Archaeological Science*, 36/4: 937-946, http://dx.doi.org/10.1016/j.jas.2008.09.009.

Gregg, M.W., Slater, G.F., in press, A new approach for the isolation, concentration, and transesterification of free fatty acids in archaeological ceramics, *Archaeometry*.

Greenfield, H.J., 1988, The origins of milk and wool production in the Old World: A zooarchaeological perspective from the Central Balkans. *Current Anthropology* 29/4: 573-593.

Greenfield, H.J., 2005, A reconsideration of the Secondary Products Revolution in south-eastern Europe: on the origins and use of domestic animals for milk, wool, and traction in the central Balkans, in *The Zooarchaeology of Fats, Oils, Milk and Dairying*, edited by J. Mulville and A.K. Outram, Oxbow Books, Oxford, pp 14-31.

Grigson, C., 1987, Different Herding Strategies for Sheep and Goats in the Chalcolithic of Beersheeva, *Archaeozoologia* I: 115-126.

Gross, M., Pramanik B N., Ganguly, A. K., 2002, *Applied electrospray mass spectrometry*, Marcel Dekker, New York.

Guasch-Jané M.R., Ibern-Gomez M., Andres-Lacueva C., Jauregui O., Lamuela-Raventos R.M., 2004, Liquid chromatography with mass spectrometry in tandem mode applied for the identification of wine markers in residues from ancient Egyptian vessels, *Analytical Chemistry*, 76/6: 1672-1677.

Guasch-Jané M.R., Ibern-Gomez M., Andres-Lacueva C., Jauregui O., Lamuela-Raventos R.M., 2006, The origin of the ancient Egyptian drink Shedeh revealed using LC/MS/MS, *Journal of Archaeological Science*, 33/1: 98-101.

Gurfinkel, D.M., Franklin, U.M., 1988, A study on the feasibility of detecting blood residue on artifacts, *Journal of Archaeological Science*, 15: 83-97.

Haaland, R. 1992, Fish, pots and grain: Early and Mid-Holocene adaptations in the Central Sudan, *African Archaeological Review*, 10/1:43-67.

Haaland, R., 2007, Porridge and pot, bread and oven: Food ways and symbolism in Africa and the Near East from the Neolithic to the present, *Cambridge Archaeological Journal*, 17/2: 165-182.

Hackford, J.E., Lawson, S., Spielmann, P.E., 1931, On an Asphalt Ring from Ur of the Chaldees, *Journal of the Institute of Petroleum Technology*, December 1931: 738.

Haber, A., Dayan, T., 2004, Analyzing the process of domestication: Hagoshrim as a case study. *Journal of Archaeological Science*, 31/11: 1587-1601.

Hally, D.J., 1983, Use Alteration of Pottery Vessel Surfaces: an important source of evidence of Vessel Function, *North American Archaeologist*, 4:3-26.

Hansson, M.C., Foley, B.P., 2008, Ancient DNA fragments inside Classical Greek amphorae reveal cargo of 2400-year-old shipwreck, *Journal of Archaeological Science*, 35/5: 1169-1176.

Harrington, J.P., 1942, Culture Element Distribution: XIX, Central California Coast, *University of California Anthropological Records*, 7/1.

Harris, D.R., Masson, V.E., Berezkin. Y.E., 1993, Investigating early agriculture in Central Asia: new research at Jeitun, Turkmenistan, *Antiquity*, 67:324-38.

Harris, D., 1996, *The Origins and Spread of Agriculture and Pastoralism in Eurasia*. Smithsonian Institution, Washington, DC.

Harris, D., 1998, The Origins of Agriculture in Southwest Asia, in the *Review of Archaeology*, 19/2: 5-21.

Hastorf, C.A., DeNiro, M.J., 1985, Reconstruction of Prehistoric Plant-production and Cooking Practices by a New Isotopic Method, *Nature*, 315/ 6019: 489-491.

Hayden, B., 1990, Nimrods, piscators, pluckers, and planters: The emergence of foodproduction. Journal of Anthropological Archaeology 9: 31-69.

Hayden, B., 1995, The emergence of prestige technologies and pottery, in Barnett, W. K., and Hoopes, J. W. (eds.), *The Emergence of Pottery: Technology and Innovation in Ancient Societies*, Smithsonian Institution Press, Washington, DC, 257-266.

Hayes, J.M., Freeman, K.H., Popp, B.N., Hoham, C.H., 1990, Compound-specific isotopic analyses: A novel tool for reconstruction of ancient biogeochemical processes, *Organic Geochemistry*, 16/4-6:1115-1128.

Hayes, J.M.. 1993, Factors controlling ^{13}C contents of sedimentary organic compounds: Principles and evidence, *Marine Geology*, 113/1-2: 111-125.

Hayes, J. M., 2001, Fractionation of Carbon and Hydrogen Isotopes in Biosynthetic Processes, *Reviews in Mineralogy and Geochemistry*, 43/1: 225-277.

Hayes, B.L., 2002, *Microwave Synthesis: Chemistry at the Speed of Light.*

Hedges, R.E.M., Housley, R.A., Bronk, C.R., Van Klinken, G.J., 1990, Radiocrabon Dates from the Oxford AMS System, *Archaeometry* Date List 11, *Archaeometry* 32: 211-237.

Helbaek, H., 1964, First Impressions of Çatahoyuk Plant Husbandry, *Anatolian Studies*, 14:121-123.

Henrickson, E., McDonald, M., 1980, Ceramic form and function: an ethnographic search and archaeological application, *American Anthropologist,* 85:630-643.

Henderson J.S, Joyce R.A, Hall G.R., Hurst W.J., McGovern, P.E., 2007, Chemical and archaeological evidence for the earliest cacao beverages, *PNAS*, 104/48:18937-18940.

Heron, C.P., Evershed, R.P., Goad, L.J., Denham, V., 1991, New Approaches to the Analysis of Organic Residues from Archaeological Remains, in *Archaeological Sciences 1989*, edited by P. Budd, B. Chapman, C. Jackson, R. Janaway, B. Ottaway, Oxbow Monograph 9, Oxford, 332-339.

Heron, C.P., Nemcek, N., Bonfield, K.M., Dixon, D., Ottaway, B.S., 1994, The Chemistry of Neolithic Beeswax, *Naturwissenschaften*, 81/6: 266-269.

Heron, C.P., Evershed, R. P., 1995, The analysis of organic residues and the study of pottery use, *Archaeological Method and Theory*, Vol. 5. Arizona: University of Arizona Press, 247-284.

Heron, C.P., 2001, Geochemical Prospection, in *The Handbook of Archaeological Sciences*, edited by D.R. Brothwell and A. M. Pollard, Wiley & Sons, p. 565-573.

Hesse, B., 1982, Animal Domestication in Oscillating Climates, *Journal of Ethnobiology,* 2 (1):1-15.

Hesse, B., 1983, Slaughter Patterns and Domestication: the Beginnings of Pastoralism in Western Iran, *Man*, 17: 403-417.

Hesse, B., 1984, These are our goats: the origins of herding in west central Iran, in *Animals and Archaeology* III, edited by Juliet Clutton-Brock and Caroline Grigson, BAR 202, Oxford, p. 243- 263.

Hesse, B., Wapnish, P., 2002, An Archaeozoological Perspective on the Cultural Use of Mammals in the Levant, in *A History of the Animal World in the Ancient Near East*, edited by B.J. Collins, Brill, Leiden, p. 457-474.

Hiebert, F.T., Dyson, R.H., 2002, Prehistoric Nishapur and the frontier between Central Asia and Iran, *Iranica Antiqua* 37: 113-149.

Hiebert, F.T., Kurbansakhatov, K., 2003, *A Central Asian Village at the Dawn of Civilization, Excavations at Anau, Turkmenistan,* University of Pennsylvania, Philadelphia.

Hillman G., Hedges, R., Moore, A., 2001, New evidence of late glacial cereal cultivation at Abu Hureyra on the Euphrates, *Holocene*, 11/ 4: 383-393.

Hodder, I., 1978, *The Spatial Organization od Culture*, Duckworth, London.

Hodder, I., 2006, Çatalhöyük: the Leopard's Tale, Thames and Hudson, London.

Hodder, I., 2007, Çatalhöyük in the context of the Middle Eastern Neolithic, *Annual Review of Anthropology*, 36: 105-120.

Hodder, I., Cessford, C., Farid, S., 2007, Introduction to Methods and Approach, *Excavating Çatalhöyük*, McDonald Institute Monographs, Volume 3, Cambridge.

Hole, F., 1974, Tepe Tula'i: an early campsite in Khuzistan, Iran, in *Paléorient,* vol. 2/2: 219-237.

Hole, F., 1977, *Studies in the archaeological history of the Deh Luran plan: The excavation of Chagha Sefid*, Memoirs of the Museum of Anthropology 9, University of Michigan, Ann Arbor.

Hole, F., 1978, Pastoral Nomadism in Western Iran, *Explorations in Ethnoarchaeology,* edited by R.A. Gould, University of New Mexico Press, Albuquerque, 127-167.

Hole, F., 1984, A Reassessment of the Neolithic Revolution, *Paléorient*, 2/10: 49-60.

Hole, F., 1987a Chronologies of the Iranian Neolithic, in *Chronologies in the Near East*, edited by O. Aurenche, J. Elvin, and F. Hours, BAR International Series, 379(i): 353-379.

Hole, F., 1987b Chronologies of the Iranian Neolithic, in *Chronologies in the Near East*, edited by O. Aurenche, J. Elvin, and F. Hours, BAR International Series, 379(i): 353-379.

Hole, F., 1987c, Archaeology of the Village Period, in *The Archaeology of Western Iran*, edited by Frank Hole, Smithsonian Institution Press, Washington, 29-78.

Hole, F., 1989, A two-part, two stage model of domestication, in *The Walking Larder,* edited by J. Clutton-Brock, Unwin Hyman, London, 91-104.

Hole, F., 1992 *The Prehistory of Herding: Some Suggestions from Ethnography*, Colloques internationaux du C.N.R.S., 580.

Hole, F., 1996, The context of caprine domestication in the Zagros region, in *The origins and spread of agriculture and pastoralism in Eurasia,* edited by D. Harris, UCL Press, London, 263-281.

Hole, F., 2000, New Radiocarbon dates for Ali Kosh, Iran, *Neolithics*, 1/00: 14.

Hole, F., 2001, A Radiocarbon Chronology for the Middle Khabur, Syria, Iraq 63: 67-98.

Hole, F., Flannery, K.V., 1961, Excavations at Ali Kosh, *Iranica Antiqua* II: 144-145.

Hole, F., Flannery, K.V., Neeley, J., 1965, Early Agriculture and Animal Husbandry in Deh Luran, Iran, *Current Anthropology,* 6/1:105-106.

Hole, F., Flannery, K.V., 1967, The Prehistory of Southwestern Iran: A Preliminary Report, *Proceedings of the Prehistoric Society*, 22/9: 147-206.

Hole, F., Flannery, K.V., Neely, J.A., 1969, *Prehistory and Human Ecology of the Deh Luran Plain,* Memoirs of the Museum of Anthropology, (1), Ann Arbor

Hornsey, I.S., 2003, *History of Beermaking and Brewing*, Royal Society of Chemists, London.

Horwitz, L.K., 1989, A reassessment of caprovine domestication in the Levantine Neolithic: Old questions;

new answers, in *People and Culture in Change*, BAR International. Series 508:(i):153-181, Oxford.

Horwitz, L.K., Ducos, P., 1998, An Investigation into the Domestication of Sheep in the southern Levant, in *Archaeozoology of the Near East III*, ARC Publications, Gronigen, 80-95.

Horwitz, L., Tchernov, E., Ducos, P.,Becker., Von Den Driesh, A., Martin, L., Garrard, A., 1999, Animal Domestication in the Southern Levant, *Paléorient*, 25/2:63-80.

Hours, F., Aurenche, O., Cauvin, J., Cauvin, M.-C., Copeland, L., Sanlavill, P., 1994, *Atlas des Sites du Proche-Orient, 14,000 – 5700 BP*, Travaux de la Maison de l'Orient mediterraéan 24, Lyon.

Housley, R.A., 1994, Eastern Mediterranean Chronologies: The Oxford AMS Contribution *Radiocarbon*, 36, 55-73.

Huber, E., 1926, *Bier und Bierbereitung bei den Volkern der Urzeir I, Babylonien und Aegypten,* Gesellschaft fur die Geschichte und Bibliographie des Brauwesens, Berlin.

Hughen, K.A., Eglinton, T.I., Xu, L., 2004, Abrupt Tropical Vegetation Response to Rapid Climate Changes. *Science*, 304, 1955-9.

Hughes, A., 2008, *Primary DNA Molecular Structure*, Connexions online electronic resource, Rice University, accessed November 8, 2008 at http://cnx.org/content/m11411/latest/.

Hutton, J., 1794, *An Investigation of the Principles of Knowledge and of the Progress of Reason, from Sense t to Science and Philosophy*, 3 volumes, Strahan and Cadell, Edinburgh.

Ikawa-Smith, F. 1976, On Ceramic Technology in East Asia, *Current Anthropology*, 17/3:211-218.

Ingold, T., 1980. *Hunters, pastoralists, and ranchers: Reindeer economies and their transformation,* Cambridge University Press, Cambridge.

Ingold, T., 1984, Time, Social Relationships and the Exploitation of Animals: Anthropological Reflections on Prehistory, in *Animals and Archaeology: Early Herders and their Flocks, Volume 3,* edited by J. Clutton-Brock & C. Grigson, BAR International Series 203, p. 3-12.

Ingold, T., 1994, From Trust to Domination: an alternative history of human-animal relations in *Animals and Human Society*, edited by A. Manning & J. Serpell, Routledge, London, p. 1-22.

Ingold, T., 2000, *The perception of the environment: essays on livelihood, dwelling and skill*, Routledge, London.

Jensen W.B., 2007, The Origin of the Soxhlet Extractor, *Journal of Chemical Education*, 84/12: 124-132.

Johnson, D., 1998, Removing beerstone: a look at alternative cleaning methods, *Modern Brewery Age* 49/12:36-39.

Johnson, O.W., 1969, *Flathead and Kootenay: The Rivers, the Tribes, and the Region's Traders*, Arthur H. Clark, Glendale, CA.

Jones, C.C., 1873, *Antiquities of the Southern Indians, Particularly of the Georgian Tribes,* Appleton, New York.

Jones, M., 2001, *The Molecule Hunt*, Penguin, London.

Kadowaki, S., Gibbs, K., Allentuck, A., Banning, E. B., 2008, Late Neolithic and Early Bronze I Occupations at at al-Basatîn, Wadi Ziqlab, Jordan, accepted for publication in *Paléorient*, 34/1:105-129.

Kafafi, Z., 1985, The first season of excavation at Abu Thawwab, *Annual of the Department of Antquitities of Jordan*, 29:31-42.

Kafafi, Z., 1986, The second season of excavation at Abu Thawwab, *Annual of the Department of Antquitities of Jordan*, 30:57-69.

Kafafi, Z., 1993, The Yarmoukians in Jordan, *Paléorient*, 19, 101-11.

Kaplan, Kaplan, J., 1954, Two Chalcolithic vessels from Palestine, in the *Palestine Exploration Quarterly*, 86:97-100.

Kaplan, J., 1965, Skin Bottles and Pottery Imitations, in the *Palestine Exploration Quarterly*, 130:145–152.

Kappe, C.O., Stadler, A., 2005, *Microwaves in Organic and Medicinal Chemistry*, Wiley-VCH Publishing: Weinheim.

Katz, S.H., 2003, Encyclopedia of food and culture, Scribner, New York.

Katz, I., Keeney, M., 1963, The isolation of fatty aldehydes from rumen-microbial lipid, *Biochimica et Biophysica Acta*, 84: 128-132.

Kendall, C., Caldwell, E. A., 1998, Fundamentals of Isotope Geochemistry, C. Kendall and J.J. McDonnell (Eds.), *Isotope Tracers in Catchment Hydrology*, Elsevier Science, Amsterdam, 51-86.

Kenrick, D.M., 1995, *Jomon of Japan: the world's oldest pottery*, Kegan Paul International, London.

Kenyon, K.M., 1957, *Digging Up Jericho*, Ernst Benn, London.

Kenyon, K.M., 1960, *Excavations at Jericho*, Oxford University Press, Oxford.

Khazanov, A.M., 1994, *Nomads and the outside world*, 2nd edition, translated by Julia Crookenden, University of Wisconsin Press, Madison.

Killick, D., Goldberg, P., 2009, A Quiet Crisis in American Archaeology, *SAA Archaeological Record*, 9/1: 6-40.

Killops S., Killops, V., 2005, *Introduction to Organic Geochemistry*, Blackwell, Malden, CA.

Kingery, W. D., Vandiver, P. B., Prickett, M., 1988, The Beginnings of pyrotechnology, part II: production and use of lime and gypsum plaster in the pre-pottery Neolithic Near East, *Journal of Field Archaeology*, 15: 219-44.

Kirkbride, D., 1973, Umm Dabaghiyah 1972: a second preliminary report, *Iraq*, 35:1 –7.

Kobayashi, T., 2004, *Jomon reflections: forager life and culture in the prehistoric Japanese archipelago*, Oxbow, Oxford.

Krause, A., 1956, *The Tlinget Indians: Results of a trip to t the Northwest Coast of America and the Bering Straits*, University of Washington Press, Seattle.

Kuhn, T.S., 1962, *The Structure of Scientific Revolutions,* University of Chicago Press, Chicago.

Kuijt, I., 2001, Lithic Inter-assemblage Variability and Cultural-Historical Sequences: A Consideration of the Pre-Pottery Neolithic A Occupation of Dhra`, Jordan, *Paléorient*, 27/1, 107-125.

Kuijt I., Finlayson B., MacKay J., 2007, Pottery Neolithic landscape modification at Dhra', *Antiquity* 81/311: 106-118.

Kuzmin, Y.V., 2006, Chronology of the earliest pottery in

East Asia: progress and pitfalls, *Antiquity*. 80:362-72.

Last, J., 1996, Surface Pottery at Çatahoyuk, *On the Surface Çatalhöyük:1993-1995*, McDonald Institute for Archaeological Research, Cambridge, 115-171.

Last, J., 2005 Pottery from the East Mound, 2005, *Changing Materialities at Çatalhöyük*: Reports from the 1995-99 Seasons, McDonald Institute for Archaeological Research, Cambridge, 169-174.

Lee-Thorp, J.A., 2008, On Isotopes and Old Bones, *Archaeometry*, 50/6:925-950.

Legge, A., 2005, Milk use in prehistory: the osteological evidence, *The Zooarchaeology of Milk and Fats*, J. Mulville & A. Outram eds., Oxbow, Oxford, 8-13.

Le Mière, M., 1983, Bouqras revisited: a preliminary report on a project in Eastern Syria, *Proceedings of the Prehistoric Society*, 49: 335-72.

Le Mière., Picon, M., 1999, Les debuts de la céramique au Proche Orient in *Palaéorient*, 24/2: 5-26.

Le Mière, M., Picon, M., 1987, Production locales et circulation des céramiques au Vie millénaire au Proche-Oriente, *Paléorient* 13/2: 133-147.

Levine, L., McDonald, M.M.A., 1977, The Neolithic and Chalcolithic periods in the Mahidasht, *Iran*, 15: 39-50.

Levine, L., Young, T.C., 1986, *A summary of the ceramic assemblages of the central western Zagros from the middle Neolithic to the late third millennium B.C. Editions du CNRS*, 1986, Paris.

Lévi-Strauss, C., 1970, *Introduction to a Science of Mythology, Vol. 1: The Raw and the Cooked*, translated by John and Doreen Weightman. London: Jonathan Cape.

Levy, T. E., 1983, Emergence of specialized pastoralism in the Levant. *World Archaeology* 15/1: 15-37.

Levy, T. E., 1992, Transhumance, Subsistence, and Social Evolution in the Northern Negev Desert, *Pastoralism in the Levant*, Prehistory Press, Madison, 65-82.

Levy, T. E., Alon, D., Grigson, C., Holl, A., Goldberg, P., Rowan, Y., Smith, P., 1991, Subterranean Negev Settlement, 7/4: 394-413.

Lev-Yadun, S., 2000, Why are underground flowering and fruiting plants more common in Israel than anywhere else in the world? *Current Science*, 79/3: 289-289.

Libby, W.F., 1951, *Radiocarbon Dating*, University of Chicago Press, Chicago.

Linton, R., 1944, North American Cooking Pots, *American Antiquity*, 9/4:369-380.

Loy, T.H., 1983, Prehistoric blood residues: detection on tool surfaces and identification of species of origin, *Science*, 220: 1269-70.

Loy, T.H., Hardy, B.G., 1992, Blood Residue Analysis of 90,000 year old stone tools from Tabun Cave, Israel, *Antiquity*, 66:24-35.

Loy, T.H., Wood, A.R.,1989, Blood Residue Analysis at Çayönü Tepesi, Turkey, *Journal of Archaeological Science*, 16:451-460.

Loupy, A., 2002, *Microwaves in Organic Synthesis*, Wiley-VCH Publishing, Weinheim.

Lovell, J., Dollfus, G., Kafafi. Z., 2004, The Middle Phases at Abu Hamid and the Wadi Rabah Horizon, *Studies in the History andArchaeology of Jordan VIII:*263-274.

Lovell, J., Dollfus, G., Kafafi. Z., 2007, Ceramics of the Late Neolithic and Chalcolithic: Abu Hamid and the Burnished Tradition, *Paléorient*, 33/1: 51-76.

Lucas, A., 1948, Ancient Egyptian Materials and Industries, E. Arnold, London.

Lucas, A., Harris, J.R., 1962, *Ancient Egyptian Materials and Industries,* 4th edition, Edward Arnold, London.

Lutz, H.F. 1922, *Viticulture and Brewing in the Ancient Orient*, Leipzig.

Lyell, C., 1830, *Principles of geology: being an inquiry how far the former changes of the earth's surface are referable to causes now in operation*, J. Murray, London.

Maisels, C.K., 1990, The Emergence of Civilization: From Hunting and Gathering to Agriculture, Cities and the State in the Near East, Routledge, London.

Malainey, M.E., Przybylski, R,, Sherriff, B.L., 1994, Identifying the former contents of late precontact period pottery vessels from western Canada using gas chromatography, *Journal of Archaeological Science*, 26/4: 425-438.

Mallon, A., Koeppel, R., Neuville, R., 1934, *Teleilat Ghassul*, The Pontifical Institute, Rome.

Manning, A.P., 1994, A Cautionary Note on the use of Hemastix and Dot-blot Assays for the Detection and Confirmation of Archaeological Blood Residues, *Journal of Archaeological Science*, 21/2: 159-162.

Maréchal, G., 1982, 'Vaiselles Blanche du Proche-Orient', *Cahier de l'Euphrate,* CNRS, Institure de Préhistoire Oriental, 3:217-251.

Matson, F.R., 1951, Ceramic Technology as an Aid to Cultural Interpretation—Techniques and Problems, *Essays on archaeological methods: proceedings of a conference held under auspices of the Viking Fund*, University of Michigan Press, Ann Arbor, 20-38.

Matson, F.R., 1965, Ceramic Ecology: an Approach to the Study of Early Cultures of the Near East, *Ceramics and Man*, ed. F.R. Matson, Wenner-Gren Foundation, Aldine, Chicago, 202-217.

Matsutani, T., 1989, Excavation at Tell Kashkashok II, 1987, Memoirs of the Institute of Oriental Culture, Tokyo, 1-33.

Matsutani, T., 1991, *Tell Kashkashok. The excavations at Tell II*, Institute of Oriental Culture, University of Tokyo, Tokyo.

McBurney, C.B., 1968, The Cave of Ali Tappeh and the Epi-Palaeolithic in N.E. Iran,*Proceedings of the Prehistoric Society*, 12: 385-413.

McCarroll, D., Loader, N.J., 2004, Stable isotopes in tree rings, *Quaternary Science Reviews,* 23:771-801.

McCormick, F., 1992, Early Faunal Evidence of Dairying, *Oxford Journal of Archaeology*, 11:201-209.

McCorriston, J., 1997, The Fiber Revolution: Textile Extensification, Alienation, and Social Stratification in Ancient Mesopotamia, *Current Anthropology*, 38/4: 517-549.

McDonald, M., 1979, *An examination of mid-holocene settlement patterns in the central Zagros region of western Iran, unpublished doctoral dissertation*, Department of anthropology, University of Toronto.

McGhee, R., 2008, Aboriginalism and the Problems of Indigenous Archaeology, *American Antiquity*, 73/4: 570-598.

McMurray, J., 2004, *Organic Chemistry*, Thomson Books, Standford, CN.

McGovern, P.E., 1996. Vin extraordinaire. The Sciences 36, 27-31.

McGovern, P.E., 1997. Wine of Egypt's golden age: an archaeochemical perspective. *Journal of Egyptian Archaeology* 83, 69-108.

McGovern, P.E., 2003. *Ancient Wine: The Search for the Origins of Viniculture*. Princeton University Press, Oxford.

McGovern, P.E., Michel, R.H., 1996. The analytical and archaeological challenge of detecting ancient wine: two case studies from the Ancient Near East. In: McGovern, P.E., Fleming, S.J., Katz, S.H. (Eds.), *The Origins and Ancient History of Wine*, Gordon and Breach, Langhorne (PA), 57-65.

McGovern, P.E., Glusker, D.L., Exner, L.J., Voigt, M.M.,1996. Neolithic resinated wine. *Nature*, 381, 480-481.

McGovern, P.E., Hartung, U., Badler, V.R., Glusker, D.L., Exner, L.J., 1997, The beginnings of winemaking and viniculture in the ancient near east and Egypt. *Expedition* 39, 3-21.

McGovern, P.E., Zhang, J., Tang, J., Zhang, Z., Hall, G.R., Moreau, R.A, Nuñez, A., Butrym, E.D., Richards, M.P., Wang, C., Cheng, Z., Zhao, Z, Wang, C., 2004, Fermented beverages of pre- and proto-historic China, *PNAS* 101:51: 17593-17598.

Meadow, R.H., 1993 [1982], Animal domestication in the Middle East: a revised view from the Eastern Margin, *Harappan Civilization* (2nd edition), edited by G. Possehl, Oxford and IBH, 295-320.

Meadow, R.H., 1996, The Origins and Spread of Pastoralism in Northwestern South Asia, in *Origins and Spread of Pastoralism in Eurasia*, edited by D.R. Harris, UCL Press, London, 309-412.

Mee, C., 2007, Cooking up the past: food and culinary practices in the Neolithic and Bronze Age Aegean, Oxbow, Oxford.

Meskell, L., Nakamura, C., King, R., 2008, Figured lifeworlds and depositional practices at Catalhoyuk, *Cambridge Archaeological Journal*, 18/2: 139-161.

Michel, F.A., 1998, The relationship of massive ground ice and the late Pleistocene history of northwest Siberia, *Quaternary International*, 45-6: 43-48.

Michel, R.H., McGovern, P.E., Badler, V.R., 1992, Chemical Evidence for Ancient Beer, *Nature*, 360/6399: 24.

Michel, R.H., McGovern, P.E., Badler, V.R., 1993, The First Wine and Beer, *Analytical Chemistry,* Vol. 65, No. 8: 408-413.

Middleditch, B.S., 1989, *Analytical artifacts: GC, MS, HPLC, TLC, and PC*, Elsevier, New York.

Mills, J.S., 1966, The Gas-Chromatographic Exanunation of Paint Media: Fatty Acid Composition and Identification of Dried oil Films, *Studies in Conservation*, 11: 92-98.

Mills, J.S., White, R., 1977, Natural Resins of Art and Archaeology Their Sources, Chemistry, and Identification, *Studies in Conservation*, 22/1: 12-31.

Mills, J.S., White, R., 1978, Organic Analysis in the Arts: Some Further Paint Medium Analyses, *The National Gallery Technical Bulletin*, 2/1:71-76.

Mirabaud, S., Christian, R., Regert, M., 2007, Molecular Criteria for Discriminating Adipose Fat and Milk from Different Species by Nano ESI MS and MS/MS of Their Triacylglycerols: Application to Archaeological Remains, *Analytical Chemistry*, 79: 6182-6192.

Mirabaud, S., 2008, personal communication with Michael Gregg at the International Symposium on Archaeometry, May 17, 2008.

Mithen, S., 1996, *The Prehistory of the Mind*, Oxford University Press, Oxford.

Molleson, T., Jones, K., Jones, S., 1993. Dietary Change and the Effects of Food Preparation on Microwear Patterns in the Late Neolithic of Abu Hureyra, *Journal of Human Evolution,* 24/6): 455-468.

Molleson, T., Jones, K., 1991. Dental Evidence for Dietary Change at Abu Hureyra, *Journal of Archaeological Science*, 18/5: 525-539.

Moore, R.C., 1958, *Introduction to Historical Geology*, McGraw Hill, New York.

Moore, A., 1982, A four-stage sequence for the Levantine \ Neolithic, ca. 8500-3750 B.C., *Bulletin of the American School of Oriental Research,* 246:1-34

Moore, A., 1995, The inception of potting in western Asia and its impact on Economy and Society, in *The Emergence of Pottery*, edited by W. Barnett and J. Hoopes, Smithsonian Institution Press, Washington.

Moore, A., Hillman, G., Legge, A. J., 2000, *Village on the Euphrates*, Oxford University Press, Oxford.

Morris, E.L., 2002, The Function and Use of Prehistoric Ceramics, *Prehistoric Britain: The Ceramic Basis*, Oxbow Books, Oxford, 54-61.

Morris, L.J., 1966, Separation of lipids by silver ion chromatography, *Lipid Research* 7:717-732.

Mortensen, P., 1962, On the Chronology of Early Village Farming Communities in Northern Iraq, *Sumer,* 18:73-80.

Mortensen, P., 1963, Early Village-Farming Occupation, In Meldgaard et al., Excavations at Tepe Guran, Luristan, *Acta Archaeologica,* 34110-121.

Mortensen, P., 1964, Additional Remarks on the Chronology of Early Village-farming Communities in the Zagros area, *Sumer*, 20:28-36

Mortensen, P., 1970, Seasonal camps and early villages in the Zagros, in *Man, Settlement, and Urbanism*, ed. P. Ucko, R. Tringham & G.W. Dimbley, Duckworth, London, p. 293-297.

Mortenson, P., 1992, The Neolithic Period in Central and Western Persia, *Encyclopedia Iranica*, Columbia University, New York (276-278.

Morton, J., Schwarz, H.P., 2004, Paleodietary implications from isotopic analysis of food residues on prehistoric Ontario ceramics, *Journal of Archaeological Science*, 31: 503-517.

Mottram, H.R., Dudd, S.R., Stott, A.W., Lawrence, G.J., Evershed, R.P.,1999, New chromatographic, mass spectrometric and stable isotope approaches to the classification of degraded animal fats preserved in archaeological pottery, *Journal of Chromatography A*, 833: 209-221.

Mottram, H.R., Evershed, R.P., 2001, Elucidation of the composition of bovine triacyglycerols using high-performance liquid chromatography-atmospheric pressure chemical ionization mass spectometry, in

Journal of Chromatography A, 926, 239-253.

Movius, H.L., 1953, Palaeolithic and Mesolithic Sites in Soviet Central Asia, *Proceedings of the American Philosophical Society*, 97/4:383-421.

Mukherjee, A.J., Berstan, R., Copley, M.S., Gibson, A.M., Evershed, R.P., 2007, Compound-specific stable carbon isotopic detection of pig product processing in British Late Neolithic pottery, *Antiquity*, 81/313:743-754.

Munro, N.D., Bar-Oz, G., 2005, Gazelle bone fat processing in the Levantine Epipalaeolithic, *Journal of Archaeological Science*, 32/2:223-239.

Myers, T.P., 1989, The Role of Pottery in the Rise of American Civilizations, in *Ceramic Ecology 1988*, edited by Charle Kolb, B.A.R., Oxford, 1-28.

Namdar, D., 2007, *Reconstruction of the Economy of the Chalcolithic Period in Israel by Assessment of Preservation and Degradation Processes of Organic Substances Adsorbed to Archaeological Ceramic Vessels*, unpublished doctoral dissertation, Department of Archaeology, University of Tel Aviv.

Newman, M.E., Yohe, R.M.,Ceri, H., Sutton, M.Q., 1993, Immunological Protein Residue Analysis of Non-lithic] Archaeological Materials, *Journal of Archaeological Science*, 20:93-100.

Niessen, W.M., 2001, *Current practice of gas chromatography--mass spectrometry*, Marcel Dekker, New York.

Nishiaki, Y., 2003, *Prehistoric Pottery from the Marv Dasht Plain, Iran*, Department of Archaeology of Western Asia, University of Tokyo Museum, Tokyo.

Nishiaki, Y., LeMiere, M., 2005, The oldest Pottery Neolithic of Upper Mesopotamia : New evidence from tell Seker al-Aheimar, the Khabur, northeast Syria, *Paléorient*, 31/2: 55-68.

Nissen, H.J., 1993, The PPNC, the Sheep, and the "Hiatus Palestinien", *Paleorient*, 19/1:177-182.

Nissen, H.J., Muheisen, M., Gebel, H.J., 1987, Report on the first two season of excavations at Basta, *Annual of the Department of Antiquities of Jordan,* Amman.

Norris, M., Oppenheim, C., 2003, Citation counts and the Research Assessment Exercise V - Archaeology and the 2001 RAE, *Journal of Documentation*, 59/6:709-730.

Noy, T., 1989, Gilgal I, a pre-pottery Neolithic site, Israel: the 1985-1987 seasons, *Paleorient*, 15:11-18.

Noy. T., Schulderein, P., Tchernov, E., 1980, Giglal, a pre-pottery Neolithic A site in the lower Jordan Valley, *Israel Exploration Journal*, 30:63-82.

Obeidat, D., 1995, *Die neolithische Keramik aus Abu Thawwab, Jordanien*, ex oriente, Berlin.

Okladnikov, A.P., 1949, Neanderthal Man and traces of his culture in Central Asia, Sovetskaia *Arkheoloyiia*, 6:5-19.

O'Leary. M.H., 1981, Carbon Isotope Fractionation in Plants, *Phytochemistry*, 20/4:553-567.

Olszewski, D.I., 1993, The Zarzian Occupation at Warwasi Rockshelter, Iran, *The Paleolithic Prehistory of the Zagros-Taurus*, edited by D.I. Olszewsky and H.L. Dibble, University of Pennsylvania Museum Symposium Series, Volume 5, Philadelphia, 207-236.

Oppenheim, A.L., Hartman, L.F., 1950, On Beer and Brewing Techniques in Ancient Mesopotamia, supplement 10, *Journal of the American Oriental Society*.

Oppenheim, C., 1997, The correlation between citation counts and the 1992 research assessment exercise ratings for British research in genetics, anatomy and archaeology, *Journal of Documentation*, 53/5: 477-487.

Outram, A.K., Stear, N.A., Bendrey, R., Olsen, S., Kasparov, A., Zaibert, V., Thorpe, N., Evershed, R.P., 2009, The Earliest Horse Harnessing and Milking, *Science*, 323: 1332-1335.

OxCal 4.0, 2009, Online radiocalibration program of the Oxford Radiocarbon Accelerator Unit, http://c14.arch.ox.ac.uk/embed.php?File=oxcal.html

Ozdogan, A., 1999, Çayönü, in *Neolithic in Turkey: the Cradle of Civilization,* edited by Mehmet Ozdogan and Nezih Basgelen, Arkeoloji Sanat Yayinlari, Istanbul, p. 36 -63.

Ozdogan, M., Ozdogan, A., 1993, Pre-Halafian Pottery of Southeastern Anatolia, in *Between the Rivers and Over the Mountains,* University of Rome, p. 87-103.

Paabo, S., Poinar, H., Serre, D., Jaenicke-Despres, V., Hebler, J., Rohland, N., Kuch, M., Krause, J., Vigilant, L., Hofreiter, M., 2004, Genetic analyses from ancient DNA, *Annual Review of Genetics*, 38: 645-679.

Palmer, C., 2002, Milk and Cereals: Identifying Food and Food Identity, Among *Fallahin* and Bedouin in Jordan, in *Levan*t, 34: 173-195.

Payne, S., 1973, Kill-off patterns in sheep and goats: the mandibles from Asvan Kale, in *Anatolian Studies* 23: 281-303.

Pearson, J. A., Buitenhuis, H., Hedges, R. E. M., Martin, L., Russell, N., Twiss, K. C., 2007, New light on early caprine herding strategies from isotope analysis: a case study from Neolithic Anatolia, *Journal of Archaeological Science* 34/12:2170-2179.

Perkins, D., 1964, Prehistoric fauna from Shanidar, Iraq, *Science*, 144:1565-1566.

Perkins, D., 1973, The Beginnings of Animal Domestication in the Near East, *American Journal of Archaeology*, 77 (3):279-282.

Perrot, J., 1955, The excavations at Tell Abu Matar, near Beersheba, *Israel Exploration Journal*, 5/1:17-40.

Perrot, J., 1964, Les deux premibres campagnes de fouilles A Munhata (1962-1963). Premiers résultats. *Syria,* XLI:323-345.

Perrot, J., 1968, Préhistoire Palestinienne, *Supplément au Dictionaire de la Bible*, 7:286-446.

Peters, D., Helmer, D., Driesch, A., Segui, M.S., 1999, Early Animal Husbandry in the Northern Levant, *Paléorient*, 25/2:27-47.

Playfair, J., 1802, *Illustrations of the Huttonian Theory of the Earth*, Cadell and Davies, London.

Pollard, A.M., Heron. C., 2008, *Archaeological chemistry, Royal Society of Chemistry,* Cambridge.

Pollard, A.M., Stern B., Batt, K., 2007, Analytical Chemistry in Archaeology, Cambridge University Press, Cambridge.

Prausnitz, M.W., 1977, The pottery of Newe Yam, *Eretz Israel* 13: 272-275.

Ranov, V.A., Davis, R.S., 1979, Toward a New Outline of the Soviet Central Asian Palaeolithic, *Current Anthropology*, 20/2: 249-270.

Reber, E.A., Evershed, R.P., 2004a, Identification of maize

in absorbed organic residues: a cautionary tale, *Journal of Archaeological Science* 31/4: 399-410.

Reber, E.A., Evershed, R.P., 2004b, How did Mississipians prepare maize? The application of compound-specific carbon isotope analysis to absorbed pottery residues from several Mississipi walley sites, *Archaeometry*, 46/1:19-33.

Renfrew, C., 2001, Production and consumption in a sacred economy: The material correlates of high devotional expression at Chaco Canyon, *American Antiquity*, 66/1: 14-25.

Rice, P.C. 1997, *Doing Archaeology: A Hands-On Laboratory Manual*, Mayfield, CA.

Rice, P.M., 1987, *Pottery Analysis: A Sourcebook*, University of Chicago Press, Chicago.

Rice, P.M., 1990, Functions and uses of archaeological ceramics, *The Changing Roles of Ceramics in Society: 26,000 BP to the Present*, ed., W.D. Kingery, Ceramics and Civilization Series, Volume V, American Ceramic Society, Westerville, OH, 1-12.

Rice, P., 1999, On the Origins of Pottery, *Journal of Archaeological Method and Theory*, Vol. 6, No. 1: 1-53.

Richards, M.P., 2003, Stable Isotope Evidence of Diet at Neolithic Çatalhöyük, *Journal of Archaeological Science*, 30:67-76.

Rindos, D., 1987, *The Origins of Agriculture: An Evolutionary Perspective*, Academic Press, New York.

Robb, J.E., 1998, The Archaeology of Symbols, *Annual Review of Anthropology*, 27:329-46.

Rollefson, G., 1984, Ain Ghazal: An Early Neolithic Community in Highland Jordan, near Amman, *Bulletin of the American Schools of Oriental Research*, 255: 3-14.

Rollefson, F.O., Simmons, A.H., Kafafi, Z., 1992, Neolithic Cultures at Ain Ghazal, Jordan, *Journal of Field Archaeology*, 19/4: 443-470.

Romanus, K., Poblome, J., Verbeke, J., Luypaerts, A., Jacobs. P., DeVos, D., Waelkins, M., 2007, An evaluation of analytical and interpretive technologies for the extraction and identification of lipids associated with pottery sherds from the site of Sagalassos, Turkey, *Archaeometry*, 49/4: 729-747.

Rosen, S., 1988, Notes on the Origins of Pastoral Nomadism: a case from the Negev and the Sinai, *Current Anthropology* 29 (3): 498-506.

Rosenberg, M., 1999, A Report on Sounding at Demirkoy Hoyuk: an Aceramic Neolithic site in Eastern Anatolia, *Anatolica*, XXIV: 195-207.

Rossell, J.B., 1998, Development of purity criteria for edible vegetable oils, in *Lipid Analysis in Oils and Fats*, edited by R.J. Hamilton, Blackie, London, 265-289.

Rottlander, R. C. A., and Hartke, I., 1982, New result of food identification by fat analysis, *Proceedings of the 22nd Symposium on Archaeometry*, University of Bradford, U.K., edited by A. Aspinall and S. E. Warren, West Yorkshire Schools of Physics and Archaeological Sciences, Bradford, 218–221.

Russell, K., 1988, *After Eden: The Behavioral Ecology of Early Food Production in the Near East and North Africa*, BAR International Series 391, Oxford.

Ryder, M. I., 1993, Sheep and goat husbandry with particular reference to textile fibre and milk production, in Domestic Animals of Mesopotamia I, *Bulletin on Sumerian Agriculture*, Cambridge, p. 9-32.

Sahlins, M., 1972, *Stone Age Economics*, Aldine, Chicago.

Samuel, D., 1996, Investigation of ancient Egyptian baking and brewing methods by correlative microscopy, *Science*, 273/5274: 488-490.

Sassaman, K.E., 1993, *Early pottery in the Southeast: tradition and innovation in cooking technology*, University of Alabama Press, Tuscaloosa.

Sauter, F., Puchinger, L., Schoop, U.D., 2003, Fat analysis sheds light on everyday life in prehistoric Anatolia: traces of lipids identified in chalcolithic potsherds excavated near Boazkale, Central Turkey, Online journal: *Studies in Organic Archaeometry XV*, http://www.arkat-usa.org/arkivoc-journal/browse-arkivoc/2003/15/.

Schmandt-Besserat, D., 1974, The use of clay before pottery in the Zagros, *Expedition*, 16/2: 11-17.

Shackley, M., 1982, Gas chromatographic identification of a resinous deposit from a 6th century storage jar and its possible identification, *Journal of Archaeological Science*, 9/3: 305-306.

Shanks, M., 2005, *The science question in archaeology*, Address to the Society for Social Studies of Science, Vancouver, (nd), online electronic resource downloaded on October 30, 2008 from website at Stanford University: http://documents.stanford.edu/michaelshanks/77.

Shennan, S.J., 1993, Settlement and Social Change in Central Europe 3500-1500 BC, *Journal of World Prehistory*, 7/2: 121-161.

Sherratt, A., 1981, Plough and pastoralism: aspects of the secondary products revolution, in *Pattern of the Past: Studies in honour of David Clarke*, edited by I. Hodder, G. Isaac, N. Hammond, Cambridge University Press, p. 261–305.

Sherratt, A., 1983, The secondary exploitation of animals in the Old World, *World Archaeology*, 15/1:90-103.

Sherratt, A, Yoffee, 1993, Introduction: the sources of archaeological theory, Archaeological theory: who sets t the agenda, Cambridge University Press, Cambridge, 1-9.

Shepard, A.O., 1957, *Ceramics for the archaeologist*, Carnegie Institution, Washington.

Shick, T., 1997, Miscellaneous finds: a note on perishable items from Netiv Hagud, in *An Early Neolithic Village in the Jordan Valley*, ed. O. Bar-Yosef and A. Gophner, American School of Prehistoric Research, Bulletin 43, Peabody Museum, Harvard University, Cambridge, MA.

Shimoyama, A., Ichikawa, A., 2000, Fatty acid analysis of pottery samples from Tel-el Kerkh, *Bulletin of the Ancient Orient Museum*, Tokyo, XXI: 33-36.

Shomer-Ilan, A., Nissenbaum, A., Waisel, Y., 1981, Photosynthetic Pathways and the Ecological Distribution of Chenopodiaceae in Israel, *Oecologia*, 48: 244-248.

Signorelli, F., Contarini, G., Annicchiarico, G., Napolitano, F., Orrù, L., Catillo, G., Haenlein, G., Moioli, B.,2008, Breed differences in sheep milk fatty acid profiles: Opportunities for sustainable use of animal genetic resources, *Small Ruminant Research*, 78/1-3: 24-31.

Simmons, A.H., Rollefson, G.O., 1984, Neolithic'Ain Ghazal (Jordan): Interim Report in the First Two Seasons, 1982-1983, *Journal of Field Archaeology*, 11/4: 387-395.

Sinopoli, C.M., 1991, *Approaches to Archaeological Ceramics*, Plenum Press, New York.

Smith, B., 1984, Chenopodium as a Prehistoric Domesticate

in Eastern North America: Evidence from Russell Cave, Alabama, *Science*, 226:165-167.

Smith, M.F., 1985, Toward an Economic Interpretation of Ceramics: Relating Vessel Shape and Size to Use, in *Decoding Prehistoric Ceramics,* edited by B.A. Wilson, Southern Illinois University Press, Carbondale.

Smith, P.E.L., 1974, Ganj Dareh Tepe, *Paléorient*, 2/1:207.

Smith, P.E.L., 1978, An Interim Report on Ganj Dareh Tepe, Iran, *American Journal of Archaeology,* 84/4:538.

Smith, P.R., Wilson, M.T., 1992, Blood Residues on ancient tool surfaces: a cautionary note, *Journal of Archaeological Science*, 19: 237-241.

Smith, P.R., Wilson, M.T., 2001, Blood Residues in Archaeology, in *Handbook of Archaeological Sciences,* edited by D.R. Brothwell and A.M. Pollard, John Wiley and Sons, London.

Solazzo, C., Fitzhugh, W., Rolando, C., Tokarski, C., 2008, Identification of Protein Remains in Archaeological Potsherds by Proteomics, *Analytical Chemistry*, 80/12: 4590–4597.

Solecki, R., 1963, Prehistory in the Shandar Valley, Northern Iraq, *Science*, 39/3551:179-193.

Spangenberg, J.E., Jacomet, S., Schibler, J., 2006, Chemical analyses of organic residues in archaeological pottery from Arbon Bleiche 3, Switzerland - evidence for dairying in the late Neolithic, *Journal of Archaeological Science*, 33/1:1-13.

Stahl, A. B., 1986, Plants Food Processing : Implications for Dietary Quality in Recent Advances in the Understanding of Plant Domestication and Early Agriculture, *Proceedings of the World Archaeological Congress*, University of Southampton, 89-101.

Stankiewicz, B.A,, Hutchins, J.C., Thomson, R., 1997, Assessment of bog-body tissue preservation by pyrolysis gas chromatography mass spectrometry, *Rapid Communications in Mass Spectrometry*, 11/17: 1884-1890.

Stekelis, M., 1950, A New Neolithic Industry: The Yarmukian of Palestine, *Israel Exploration Journal*, 1-24.

Stern, B., Heron, C. P., Bourriau, J., Serpico, M., 2000, A comparison of methods for establishing fatty acid concentration gradients across potsherds: A case study using Late Bronze Age Canaanite amphorae, *Archaeometry*, 42:399-414.

Stern, B., Heron, C., Tellefsen, T., 2008, New investigations into the Uluburun resin cargo, *Journal of Archaeological Science*, 35/8: 2188-2203.

Stordeur, D. 2000, Jerf el Ahmar et l'émergence du Néolithique au Proche Orient. In: Guilaine J (ed) Premiers Paysans du monde. *Naissances des agricultures,* Errance edition. Collection des Hesperides, Paris, 33–60.

Stott, A.W., Evershed, R.P., Jim. S., Jones, V., Rogers, J.M., Tuross, N., Ambrose, S., 1999, Cholestorol as a New Source of Palaeodietary Information: Experimental Approaches and Archaeological Applications, *Journal of Archaeological Science,* 26: 705-716.

Stuckenrath, R., 1963, University of Pennsylvania radiocarbon dates VI, *Radiocarbon*, 5:82-103.

Sumner, W.M., 1972, *Cultural Developments in the Kur River Basin. Iran, and Archaeological Analysis of of Settlement Patterns*, PhD dissertation, Department of Anthropology, University of Pennsylvania.

Tani, Y., 2005, Early Techniques as the forerunner of milking practices, in *The Zooarchaeology of Fats, Oils, Milk and Dairying,* edited by J. Mulville and A.K. Outram, Oxbow Books, Oxford, pp 114-120.

Tauber, H., 1968, Copenhagen Radiocarbon Dates IX, *Radiocarbon*, 10, 295-327.

Terrell, J., Barut, S., Cellinese, N., Curet, A., Denham, T., Kusimba, C., Latinis, K., Oka, R., Palka, J., Pohl, M., Pope, K., Williams, P., Haines, H., Staller, J., Hart, J., 2003, Domesticated Landscapes: The Subsistence Ecology of Plant and Animal Domestication, *Journal of Archaeological Method and Theory*, 10/4: 323-368.

Theya, M., Jones, K., Jones, S., 1993, Dietary change and the effects of food preparation on microwear patterns in the Late Neolithic of Abu Hureyra, northern Syria *Journal of Human Evolution*, 24/6: 455-468.

Thissen, L., 2002, CANeW ^{14}C databases and ^{14}C charts, Anatolia, 10000 - 5000 calBC, *The Neolithic of Central Anatolia. Internal Developments and External Relations during the 9th - 6th Millennia calBC*, Proceedings of the CANeW Table Ronde, Istanbul 23-24 November 2001, Istanbul, Ege Publishing Co., Istanbul, 299-337.

Thoms, A.V., 2008, The fire stones carry: Ethnographic records and archaeological expectations for hot-rock cookery in western North America, *Journal of Anthropological Archaeology*, 27/4: 443-460.

Tite, M.S., Kilikoglou, V., Vekinis, G., 2001, Strength, toughness and thermal shock resistance of ancient ceramics, and their influence on technological choice, *Archaeometry,* 43/3 301-324.

Tomkins, P., 2007, Community and Competition: The social life of food containers at Aceramic and Early Neolithic Knossos Crete, in *Cooking up the past: food and culinary practices in the Neolithic and Bronze Age Aegean*, edited by C. Mee, Oxbow, Oxford, 174-199.

Twiss, K.C. 2008, Transformations in an early agricultural society: Feasting in the southern Levantine Pre-Pottery Neolithic, *Journal of Anthropological Archaeology*, 27: 418–442.

Trigger, B.G., 1970, Aims in Prehistoric Archaeology, *Antiquity*, 44:26-37.

Trigger, B.G., 1988, Archaeology's Relation with the Physical and Biological Sciences: A Historical Review, *Proceedings of the 26th International Archaeometry Symposium*, 1-9, Department of Physics, University of Toronto, Toronto.

Trigger, B.G., 1989, Archaeology and Anthropology: Current and Future Relations, *Canadian Journal of Archaeology*, 13

Trigger, B.G., 2003, The social construction of ancient cities, *Cambridge Archaeological Journal,* 13/2: 281-283.

Trigger, B.G., 2006, *History of Archaeological Thought*, 2nd edition, Cambridge University Press, Cambridge.

Trudinger, C.M., Enting, I.G., Francey, D.M., Etheridge, D.M., Rauner, P.J., 1999, Longterm variability in the global carbon cycle inferred from a high-precision CO_2 and $\partial^{13}C$ ice-core record, *Tellus*, 51B: 233-248.

Tsuneki, A., Miyake, Y., 1996, The earliest pottery sequence in the Levant: new data from Tell el-Kherk 2, Northern Syria, *Palérient*, 22:109-23.

Uerpmann, H.P., 1987, *The Ancient Distribution of*

Ungulate Mammals in the Middle East. Dr. Ludwig Reichert Verlag, Wiesbaden.

Ulberth, F., Henninger, M., 1992, One-Step Extraction/Methylation Method for Determining Fatty Acid Composition of Processed Foods, *Journal of the American Oil Chemists' Society*, 69/2:174-177.

Vaks, A., Bar-Matthews, M., Ayalon, A., Matthews, A., Frumkin, A., Dayan, U., Halicz, L., Almogi-Labin, A., Schilman, B., 2006, Paleoclimate and location of the border between Mediterranean climate region and the Saharo-Arabian Desert as revealed by speleothems from the northern Negev Desert, Israel, *Earth and Planetary Science Letters*, 249/3-4: 384-399.

Vandiver, P.B., Soffer, O., Klima, B., 1990, *The Changing Roles of Ceramics in Society: 26,000 BP to the Present*, ed., W.D. Kingery, Ceramics and Civilization Series, Volume V, American Ceramic Society, Westerville, OH, 13-82.

Van Zeist, W., Bottema, S., 1991, *Late Quaternary Vegetation of the Near East,* Ludwig Reichert Verlag, Weisbaden.

Van Zeist, W., Smith, P.E.L., Palfenier-Vetger, R.,Suwijn, M.,Casparie, W.A., 1984, An Archaeobotanical Study of Ganj Dareh Tepe, Iran, *Palaeohistoria*, Vol. 26: 201-224.

Van Zeist, W., de Roller, G.J., 1995, Plant Remains from Asikli Höyük, a pre-pottery Neolithic site in Anatolia, *Vegetation History and Archaeobotany* 4:179-185.

Van Zeist, W., Woldring, A., 1978, Post-glacial Pollen Diagram from Lake Van in East Anatolia, *Review of Palaeobotany and Palynology* 26/1-4: 249-276.

Vernon, R.G., 1981, Lipid metabolism in the rumen, in *Lipid Metabolism in the Adipose Tissue of Ruminant Animals*, ed. W. Christie, Pergamom, Oxford, 279-362.

Vigne, J.D., Dollfus, G., Peters, J., 1999, Beginning of Herding in the Near East: New Data and New Ideas, translated by H.T. Wright, *Paléorient* 25/2, p.9-10.

Vitelli, K. D., 1989, Were pots first made for food? Doubts from Franchthi. *World Archaeology,* 21: 17-29.

Vitelli, K. D., 1993, *Franchthi Neolithic Pottery,* Indiana University Press, Blommington.

Vitelli, K. D., 1995, Pots, potters, and the shaping of Greek Neolithic society, in Barnett, W. K., and Hoopes, J. W. (eds.), *The Emergence of Pottery: Technology and Innovation in Ancient Societies,* Smithsonian Institution Press, Washington, DC, 55-63.

Vitelli, K. D., 1999, "Looking up" at early ceramics in Greece. in Skibo, J. M., and Feinman,G. (eds.), *Pottery and People: Dynamic Interactions,* University of Utah Press, Salt LakeCity, 184-198.

Vogel, J.C., Fuls, A., Danin, A., 1986, Geographical and environmental distribution of C_3 and C_4 grasses in the Sinai, Negev, and Judean deserts, *Oecologia*, 70:258-265.

Voigt, M.M., 1983, *Hajji Firuz Tepe, Iran: the Neolithic settlement*, Monograph 50, The University Museum, University of Pennsylvania, Philadelphia.

Voigt, M., 1992, The Neolithic Period in Northwestern Persia, *Encyclopedia Iranica*, Columbia University, New York, 275-276.

Voigt, M., Dyson, R.H., 1992, The Chronology of Iran, ca. 8000-2000 BC, *Chronologies in Old World Archaeology*, ed. R.W. Ehrich, University of Chicago Press, Chicago, 122-178.

Wahlen, M., 1994, Carbon dioxide, carbon monoxide, and methane in the atmosphere: abundance and isotopic composition, in *Stable Isotopes in Ecology and Environmental Science*, ed. K Lajtha and R.H. Michener, Elsevier, London, 93-113.

Wasse, A., 2001, The Wild Goats of Lebanon: Evidence for Early Domestication? *Levant*, 21-34.

Warinner, C., Tuross, N., 2009, Alkaline Cooking and Stable Isotope Diet-Tissue Discrimination in Swine: Archaeological Implications, *Journal of Archaeological Science*, DOI: 10.1016/j.jas.2009.03.034.

White, R. E., 2006, *Principles and practice of soil science: the soil as a natural resource*, Blackwell, Malden, MA.

Wick, L., Lemcke, G., Sturm, M., 2003, Evidence of Late Glacial and Holocene climatic change and human impact in eastern Anatolia: high-resolution pollen, charcoal, isotopic and geochemical records from the laminated sediments of Lake Van, Turkey, *Holocene*, 13/5: 665-675.

Wollstonecroft, M.M., Ellis, P.R., Hillman, G.C., Fuller, D.Q., 2008, Advances in plant food processing in the Near Eastern Epipalaeolithic and implications for improved edibility and nutrient bioaccessibility: an experimental assessment of Bolboschoenus maritimus, *Vegetation History and Archaeobotany*, 17/1: 19-27.

Woodbury, S.E., Evershed, R, P., Rossell, J.B., Griffith, R.E,, Farnell, P., 1995, Dectection of vegetable oil adultaration using gas-chromatography combustion isotope ratio mass-spectrometry, *Analytical Chemistry*, 67/15: 2685-2690.

Wrangham, R.W., 1999, The raw and the stolen - Cooking and the ecology of human origins, *Current Anthropology*, 40/5: 567-594.

Wright, H.T., 1981, *An Early Town on the Deh Luran Plain: Excavations at Tepe Farukhabad*, Memoir No. 13 of the University of Michigan Museum of Anthropology, Ann Arbor.

Wright, K. I., 1994, Ground-stone tools and hunter gatherer subsistence in southwest Asia: implications for the transition to farming, *American Antiquity*, 59/2: 238-63.

Wright, K. I., 2000, The social origins of cooking and dining in early villages of Western Asia, *Proceedings of the Prehistoric Society*; 66: 89-121.

Yoffe, N., Sherratt, A., 1993, Introduction: the sources of archaeological theory, *Archaeological Theory: Who sets the agenda?* Cambridge University Press, Cambridge, 1-9.

Zaretskaya, N.E., Zhilin, M.G., Karmanov, V.N., Uspenskaya, O.N., 2005, Radiocarbon dating of wetland meso-neolithic archaeological sites within the Upper Volga and Middle Vychegda, *Geochronometria* 24: 117-131.

Zarins, J., 1990, Early Pastoral Nomadism and the Settlement of Lower Mesopotamia, *Bulletin of the American Schools of Oriental Research,* 280: 31-65.

Zhang, C. 2002a. Early pottery and rice phytolith remains from Xianrendong and Diaotonghuan sites, Wannian, Jiangxi Province, in *The Origins of Pottery and Agriculture*, ed. Y. Yasuda, New Roll Books and Lustre Press, Delhi, 185-91.

Zhang, 2002b. The discovery of early pottery in China. *Documenta Praehistorica,* 29: 29-35.

Zeder, M., 1999, Animal Domestication in the Zagros: A Review of Past and Current Research, *Paléorient,* 25/2:11-25.

Zeder, M., 2006, Central Questions in the Domestication of Plants and Animals, *Evolutionary Anthropology* 15:105-117.

Zeder, M., Hesse, B., 2000, The initial domestication of goats (*capra hircus*) in the Zagros Mountains 10,000 years ago, *Science,* March 24; 287: 2254-2257.

Zeder, M.A., Bradley D., Emshwiller, E., Smith, B.D, (eds.) 2006, *Documenting Domestication: New Genetic and Archaeological Paradigms,* University of California Press, Berkeley.

Zimmerman, D.W., Huxtable, J., 1971, Themoluminescense dating of Upper Palaeolithic fired clay from Dolni Vestonice, *Archaeometry,* 13/1: 29-52.

Zohary, D., Hopf, M., 2000, *Domestication of Plants in the Old World,* Oxford University Press, Oxford.Abu

Appendices

Appendix A.1.1

Pottery fragments examined at the Department of Archaeological Sciences, University of Bradford, using 'conventional' solvent extraction and saponification techniques. Pottery fragments yielding organic residues are highlighted in these appendices in bold text. Potsherds that did not yield measurable abundances of lipids through conventional solvent extraction or saponification techniques, but that did subsequently yield results through use of the microwave-assisted liquid chromatography protocol, are highlighted with a light grey screen here and in Appendix A.1.4. In these appendices ND and FA are abbreviations for No Data and Fatty Acids.

Sample	Excavation number	Extraction method	Lipid classes detected
AH1	AH.73.244	Solvent extracted	ND
AH2	AH.73.131	Solvent extracted	ND
AH3	AH.73.1126	Solvent & saponification	ND
AH4	AH.73.107	Solvent extracted	ND
AH5	AH.73.186	Solvent extracted	ND
AH6	AH.73.246	Solvent extracted	ND
AH7	AH.73.130.E2.6.67	Solvent extracted	ND
AH8	AH.73.208.E2/5.71	Solvent extracted	ND
AH9	AH.73.242.E2.7.82	Solvent extracted	ND
AH10	AH.73.1183.E4.29.75	Solvent extracted	ND
AH11	AH.73.186.E2.4.36	Solvent extracted	ND

Abu Hureyra: Two conventional radiocarbon dates calibrated using OxCal 4.0 provide dates for the pottery-bearing levels anywhere between 7400 and 6200 cal BC; 68% confidence (Housely 1994; Moore et al. 2000).

Sample	Excavation number	Extraction method	Lipid classes detected
AK1	**A98/70-80**	**Solvent extracted**	**Hopanes, terpanes**
AK2	**A99/60-70**	**Solvent extracted**	**Hopanes, terpanes**
AK3	O2/55-660	Solvent extracted	ND
AK4	A89/80-100	Solvent extracted	ND
AK5	A84/90-100	Solvent extracted	ND
AK6	A98/80-100	Solvent extracted	ND
AK7	A97/110-120	Solvent extracted	ND

Ali Kosh: Relatively recent AMS dating of animal bone places the earliest pottery-bearing level at this site between 7300 and 7000 cal BC (Hole 2000).

Sample	Excavation number	Extraction method	Lipid classes detected
CS1	**SA/B1/90**	**Solvent extracted**	**Hopanes, terpanes**
CS2	**SA/A4/391**	**Solvent extracted**	**Hopanes, terpanes**
CS3	SC/B17/301	Solvent extracted	ND
CS4	SA/C4/413	Solvent extracted	ND
CS5	SA/C5/391	Solvent extracted	ND
CS6	AB/1-4/212	Solvent extracted	ND
CS7	FA/D5/3-1	Solvent extracted	ND
CS8	SA/A5/413	Solvent extracted	ND
CS9	SA/O61/351	Solvent extracted	ND
CS10	SH/E/ST	Solvent extracted	ND
CS11	SA/65/313	Solvent extracted	ND
CS12	SA/15/279	Solvent extracted	ND
CS13	SA/C5/229	Solvent extracted	ND
CS14	212/A81-4	Solvent extracted	ND
CS15	SA/AS/416	Solvent extracted	ND

Chageh Sefid: Two conventional radiocarbon dates calibrated using OxCal 4.0 provide dates for the first pottery horizon at this ranging between 8170 and 6700 cal BC; 68% confidence (Hole 1977; Hole 1987a).

Çayönü:
Two conventional radiocarbon dates calibrated using OxCal 4.0 provide dates for the levels overlying the first pottery horizon ranging between 5500 and 4650 cal BC; 68% confidence (Çambel 1981; Thissen 2002)

Sample	Excavation number	Extraction method	Lipid classes detected
CU1	CT89-P26H 1-1	Solvent extracted	ND
CU2	CT86-20N 6-25	Solvent extracted	ND
CU3	CT89-P25I 1-9	Solvent extracted	ND
CU4	CT89-P25I 2-21	Solvent extracted	ND
CU5	**CT91-P25I PS 448**	**Solvent & saponification**	**FA — animal ratios**
CU6	CT91-P25I 6-78	Solvent extracted	ND
CU7	CT90-P25I 5-50	Solvent extracted	ND
CU8	CT90-P26I 1-8	Solvent extracted	ND
CU9	CT89-P25I 2-22	Solvent extracted	ND
CU10	CT94-P25I 6-71	Solvent extracted	ND
CU11	CT90-P27K 3-14	Solvent extracted	ND
CU12	CT87-F92 D5 2-3/14	Solvent extracted	ND
CU13	CT87-F Whitewear	Solvent extracted	ND
CU14	CT 70-29L P 2-18	Solvent extracted	ND
CU15	CT87-P25K 1-2 403	Solvent extracted	ND
CU17	CT90-P25H 4-40	Solvent extracted	ND
CU18	CT87-F93 D5 2-3/11	Solvent extracted	ND
CU19	CT90-P26H 4-27	Solvent extracted	ND

Faruhkabad:
4750 - 4400 cal BC (Crane & Griffin 1972; Hole 1987a)

Sample	Excavation number	Extraction method	Lipid classes detected
FK1	80673	Solvent extracted	ND
FK2	60291	Solvent extracted	ND
FK3	60501	Solvent extracted	ND
FK4	60693	Solvent extracted	ND

Kashkashok:
6600 - 5400 cal BC (Matsutani 1991)

Sample	Excavation number	Extraction method	Lipid classes detected
KA1	K120 M63 6/5	Solvent extracted	ND
KA2	Kash A	Solvent extracted	ND
KA3	Kash B	Solvent extracted	ND
KA4	K120 M33 6/5	Solvent extracted	ND

Toll-e Bashi:
6000 - 5750 cal BC; (Bernbeck et al. 2003; Gregg in press)

Sample	Excavation number	Extraction method	Lipid classes detected
TB1	RN766	Solvent extracted	ND
TB2	RN793	Solvent extracted	ND
TB3	RN771	Solvent extracted	ND
TB4	RN1059	Solvent extracted	ND
TB5	RN1677	Solvent extracted	ND
TB6	RN1188	Solvent extracted	ND
TB7	RN611	Solvent extracted	ND
TB8	RN1045	Solvent extracted	ND
TB9	RN1767	Solvent extracted	ND
TB10	RN545	Solvent extracted	ND
TB11	RN794	Solvent extracted	ND

Sample	Excavation number	Extraction method	Lipid classes detected	
TG1	H55.1	Solvent extracted	ND	**Tepe Guran:**
TG2	H55.2	Solvent extracted	ND	**6800 - 6450 cal BC** (Tauber 1968; Hole 1987a)

Sample	Excavation number	Extraction method	Lipid classes detected	
TS1	No # 'Tadpole' ware	Solvent extracted	ND	**Tepe Sarab:**
TS2	**No # thick base**	**Solvent extracted**	**ND**	**7000 - 6300 cal BC**
TS2S	**No # thick base**	**Solvent & saponification**	**FA — plant ratios**	(Stuckenrath 1963; Hole
TS3	No # thick base	Solvent extracted	ND	1987a)
TS4	No # body sherd	Solvent & saponification	ND	
TS5	No # body sherd	Solvent extracted	ND	
TS6	No # thick base	Solvent & saponification	ND	

Appendix A.1.2
Pottery fragments subsequently examined at the Department of Chemistry, University of Toronto using a 'conventional' solvent extraction technique.

Sample	Excavation number	Extraction method	Lipid classes detected	
AM1	1754-1242	Solvent extracted	ND	**Abu Matar:**
AM2	1754-2136	Solvent extracted	ND	**4500 - 3700 cal BC**
AM3	1754-1222	Solvent extracted	ND	(Gilead 1994)
AM4	1754-1217	Solvent extracted	ND	
AM5	1754-1004	Solvent extracted	ND	
AM6	1754-1233	Solvent extracted	ND	
AM7	CF1	Solvent extracted	ND	
AM8	1754-1162	Solvent extracted	ND	
AM9	1764-1247	Solvent extracted	ND	
AM10	1754-1214	Solvent extracted	ND	
AM11	1754-1289B	Solvent extracted	ND	
AM12	1754-132-1265CF2	Solvent extracted	ND	
AM13	1754-1182	Solvent extracted	ND	
AM14	CF3	Solvent extracted	ND	

Sample	Excavation number	Extraction method	Lipid classes detected	
AT1	85.A.III.6.25.10083	Solvent extracted	ND	**Abu Thawwâb:**
AT2	84.A.III.6/5.B	Solvent extracted	ND	**6500 - 6000 cal BC**
AT3	84.A.III.6/6	Solvent extracted	ND	(Kafafi 1993)
AT4	84.A.III.6/5	Solvent extracted	ND	
AT5	85.A.III.6.17.7829	Solvent extracted	ND	
AT6	85.A.III.6.13.987	Solvent extracted	ND	
AT7	85.A.III.6.25.9908	Solvent extracted	ND	
AT8	85.A.III.6.17.3700	Solvent extracted	ND	
AT9	85.A.III.6.11.1798	Solvent extracted	ND	
AT10	85.A.III.6.25.9968	Solvent extracted	ND	

	Sample	Excavation number	Extraction method	Lipid classes detected
Dhra': 6000 - 5700 cal BC (Kuijt 2001; Kuijt et al 2007)	DH1	2002.1.1050.88E.97N	Solvent extracted	ND
	DH2	C.1163.1050	Solvent extracted	ND
	DH3	C.1222.1063	Solvent extracted	ND
	DH4	C.1336.1050	Solvent extracted	ND
	DH5	C.1176.1050	Solvent extracted	ND
	DH6	C.1417.1004	Solvent extracted	ND
	DH7	C.1440.1073	Solvent extracted	ND
	DH8	C.1645.10001	Solvent extracted	ND
	DH9	C.1642.1001	Solvent extracted	ND
	DH10	C.1533.1008	Solvent extracted	ND
	DH11	C.1855.1020	Solvent extracted	ND
	DH12	C.1643.1001	Solvent extracted	ND
	DH13	C.1109.1045	Solvent extracted	ND
	DH14	C.1001.1062	Solvent extracted	ND
	DH15	C.1554.1020	Solvent extracted	ND
	DH16	C.1762.1020	Solvent extracted	ND
	DH17	C.1581.1020	Solvent extracted	ND
	DH18	C.1347.1020	Solvent extracted	ND
	DH19	C.1053.1092	Solvent extracted	ND
	DH20	C.1219.1062	Solvent extracted	ND
	DH21	C.1799.1020	Solvent extracted	ND
	DH22	C.1257.1020	Solvent extracted	ND
	DH23	C.1233.1062	Solvent extracted	ND
	DH24	C.1427.1004	Solvent extracted	ND

	Sample	Excavation number	Extraction method	Lipid classes detected
Munhata: 6500 - 5800 cal BC (Gopher & Gophna 1993)	MN1	56.4	Solvent extracted	ND
	MN2	57.3	Solvent extracted	ND
	MN3	57.1	Solvent extracted	ND
	MN4	69.12	Solvent extracted	ND
	MN5	74.11	Solvent extracted	ND
	MN6	67.11	Solvent extracted	ND
	MN7	56.1	Solvent extracted	ND
	MN8	58.12	Solvent extracted	ND
	MN9	58.1	Solvent extracted	ND
	MN10	69.1	Solvent extracted	ND
	MN11	68.7	Solvent extracted	ND
	MN12	68.9	Solvent extracted	ND
	MN13	68.4	Solvent extracted	ND

	Sample	Excavation number	Extraction method	Lipid classes detected
Nevatim: 4500-3700 cal BC (Gilead & Fabian 2001)	NEV1	G96-95 1078B	Solvent extracted	ND
	NEV2	G99-95 1052	Solvent extracted	ND
	NEV3	G96-95 1078A	Solvent extracted	ND
	NEV4	G96-95 1015	Solvent extracted	ND

Sample	Excavation number	Extraction method	Lipid classes detected
NY1	26.92.21.206	Solvent extracted	ND
NY2	23.94.46.78	Solvent extracted	ND
NY3	21.95.44.471	Solvent extracted	ND
NY4	21.921.21.20	Solvent extracted	ND
NY5	26.92.21.258	Solvent extracted	ND
NY	26.92.21.258	Solvent extracted	ND
NY6	21.94.44.15.94.B	Solvent extracted	ND
NY7	21.94.44.15.4.A	Solvent extracted	ND
NY8	21,94.46.27.B	Solvent extracted	ND
NY9	21.94.46.27.A	Solvent extracted	ND
NY10	30.93.9.197	Solvent extracted	ND
NY11	21.94.47.74	Solvent extracted	ND
NY12	21.94.44.27.B-5	Solvent extracted	ND
NY13	21.94/44.22.B-1	Solvent extracted	ND
NY14	21.94.47.165.B	Solvent extracted	ND
NY15	21.94.47.160.A	Solvent extracted	ND
NY16	21.94.44.473	Solvent extracted	ND
NY17	30.93.54.26	Solvent extracted	ND
NY18	30.33.9.343	Solvent extracted	ND
NY19	21.94.57.57	Solvent extracted	ND
NY20	26.92.2.8	Solvent extracted	ND
NY21	21.94.44.333	Solvent extracted	ND
NY22	26.92.21.174	Solvent extracted	ND
NY23	15.91.56.5	Solvent extracted	ND
NY24	21.94.7.57	Solvent extracted	ND
NY25	53.95.1.94	Solvent extracted	ND
NY26	21.94.47.202	Solvent extracted	ND
NY27	21.94.44.3	Solvent extracted	ND
NY28	21.94.44.279	Solvent extracted	ND
NY29	26.92.21.1246	Solvent extracted	ND
NY30	25.92.9.12	Solvent extracted	ND
NY31	21.94.44.22.B-4	Solvent extracted	ND
NY32	21.94.44.280	Solvent extracted	ND
NY33	21.94.47.196	Solvent extracted	ND

Newe Yam:
5500 - 5000 cal BC
(Galili 2004)

Sample	Excavation number	Extraction method	Lipid classes detected
SH1	7.35.1	Solvent extracted	ND
SH2	7.33.3	Solvent extracted	ND
SH3	7.19.5	Solvent extracted	ND
SH4	7.34.2	Solvent extracted	ND
SH5	7.39.5	Solvent extracted	ND
SH6	7.35.3	Solvent extracted	ND
SH7	7.24.4	Solvent extracted	ND
SH8	7.35.2	Solvent extracted	ND
SH9	7.35.4	Solvent extracted	ND
SH10	3.36.5	Solvent extracted	ND
SH11	7.38.11	Solvent extracted	ND
SH12	7.38.11	Solvent extracted	ND
SH13	7.36.3	Solvent extracted	ND
SH14	7.33.4	Solvent extracted	ND
SH15	7.33.2	Solvent extracted	ND
SH16	7.19.7	Solvent extracted	ND

Sha'ar Hagolan:
6500 - 5800 cal BC
(Garfinkel 1999b)

	Sample	Excavation number	Extraction method	Lipid classes detected
Tubna: 5000 - 4800 cal BC (Banning 1997; Banning 2007)	WZ121/1	826024	Solvent extracted	ND
	WZ121/2	826023	Solvent extracted	ND
	WZ121/3	826925	Solvent extracted	ND
	WZ121/4	826043	Solvent extracted	ND
	WZ121/5	826032	Solvent extracted	ND
	WZ121/6	290020	Solvent extracted	ND
	WZ121/7	826031	Solvent extracted	ND
	WZ121/8	826042	Solvent extracted	ND
	WZ121/9	290029	Solvent extracted	ND
	WZ121/10	826021	Solvent extracted	ND
	WZ121/11	290023	Solvent extracted	ND
	WZ121/12	826015	Solvent extracted	ND
	WZ121/13	962010	Solvent extracted	ND
	WZ121/14	826015	Solvent extracted	ND
	WZ121/15	789007	Solvent extracted	ND
	WZ121/16	836039	Solvent extracted	ND
	WZ121/17	962006	Solvent extracted	ND
	WZ121/18	962007	Solvent extracted	ND
	WZ121/19	290035	Solvent extracted	ND
	WZ121/20	450007	Solvent extracted	ND
	WZ121/21	962008	Solvent extracted	ND
	WZ121/22	826020	Solvent extracted	ND

	Sample	Excavation number	Extraction method	Lipid classes detected
Tabaqat al-Bûma: 5700 - 5100 cal BC (Banning et al. 1994; Banning 2007)	WZ200/1	M9.007.950080B2	Solvent extracted	ND
	WZ200/2	A9.007.9500…ND	Solvent extracted	ND
	WZ200/3	A8.4.005.4500P4	Solvent extracted	ND
	WZ200/4	A7.8.952107	Solvent extracted	ND
	WZ200/5	A8.4.450031	Solvent extracted	ND
	WZ200/6	A13.450087	Solvent extracted	ND
	WZ200/7	A9.007.45008085	Solvent extracted	ND
	WZ200/8	A9.007.45008081	Solvent extracted	ND
	WZ200/9	A7.8.952113	Solvent extracted	ND
	WZ200/10	A7.8.952111	Solvent extracted	ND
	WZ200/11	A8.4.450030	Solvent extracted	ND
	WZ200/12	A9.007.45008080A	Solvent extracted	ND
	WZ200/13	A9.007.45008080B4	Solvent extracted	ND
	WZ200/14	A7.8.952112	Solvent extracted	ND
	WZ200/15	A9.008.450.081	Solvent extracted	ND

	Sample	Excavation number	Extraction method	Lipid classes detected
al-Basatîn: 5750 - 5200 cal BC (Banning et al. 2004; Banning 2007)	WZ135/1	Q41.22.202453	Solvent extracted	ND
	WZ135/2	Q41.26.202557	Solvent extracted	ND
	WZ135/3	P41.35.15	Solvent extracted	ND
	WZ135/4	Q41.31.202407	Solvent extracted	ND
	WZ135/5	Q41.69.ND	Solvent extracted	ND
	WZ135/6	Q41.26.202466	Solvent extracted	ND
	WZ135/7	P33/009	Solvent extracted	ND
	WZ135/RC1	**Q41.16.202466**	**Solvent extracted**	**No lipids but 14C yields**
	WZ135/RC2	**Q41.16.202577**	**Solvent extracted**	**No lipids but 14C yields**

Appendix A.1.3
Pottery fragments examined at the School of Geography and Earth Sciences at McMaster University in a pilot study using microwave-assisted solvent extraction and liquid chromatography separation techniques outlined in chapter 4. Pottery fragments yielding organic residues are highlighted in these appendices in bold text.

Sample	Excavation number	Extraction method	Lipid classes detected	
WZ135/3/micro	**Q33.32.826851**	**Microwave extracted**	**FA – animal ratios**	**al-Basatîn:**
WZ135/4/micro	Q33.29.826830a	Microwave extracted	ND	**5700-5200 cal BC**
WZ135/5/micro	**Q33.29.826830b**	**Microwave extracted**	**FA – animal ratios**	**(Banning et al. 2004;**
WZ135/6/micro	**P33.51.789094**	**Microwave extracted**	**FA – animal ratios**	**Banning 2007)**
WZ135/7/micro	**X37.10.450419**	**Microwave extracted**	**FA – animal ratios**	
WZ135/8/micro	**Q33.32.826779a**	**Microwave extracted**	**FA – animal ratios**	
WZ135/9/micro	**Q33.32.826779b**	**Microwave extracted**	**FA – animal ratios**	
WZ135/10/micro	**P33.52.942213**	**Microwave extracted**	**FA – animal ratios**	
WZ135/11/micro	**Q41.22.202453**	**Microwave extracted**	**FA – animal ratios**	
WZ135/12/micro	Q35.10.ND	Microwave extracted	ND	

Appendix A.1.4
Pottery fragments subsequently examined at the School of Geography and Earth Sciences at McMaster University using microwave-assisted solvent extraction and liquid chromatography separation techniques outlined in chapter 4. Pottery fragments yielding organic residues are highlighted in these appendices in bold text. Potsherds that did not yield measurable abundances of lipids through conventional solvent extraction or saponification techniques, but that did subsequently yield results through use of the microwave-assisted liquid chromatography protocol, are highlighted with a light grey screen here and in Appendix A.1.1. Variations in temperature programming of the gas chromatography column as noted in section 5.4 are designated by three numerical groupings in the GC Run column in the table for each archaeological site.

Sample	Excavation number	Extraction method	Lipid classes detected	GC Run	
AH1micro	**AH.73.244**	**Microwave extracted**	**FA – animal ratios**	**2**	**Abu Hureyra**
AH2micro	**AH.73.131**	**Microwave extracted**	**FA – animal ratios**	**2**	
AH3micro	**AH.73.1126**	**Microwave extracted**	**FA – animal ratios**	**2**	
AH4micro	**AH.73.107**	**Microwave extracted**	**FA – animal ratios**	**2**	
AH5micro	**AH.73.186**	**Microwave extracted**	**FA – animal ratios**	**2**	
AH6micro	**AH.73.246**	**Microwave extracted**	**FA – animal ratios**	**2**	
AH7micro	AH.73.1126	Microwave extracted	FA – animal ratios	2	

Two conventional radiocarbon dates calibrated using OxCal 4.0 provide dates for the pottery-bearing levels between 7400 and 6200 cal BC; 68% confidence (Housely 1994; Moore et al. 2000)

Sample	Excavation number	Extraction method	Lipid classes detected	GC Run	
AK1micro	A98/70-80	Microwave extracted	ND	1	Ali Kosh
AK2micro	A84/90-100	Microwave extracted	ND	1	
AK3micro	A98/70-80	Microwave extracted	ND	1	
AK4micro	A96/60-70	Microwave extracted	ND	1	
AK5micro	A25/90-100	Microwave extracted	ND	1	
AK6micro	**A16/50-60**	**Microwave extracted**	**FA – animal ratios**	**1**	

Relatively recent AMS dating of animal bone places the earliest pottery-bearing level at this site between 7300 and 7000 cal BC (Hole 2000)

	Sample	Excavation number	Extraction method	Lipid classes detected	GC Run
Çayönü: 5500-4650 cal BC (Çambel 1981; Thissen 2002)	CU3micro	CT89-P25I 1-9	Microwave extracted	FA — plant ratios	1
	CU5micro	**CT91-P25I PS 448**	**Microwave extracted**	**FA — animal ratios**	**1**
	CU9micro	**CT89-P25I 2-22**	**Microwave extracted**	**FA — plant ratios**	**1**
	CU10micro	CT94-P25I 6-71	Microwave extracted	ND	1
	CU11micro	**CT90-P27K 3-14**	**Microwave extracted**	**FA — plant ratios**	**1**
	CU13micro	CT87-F Whitewear	Microwave extracted	ND	1
	CU14micro	**CT 70-29L P 2-18**	**Microwave extracted**	**FA — plant ratios**	**1**
	CU15micro	**CT87-P25K 1-2 403**	**Microwave extracted**	**FA — plant ratios**	**1**

	Sample	Excavation number	Extraction method	Lipid classes detected	GC Run
Dalma Tepe: 5000-4800 cal BC (Stuckenrath 1963)	**DA1micro**	**60.70.730**	**Microwave extracted**	**FA — animal ratios**	**3**
	DA2micro	III.IV.3.61.27.261	Microwave extracted	ND	3
	DA3micro	61.27.39	Microwave extracted	ND	3

	Sample	Excavation number	Extraction method	Lipid classes detected	GC Run
Hajji Firuz: 6150-5750 cal BC (Voigt 1983)	HF1micro	G11.41A	Microwave extracted	ND	3
	HF2micro	G11.	Microwave extracted	FA — animal ratios	3
	HF3micro	**G11.51**	**Microwave extracted**	**FA — animal ratios**	**3**
	HF4micro	**G11.515**	**Microwave extracted**	**FA — animal ratios**	**3**
	HF5micro	**V.L7.21**	**Microwave extracted**	**FA — animal ratios**	**3**
	HF6micro	IV.B2.22	Microwave extracted	ND	3
	HF7micro	V1.8	Microwave extracted	ND	3
	HF8micro	V.F.33	Microwave extracted	ND	3
	HF9micro	G.11.4	Microwave extracted	ND	3
	HF10micro	IV.3&4	Microwave extracted	ND	3

	Sample	Excavation number	Extraction method	Lipid classes detected	GC Run
Newe Yam: 5500-5000 cal BC (Galili 2004)	NY1micro	ND	Microwave extracted	ND	1
	NY2micro	**ND**	**Microwave extracted**	**FA — animal ratios**	**1**
	NY3micro	ND	Microwave extracted	ND	1
	NY4micro	**ND**	**Microwave extracted**	**FA — animal ratios**	**1**
	NY5micro	ND	Microwave extracted	ND	1
	NY6micro	ND	Microwave extracted	ND	1
	NY7micro	**ND**	**Microwave extracted**	**FA — animal ratios**	**1**
	NY8micro	ND	Microwave extracted	ND	1
	NY9micro	ND	Microwave extracted	ND	1
	NY10micro	ND	Microwave extracted	ND	1

Sample	Excavation number	Extraction method	Lipid classes detected	GC Run
TB1micro	RN766	Microwave extracted	ND	1
TB2micro	**RN793**	**Microwave extracted**	**FA — animal ratios**	**2**
TB3micro	RN771	Microwave extracted	ND	1
TB4micro	**RN1059**	**Microwave extracted**	**FA — plant ratios**	**1**
TB5micro	RN1677	Microwave extracted	ND	1
TB9micro	RN1767	Microwave extracted	ND	1
TB10micro	**RN545**	**Microwave extracted**	**FA — animal ratios**	**2**

Toll-e Bashi: 6000-5750 cal BC (Bernbeck et al. 2003; Gregg in press)

Sample	Excavation number	Extraction method	Lipid classes detected	GC Run
TS1micro	**No # 'Tadpole' ware**	**Microwave extracted**	**FA — animal ratios**	**1**
TS2micro	**No # thick base**	**Microwave extracted**	**FA — animal ratios**	**1**
TSROM1micro	**No # ROM fragment**	**Microwave extracted**	**FA — animal ratios**	**1**
TSROM2micro	No # ROM fragment	Microwave extracted	ND	1

Tepe Sarab

Four conventional radiocarbon dates calibrated using OxCal 4.0 provide dates for the pottery horizons at this site ranging between 8700 and 5800 cal BC; 68% confidence (Hole 1977; Hole 1987a), or 6800 - 6500 calBC (Stuckenrath 1963; Hole 1987a)

Appendix A.1.5

I obtained a fragment of a large pottery churn called a *dugran* from Naci and Besime Kayan of Kizilkaya, Turkey, a small farming and herding community in central Anatolia, in the fall of 2005. This churn had been used in the manufacture of raw butter *çig tereyagi*, yogurt *aryan* and curd cheese *cökelik* during the 1980s and 1990s, and then discarded in an outbuilding adjacent to the Kayan household. In a study of subsistence practices and plant use in central Anatolia, ethnobotanist Füsün Ertug has noted that dried stomach of sheep was used as a cheese starter by pastoralists at the modern village of Gordion, but that this did not appear to be a common practice at Kizilkaya (Ertug-Yaras 1997: 346, 352). The possible use of sheep stomach or an animal udder as a starter for cheese or yogurt may explain the more positive $\partial^{13}C$ values of $C_{18:0}$ obtained from residues surviving in this vessel than that of sheep butter from the Jordan Valley.

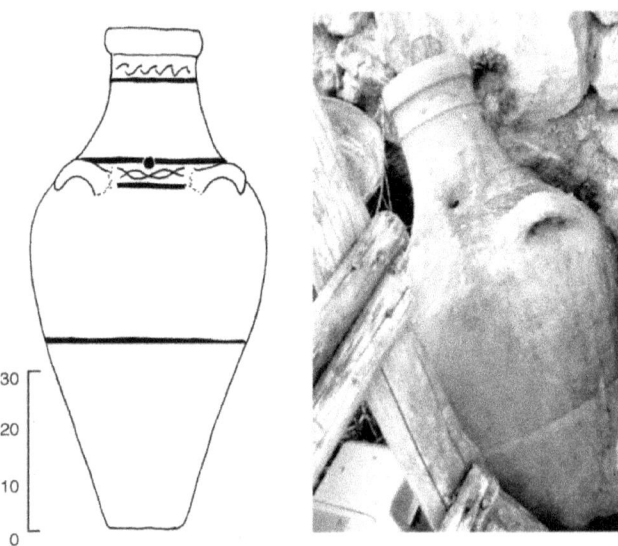 

Figure A.1.5
a. Illustration of a *dugran* pottery churn (after Ertug-Yaras 1997:Pl.126a). b. A fragment of this *dugran* pottery churn was obtained from an outbuilding adjacent to the household of Naci and Besime Kayan in Kizilkaya, Turkey in the fall of 2005 (photo by the author).

c. A woman using a *dugran* to churn butter in Kizilkaya during the early 1990s. (photo by Füsün Ertug; reproduced by permission).

Appendix A.1.6

The majority of pottery fragments (77%) examined in this study are body sherds. Consequently, I did not consider any possible correlation between pottery use and vessel size and form. However, in this appendix I have included 65 vessel profiles I was able to identify along with brief descriptions of the pottery fragments and the characteristic pottery assemblages recovered from the corresponding ceramic horizons of the archaeological sites.

A.1.6.1 *Soft-ware pottery fragments from Tepe Guran and Tepe Sarab in western Iran*

I was unable to examine soft-ware pottery from excavations at Ganj Dareh, but did obtain 8 lightly fired, chaff-tempered soft-ware potsherds from Peder Mortensen at the Carsten Niebuhr Institute in Copenhagen. A soft-ware pottery horizon has been identified in the basal levels of a number of Middle to Late Neolithic settlements over a broad geographic area adjacent to the foothills of the Zagros mountains including the sites of Jarmo, Ganj Dareh, Tepe Guran, and Tepe Sarab (Braidwood 1961,1962; Smith 1974, 1978; Mortensen 1962, 1963; Dyson 1965). Mortensen provided me with two fragments (TG1, TG2) from his excavations of the early ceramic levels at Tepe Guran (Mortensen 1962, 1963, Melgaard et al. 1964), and six base and body sherd fragments (TS1-TS6) from Robert Braidwood's excavations at Tepe Sarab (Braidwood 1961), including a single 'Tadpole' ware body fragment (TS1). No excavation numbers were available for the Tepe Sarab materials, but the Tadpole wares are known only from the stratigraphically early SI excavation units at Tepe Sarab (McDonald 1979). The forms characteristic of the Tepe Guran assemblage are thick-walled circular or oval bowls or beakers with slightly curved or vertical sides and rounded or flat bases (Mortensen 1962, 1963; Dyson 1965). The pottery assemblage at Tepe Sarab is dominated by flat-based open bowls with vertical and concave sides in the SI levels (McDonald 1979) while bowls with flaring and carinated walls and closed, round-bodied vessels are also known from the stratigraphically later SV excavation units (Henrickson and McDonald 1983).

Due to the absence of groundstone tools in its basal levels and the presence of ephemeral brush huts underlying mudbrick architecture, Tepe Guran was interpreted by Mortensen as an intermontaine valley home base for seasonal herders (Melgaard et al. 1964: 106). Circular depressions in Tepe Sarab's earliest levels were viewed by Braidwood (1962) as evidence that the highland settlement was only occupied by a specialized task group during the summer months of the year. Conventional radiocarbon dates place the soft-ware horizon between 6811 and 6445 cal BC at Tepe Guran (Tauber 1969; OxCal 2009, 68% confidence) and between 7031 and 6392 cal BC at Tepe Sarab (Stuckenrath 1963; OxCal 2009, 68% confidence).

No pottery fragments from Tepe Guran yielded organic compounds through conventional solvent extraction techniques. A single fragment (TS2) yielded measureable abundances of fatty acids through 'conventional' solvent extraction, saponification and microwave-assisted solvent recovery methods. The Tadpole ware fragment (TS1) that did not yielded fatty acids through conventional solvent extraction, yielded fatty acids through the microwave assisted protocol (TS1micro), as did another Tepe Sarab fragment (TS1ROMmicro) from the collections at the Royal Ontario Museum.

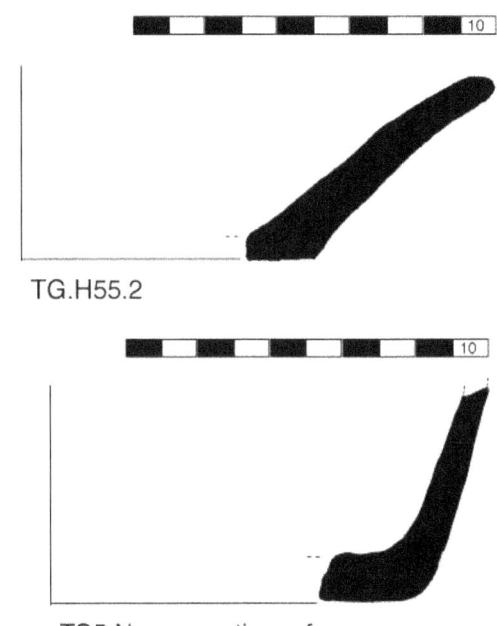

TG.H55.2

TS5 No excavation reference

Figure A.1.6.1
Profiles of soft-ware bowls identified from two of eight pottery fragments obtained from Peder Mortensen from the sites of Tepe Guran (top) and Tepe Sarab (above) in western Iran.

A.1.6.2 *Pottery fragments from additional early pottery horizons in western Iran*

I obtained 38 pottery fragments from six other early agricultural settlements in western Iran from the sites of Ali Kosh, Chageh Sefid, Furukhabad, Toll-eBashi, Hajji Firuz and Dalma Tepe. There are many typological and stylistic parallels between vessels from a broad geographic area adjacent to the foothills of the Zagros mountains during the Middle to Late Neolithic periods (Braidwood 1962; Dyson 1965; Hole et al. 1965), and useful summaries comparing similarities and differences in vessel form and decoration can be found in Voigt and Dyson (1992).

A.1.6.2.1 *Ali Kosh and Chageh Sefid*

Frank Hole of the Department of Anthropology at Yale University provided me with 12 pottery fragments (AK1 – AK7; CS1 – CS5) from his excavations of the earliest pottery-bearing levels at the aceramic to ceramic settlements of Ali Kosh and Chageh Sefid in southwestern Iran. These sites are located in the Deh Luran plain near the foothills of the Zagros mountains in Khuzistan. Vessels from the earliest pottery bearing levels at these sites (Mohammad Jaffar phase) greatly resemble the more highly-fired pottery from later occupation levels at Jarmo, Tepe Guran and Tepe Sarab (Hole et al. 1965:106). Most pots are small to medium open bowls, both plain and painted with geometric chevron designs, but there are also plain, medium-sized, closed, globular, hole-mouth vessels. Hole and his colleagues, Kent Flannery and James Neeley (1965), have interpreted the increase in faunal remains of sheep and goat accompanying the advent of pottery and the apparent decline in the cultivation and processing of cereal grains in the Mohammad Jafar phase as a preference for pastoralism over agriculture by the inhabitants of the Deh Luran plain during this period. Two relatively new AMS radiocarbon dates from the Mohammad Jaffar phase at Ali Kosh place this early pottery horizon between 7313 and 7040 cal BC (Zeder and Hesse 2000; Hole 2000; OxCal 2009, 68% confidence).Four pottery fragments from Ali Kosh (AK1, AK2) and Chageh Sefid (CS1, CS2) yielded molecular compounds consistent with bitumen through conventional solvent extraction techniques, and a single fragment (AK6micro) yielded measurable abundances of fatty acids through the microwave-assisted solvent recovery method.

A.1.6.2.2 *Farukhabad*

I also obtained four pottery fragments (FK1 – FK4) from the early occupation levels of the large tell at Furukhabad in the Deh Luran plain from Henry Wright of the Department of Anthropology at the University of Michigan. The pottery assemblage of the Bayat ceramic horizon from which these sherds were recovered is dominated by plain and painted open bowls and hole-mouth jars (Wright 1981) similar to those from the corresponding ceramic horizon at Ali Kosh and Chageh Sefid (Hole et al. 1969). A single radiocarbon determination from charcoal places this horizon between 4750 and 4400 cal BC (Crane and Griffin 1973; OxCal 2009, 68% confidence). None of the fragments from Farukhabad yielded diagnostic molecular compounds through conventional solvent extraction techniques, and no further extractions were undertaken using the microwave-assisted solvent recovery protocol.

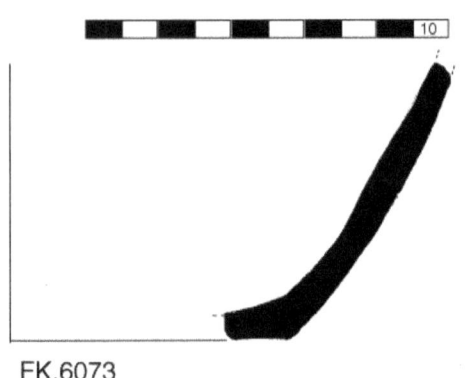

FK.6073

Figure A.1.6.2.2
Profile of a bowl fragment recovered from the early occupation level (Bayat phase) of the large tell at Farukhabad in the Deh Luran plain in southwestern Iran.

A.1.6.2.3 *Toll-e Bashi*

As a member of an international excavation team led by Reinhardt Bernbeck of Binghamton University, I recovered 11 pottery fragments specifically for organic residue analysis from the earliest pottery horizon at Toll-e Bashi in southwestern Iran. Excavations were undertaken at this low-lying tell in the Kor River basin near Marv Dasht after a small portion of the site was exposed through intensive agricultural activity. Two distinct chronological phases were identified at the site (Bernbeck et al. 2003), with the pottery from the earliest phase sharing many typological similarities with that of the nearby site at Tall-i Mushki and pottery from the later phase resembling that from the nearby site at Tall-i Jari (Fukai et al. 1973; Nishiaki 2003). AMS radiocarbon dates of faunal remains place the Mushki period occupation of the site between 6200 and 5700 cal BC (Bernbeck et al. in press). Although the pottery assemblage from this early phase is very fragmentary, it appears to be dominated by medium-sized, thick-walled, straw tempered, "bag-shaped" and beaker-like open vessels (Bernbeck in press). Tray-like vessels with thick walls and large basins are also well represented with only a small proportion of hole-mouth vessels (Bernbeck in press). None of the pottery fragments from Toll-e Bashi yielded diagnostic molecular compounds through conventional solvent extraction techniques, but three potsherds (TB2micro, TB4micro, TB10micro) yielded measurable abundances of fatty acids through the microwave-assisted solvent recovery method.

TB RN766

Figure A.1.6.2.3
Profile of a tray fragment recovered by the author from the early Mushki period occupation at Toll-e Bashi.

A.1.6.2.4 *Hajji Firuz and Dalma Tepe*

Mary Voigt of the Department of Anthropology at the College of William and Mary provided me with 13 pottery fragments (HF1micro – HF10micro; DA1micro – DA3micro) recovered from the sites of Hajji Firuz and Dalma Tepe near Lake Urmia in the province of Azerbaijan, northwestern Iran. Both sites were excavated as part of the University of Pennsylvania Museum's Hasanlu Project led by Robert Dyson. Dalma, a small mound located about 5 km southwest of Hasanlu, was excavated by Charles Burney in 1958 and 1959 and by T. Cuyler Young in 1961. In addition to conducting large-scale excavations of the Late Bronze Age and Iron Age city at Hassanlu, Dyson also undertook smaller excavations at the nearby Neolithic tell at Hajji Firuz in 1958, 1960 and 1961. Voigt and Dyson co-directed the 1968 excavations at Hajji Firuz. Voigt has subsequently published the findings of all four excavation seasons in a monograph (Voigt 1983).

The chaff-tempered pottery assemblage from the Hajji Firuz and Dalma Tepe excavations is dominated by small to medium-sized closed bowls, many decorated with red linear designs. Red-slipped and burnished pots are also common (Voigt 1983). Many technological and stylistic similarities have been noted to vessels from the western Zagros, such as were recovered from late Neolithic levels at Tepe Guran and Tepe Sarab (Young 1962; Voigt 1983, 1992). However, Voigt also points to parallels in the Jarmo Operation II horizon

(Voigt 1983:160-63), and to forms such as husking trays, carinated bowls, and collared jars linking pottery from Hajji Firuz to early Hassuna sites in upper Mesopotamia (Voigt 1992:174). Since Voigt had speculated in her 1983 excavation monograph (159) that the shape and size of medium and large closed bowls (form class 14 and 15) would have been well suited to the fermenting of yogurt, we chose non-diagnostic pottery fragments from collections housed at the University of Pennsylvania museum that Voigt thought were likely to have been from these vessel forms. Three body sherds from Hajji Firuz (HF3micro, HF4micro and HF5micro) and one from Tepe Dalma (DA1micro) yielded measurable abundances of fatty acids through the microwave-assisted solvent recovery method.

A.1.6.3 *Proto-Hassuna 'husking' tray pottery fragments from upper Mesopotamia*

In addition to the pottery fragments from Farukhabad in Iran, Henry Wright also provided me with four 'husking tray' fragments from Tell Kashkashok II (KA1 – KA4). Two of these fragments had recognizable shapes (Figure A.1.6.3.1), while two others were amorphous in form. The pottery assemblage from this small mound in the Khabur basin in Syria is dominated by plain and painted open bowls and hole-mouth jars, but carinated closed forms and 'husking' trays are also a characteristic form of Proto-Hassuna ware (Matsutani 1981, 1991; Nishiaki and Le Miére 2005). Wright was interested in obtaining direct evidence of the hypothesized uses of these trays for drying and processing cereal grain (Kirkbride 1973; Maisels 1990) or possibly as portable ovens (Voigt 1983). Matsutani (1991) placed occupation of the site on the Middle Khabur between 6600 - 5400 cal BC. However, Frank Hole has subsequently noted that the youngest radiocarbon date is stratigraphically inconsistent with the three other conventional radiocarbon dates and therefore unreliable (Hole 2001). My recalibration of the three radiocarbon determinations places occupation anywhere between 7000 and 6200 cal BC (OxCal 2009, 68% confidence). Yoshihiro Nishiaki and Marie Le Miére (2005) have recently identified a distinctive earlier pottery type (that they term as Pre-Proto-Hassuna) at the site of Seker al Aheimar in the Khabur basin. This undecorated ware is characterized by simple closed or vertically-sided forms, or hole-mouth jars with convex bodies and flat bottoms. Unlike the chaff - and mineral-tempered pottery from the overlying Proto-Hassuna levels at the site, the Pre-Proto-Hassuna ware is exclusively mineral-tempered. Eight radiocarbon dates from the stratigraphic levels containing this pottery type cluster between 7000 and 6500 cal BC while nine dates from the overlying Proto-Hassuna levels cluster between 6500 and 6000 cal BC. None of the 'husking' tray fragments from Kashkashok yielded diagnostic molecular compounds through conventional solvent-extraction techniques, and no further extractions were undertaken using the microwave-assisted solvent recovery protocol.

A.1.6.4 *Abu Hureyra*

Andrew Moore of the School of Humanities at the Rochester Institute of Technology provided me with 11 pottery fragments (AH1 – AH11) from the earliest pottery bearing levels at Abu Hureyra in northern Syria. Abu Hureyra is a Middle Epipalaeolithic and late Neolithic settlement excavated in

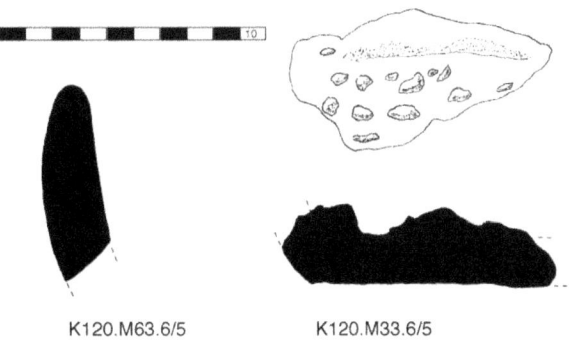

K120.M63.6/5 K120.M33.6/5

Figure A.1.6.3.1
Two Proto-Hassuna 'husking tray' fragments from the site of Kashkashok obtained from Henry Wright.

1973 by Moore in advance of construction of a dam in the middle Euphrates River valley. The chaff-tempered pottery fragments were labeled as dark-faced burnished ware by the excavator, but none exhibited evidence of burnishing or were dark in color. All of these pottery fragments were body sherds, providing no indication of vessel form. The color of the clay fabric of the majority of these potsherds is 6/2/7.5 YR, however three fragments have a lighter clay slip (8/2/7.5 YR) applied to their exterior surface. The color of the clay fabric core of three potsherds is 4/1/7.5 YR, suggesting the vessels were fired in an oxidizing environment. Dark stains on the exterior surface of pottery fragment AH3 (AH 73 1126) supports the excavator's contention (Moore 1995) that pottery vessels were used in cooking through direct placement in or over the coals of a fire. This chaff-tempered pottery assemblage from Abu Hureyra is dominated by rounded and straight-walled bowls and hole-mouth jars (Le Moore 1995). Most pottery fragments are undecorated, but a small percentage are burnished, or have fugitive red wash or linear geometric patterns, similar to potsherds recovered from the earliest pottery levels at Umm Dabaghiyah. Athough two conventional radiocarbon dates place the pottery-bearing levels at Abu Hureyra between 7400 and 6200 cal BC (Moore et al. 2000; OxCal 2009; 68% confidence), as I have noted pottery does not become traditional at most settlements built alongside the Middle Euphrates and Balikh river valleys until approximately 6800 cal BC (Akkermans and Schwartz 2003). None of the pottery fragments from Abu Hureyra yielded diagnostic molecular compounds through conventional solvent-extraction techniques. However, six potsherds (AH1micro – AH6micro) yielded measurable abundances of fatty acids through the microwave-assisted solvent-recovery method.

A.1.6.5 *Çayönü*

Asli Erim (Özdagan) of the University of Istanbul provided me with 19 pottery fragments from the earliest pottery-bearing levels at the site of Çayönü in southeastern Turkey. These fragments had been recovered by Erim and Mehmet Özdagan from a small area in the northern section of the large mound containing a pottery horizon (3) directly overlying the earlier aceramic occupation (Özdagan and Özdagan 1993:95). In their preliminary report of Pre-Halafian pottery from recovered the site, Özdagan and Özdagan (1993:100) note that no vessel forms were reconstructable, but the fragments evidently came from thick sided, simple bowls or jars with large flat bases. Two of the pottery fragments provided to me by Erim had recognizable forms of a 'sieve' and a shallow bowl or tray (Figure A.1.6.5.1). Potsherds with a dark, burnished surface were recovered from a later ceramic horizon that two conventional radiocarbon dates place between 5500 and 4650 cal BC (Çambel 1981; Thissen 2002; OxCal 2009, 68% confidence). Only one of the pottery fragments from Çayönü (CU5; CT91.P25.PS448l; Figure A.1.6.5.1) yielded diagnostic molecular compounds through conventional solvent extraction techniques. However, this fragment and four other potsherds (CU5micro, CU9micro, CU11micro, CU14micro, CU15miicro) yielded measurable abundances of fatty acids through the microwave-assisted solvent recovery method.

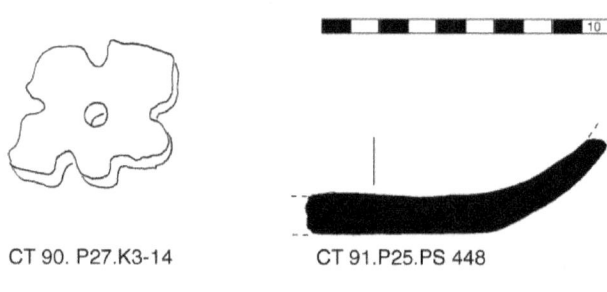

CT 90. P27.K3-14   CT 91.P25.PS 448

Figure A.1.6.5.1
Two of the 19 potsherds from the pottery-bearing horizon directly overlying the aceramic occupation at Çayönü provided to me by Asli Erim had recognizable forms of a 'sieve' and a shallow bowl or tray.

A.1.6.6 *Yarmoukian, Jericho IX, and Wadi Rabah pottery from the southern Levant*

In this study I have examined pottery fragments from eight Late Neolithic and Chalcolithic sites in the southern Levant. As I have noted in section 1.2.1, when pottery emerges in this region it appears as a more fully developed container technology than in other parts in the Middle East. Crude pottery fragments and unfired clay vessels were recovered from a small number of Middle to Late PPNB contexts (Rollefson and Simmons 1985; Nissen et al. 1987), but pottery did not become common in the region until the Yarmoukian period beginning between 6527 and 6376 cal BC (68% confidence; Banning 2007). Edward Banning's recent analysis of radiocarbon dates associated with Late Neolithic and Chalcolithic pottery in the southern Levant suggests that Yarmoukian sites are consistently older than those containing Wadi Rabah assemblages, but due to typological similarities between Jericho IX and Yarmoukian ceramic horizons, it appears that these may be "at least partly contemporary" with one another (Banning 2007:88).

A.1.6.6.1 *Yarmoukian potsherds from Munhata, Sha'ar Hagolan and Abu Thawwab*

I obtained 39 pottery fragments from the Yarmoukian sites of Munhata (MN1 – MN13), Sha'ar Hagolan (SH1 – SH16) and Abu Thawwab (AT1 – AT10). The potsherds from level 2b at Munhata and those from Sha'ar Hagolan were provided to me by Yosef Garfinkel of the Institute of Archaeology at the Hebrew University in Jerusalem. Those from Abu Thawwab were provided by Zeidan Kafafi of the Institute of Archaeology at Yarmouk University. Yarmoukian pottery vessels come in a full range of shapes and sizes, in decorated and undecorated forms: finewares, coarsewares, with and without handles, mineral and vegetable tempers, both painted and incised. Detailed characteristics of Yarmoukian pottery assemblages can be found in Garfinkel (1994; 1999a) and Obeidat (1995). Excavation reports on these sites can be found in Stekelis (1950), Perrot (1964), Coughenour (1976), Gillet and Gillet (1983), Kafafi (1985, 1986), Garfinkel (1997), Garfinkel and Miller (2001). None of the Yarmoukian pottery fragments from these three sites yielded diagnostic molecular compounds through conventional-solvent extraction techniques, and no further extractions were undertaken using the microwave-assisted solvent-recovery protocol.

A.1.6.6.2 *Jericho IX pottery fragments from Dhra'*

Twenty-four Jericho IX (Lodian) pottery fragments recovered from the Late Neolithic occupation of Dhra' near the Lisan of the Dead Sea in central Jordan were provided to me by Ian Kuijt of Notre Dame University and Bill Finlayson of the British Council for Research in the Levant. A general description of the fabric and decoration and preliminary typologies of the pottery vessels can be found in Finlayson et al. (2003). The pottery assemblage is dominated by slipped, painted and burnished wares with a coarse orange-colored, mineral-tempered fabric. Closed and open bowls, basins, pithoi, and necked and hole-mouth jars are all common. Vessels with handles are rare. A single radiocarbon date (Kuijt 2001; Kuijt et al. 2007) associated with this ceramic horizon places the Jericho IX occupation of the site around 5874 - 5763 cal BC (68% probability; Banning 2007). None of the Jericho IX pottery fragments from Dhra' yielded diagnostic molecular compounds through conventional solvent extraction techniques, and no further extractions were undertaken using the microwave-assisted solvent recovery protocol.

A.1.6.6.3 *Wadi Rabah pottery fragments from Tabaqat al-Bûma and al-Basatîn*

I also examined 48 pottery fragments from the Late Neolithic sites of Tabaqat al-Bûma (WZ200) and al-Basatîn (WZ135) as part of Edward Banning's ongoing investigation of the late prehistory of Wadi Ziqlab in the al Koura district of northern Jordan (Banning et al. 1998; Banning et al. 2004; Banning et al. 2006; Banning 2007; Gregg et al. 2009). During the 2004 excavations at al-Basatîn, I recovered 9 pottery fragments specifically for organic residue analysis (WZ135/1 WZ135/7; WZ135/RC1, WZ135/RC2). Radiocarbon assays on visible charred organic residues on the interior surface of two of these fragments (WZ135/RC1, WZ135/RC2) yielded dates of 5644-5538 cal BC and 5620-5483 cal BC respectively (68% confidence; Banning 2007). However, none of these potsherds yielded measurable quantities of diagnostic lipids through use of 'conventional' solvent extraction techniques.

10 additional pottery fragments (WZ135/3 micro-WZ135/12micro) exhibiting visible evidence of charred organic residues on their interior surface were recovered specifically for organic residue analysis from the 2006 excavations at al-Basatîn by my colleagues Seiji Kadowaki and Kevin Gibbs. Eight of these 10 fragments yielded diagnostic compounds through use of the microwave-assisted liquid chromatography

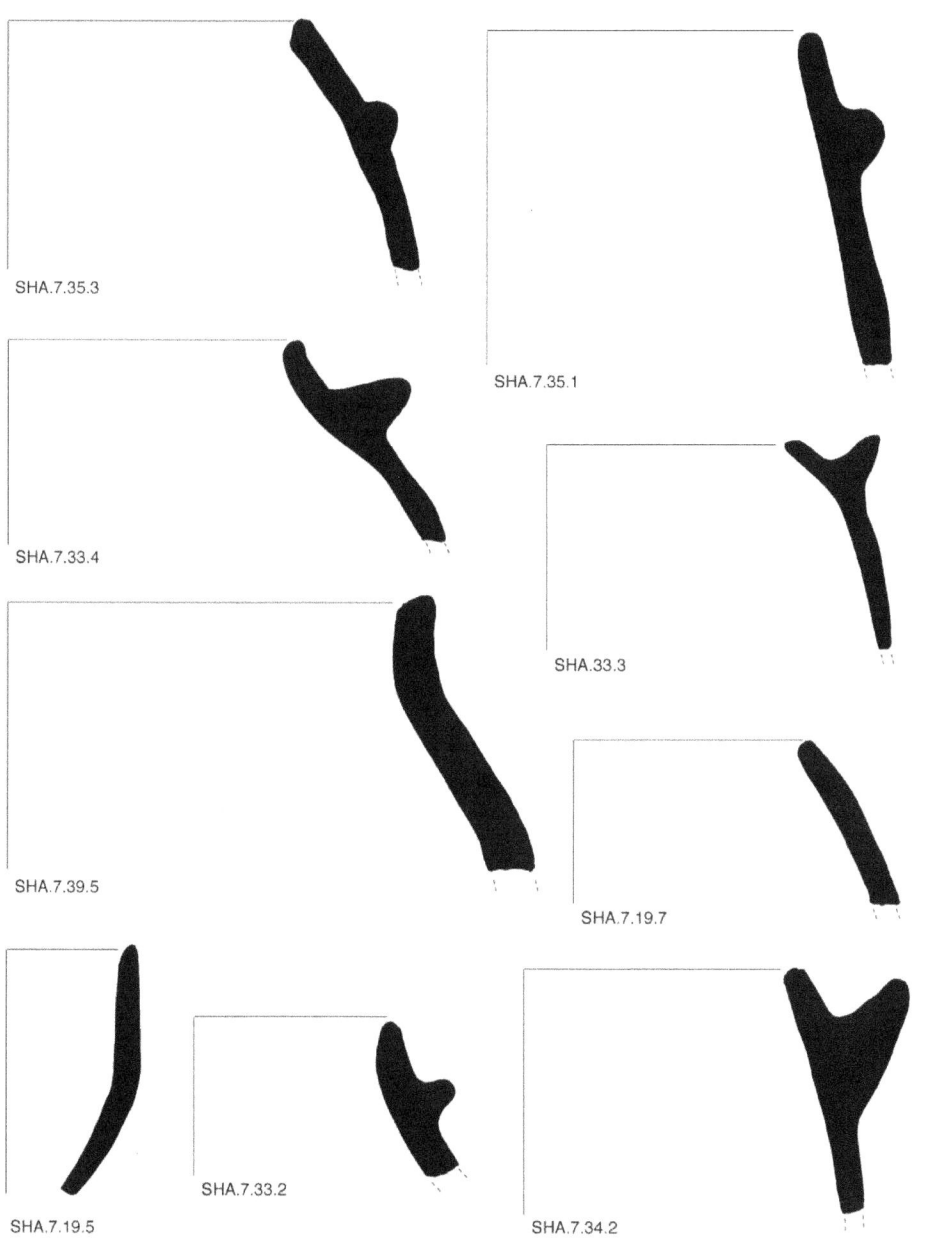

Figure A.1.6.6.1
Nine of 16 Yarmoukian potsherds from Sha 'ar Hagolan had diagnostic vessel profiles. None of the pottery fragments from Munhata or Abu Thawwab displayed evidence of vessel size or

protocol outlined in chapter 4 (Gregg et al. 2009). All of these pottery fragments were body sherds providing no indication of vessel form. However, where form is evident in other vessel fragments from the al-Basatîn assemblage, cups, bowls and hole-mouth jars appear common (Gregg et al. 2009).

I also examined fifteen pottery fragments recovered from Banning's earlier excavations at the nearby site at Tabaqat al-Bûma (Banning et al. 1994, 2004, in press). Like the al-Basatîn ceramic assemblage, the Tabaqat al-Bûma pottery is handmade, crudely constructed and poorly fired, and shows similarities in form, surface treatment and decoration to assemblages of the Wadi Rabah culture in northern and western Israel (Garfinkel and Matskevich 2002). Radiocarbon determinations from the relevant LN3, LN4 and LN5 phases at the site have yielded dates between 5700 and 5100 cal BC (Banning 2007). None of the pottery fragments from Tabaqat al-Bûma yielded diagnostic molecular compounds through conventional solvent extraction techniques, and no further extractions were undertaken on the pottery fragments using the microwave-assisted recovery protocol.

A.1.6.6.4 *Wadi Rabah and Jericho IX pottery fragments from Newe Yam*

I obtained 43 pottery fragments from the submerged Late Neolithic Mediterranean coastal settlement of Newe Yam for analysis from Ehud Galili of the Marine Archaeology Branch of the Israel Antiquities Authority. A detailed assessment of the ceramic assemblage has not been undertaken since Galili's excavation of the site between 1992 and 1995, but pottery from different parts of the site has been assigned to Jericho IX (Lodian) and Wadi Rabah cultural groupings (Galili et al. 1998). Following the initial exposure of the site by a storm surge in the early 1970s, Moshé Prausnitz (1973:273) suggested that many components of the fragmented ceramic assemblage had "close resemblances to pottery from Tell Halaf prior to the Halafian painted pottery", and typological affinities with northern Levantine Dark Faced Burnish Ware from Robert Braidwood's survey and test excavations in the Amuq plain (Braidwood 1960). A single radiocarbon date places occupation of Newe Yam between 5527 and 4996 cal BC (Banning 2007; 68% confidence).

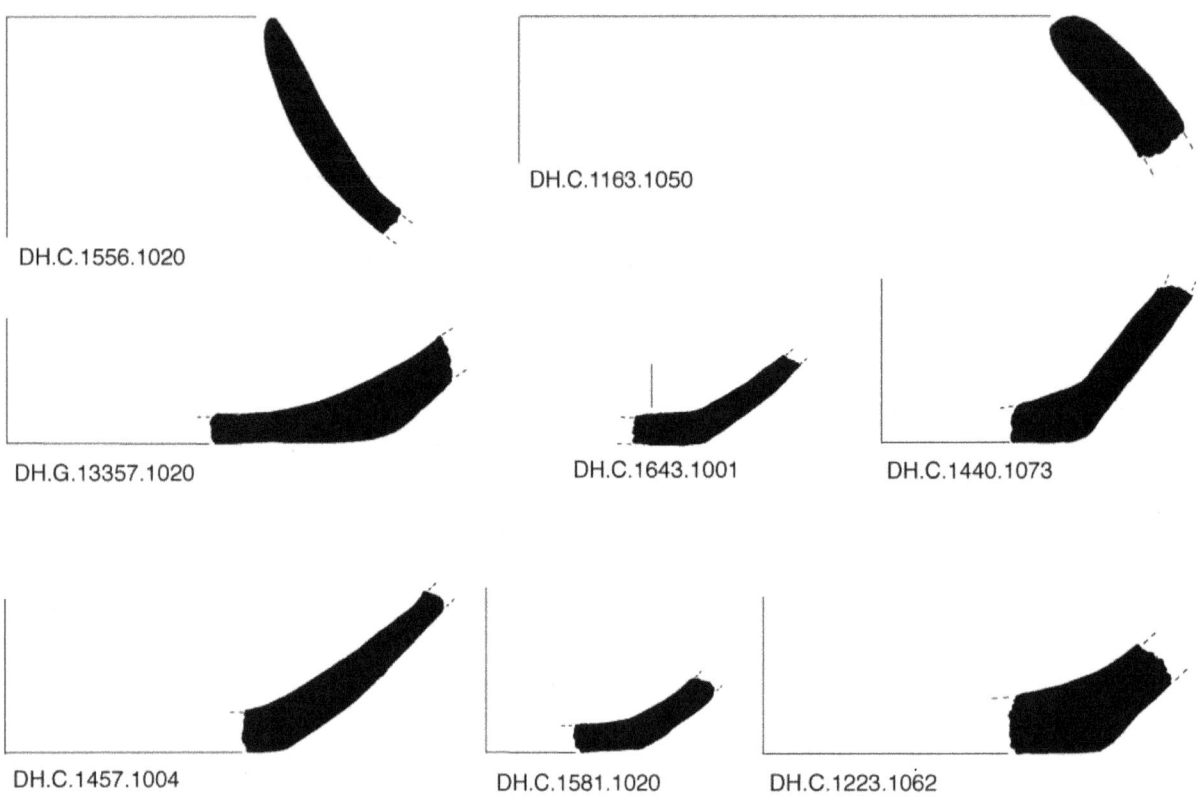

Figure A.1.6.6.2
Eight of 24 Jericho IX potsherds from Dhra' had diagnostic vessel profiles including those of shallow bowls, necked vessels and hole-mouth jars.

In 2005, Galili provided me with 33 potsherds (NY1 – NY33) but residue extraction using conventional solvent-recovery techniques was unsuccessful. In 2007, Galili provided me with 10 additional pottery fragments (NY1micro – NY10 micro), three of which yielded fatty acids through use of the microwave-assisted liquid chromatography protocol. All of these 10 pottery fragments were body sherds displaying no evidence of vessel size or form.

Twenty-five of 33 pottery fragments provided to me in 2005 showed evidence that the ceramic assemblage from Newe Yam included a full range of shapes and sizes.

Figure A.1.6.6.4:
Profiles of pottery fragments from Newe Yam (to the right and next three pages)

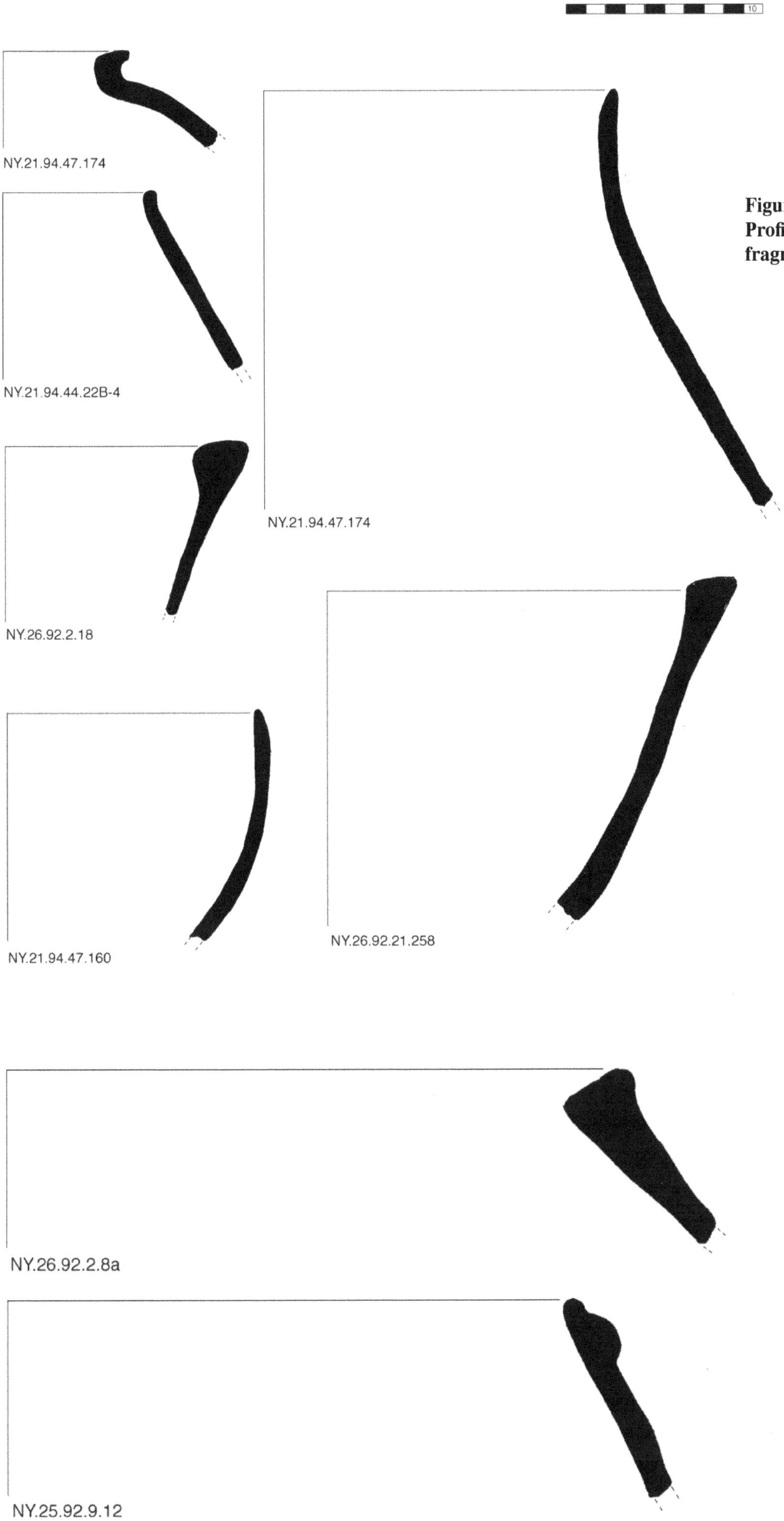

Figure A.1.6.6.4
Profiles of pottery fragments from Newe Yam

Figure A.1.6.6.4
Profiles of pottery fragments from Newe Yam

NY.30.93.54.26

NY.21.94.47.160

NY.26.92.21.1246

NY.21.94.44.1279

NY.21.94.57.57

NY.21.94.44.271

NY.21.94.47.196

NY.21.94.7.57

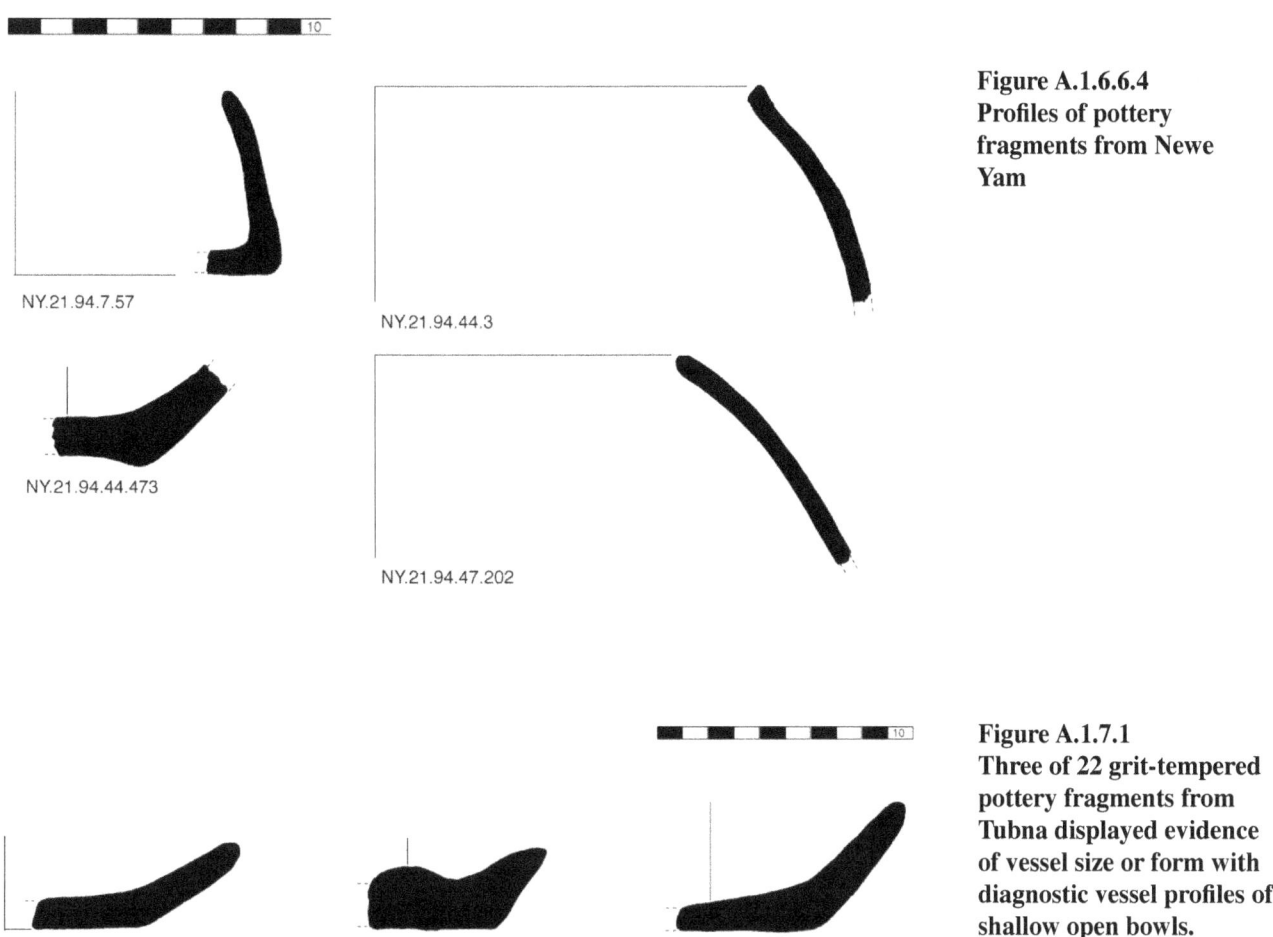

Figure A.1.6.6.4
Profiles of pottery fragments from Newe Yam

Figure A.1.7.1
Three of 22 grit-tempered pottery fragments from Tubna displayed evidence of vessel size or form with diagnostic vessel profiles of shallow open bowls.

A.1.7 *Middle Chalcolithic pottery fragments from Tubna*

I also examined 22 pottery fragments recovered specifically for organic residue analysis from Tubna (WZ121/1 – WZ121/22) by one of Edward Banning's former graduate students, Alicia Beck. The grit-tempered pottery from Tubna has many forms and stylistic parallels to Middle Chalcolithic assemblages from Pella, Abu Habil, and Abu Hamid (Banning et al. 1997; Lovell et al.2004; Lovell et al. 2007). Like the assemblages from these sites, it does not contain distinctive vessels characteristic of Ghassulian pottery assemblages, such as cornets or churns (Banning 2007). No dates have been directly associated with the pottery assemblage from Tubna, but radiocarbon determinations from the basal levels of the site place the earliest occupation between 5007 and 4808 cal BC (Banning 2007). None of the pottery fragments from Tubna yielded diagnostic molecular compounds through conventional solvent extraction techniques, and no further extractions were undertaken on the pottery fragments using the microwave-assisted recovery protocol.

A.1.6.8 *Late Chalcolithic 'churn' fragments from Abu Matar and Nevatim, Israel*

I obtained 18 Chalcolithic 'churn' fragments from the sites of Abu Matar (AM1-AM14) and Nevatin (NEV 1- NEV4) from Steven Rosen of the Institute of Archaeology at Ben-Gurion University of the Negev. Similar fragments from vessels recovered from Teleilat-Ghassul were described as 'bird vases' by Mallon et al. (1934), and subsequently as 'churns' by Kaplan (1954; 1965). Although these vessels are known to vary in size and form, the barrel-shaped body of a typical 'churn' is 60 cm long with two loop handles and a bow-shaped vertical neck resembling a cup. In some smaller 'churns' a holed clay strainer is located in the base of the neck (Garfinkel 1999a). Similarities in the form of these vessels to skin bags used in the processing of dairy foods have been used to support the hypothesis that specialized pastoralism emerged in the Levant during the Late Chalcolithic (Levy 1983; 1992).

A complex of subterranean and overlying rectilinear architecture was excavated Abu Matar in the Beersheva valley by Jean Perrot (1955) from 1952-54, and subsequently by Isaac Gilead and Steven Rosen in 1990 and 1991 (Gilead et al. 1992). No radiocarbon assays have been undertaken on materials from Abu Matar but, based on the similarities of pottery and architectural forms at Shiqmin, Gilead (1994) places occupation of the site between 4400 and 4200 cal B.C. In addition to the materials from Abu Matar, Rosen also provided me with four 'churn' fragments from the Late Chalcolithic site at Nevatim in the northern Negev desert (Gilead and Fabian 2001). None of the 'churn' fragments from Abu Matar or Nevatim yielded diagnostic molecular compounds through conventional solvent-extraction techniques, and no further extractions were undertaken using the microwave-assisted solvent-recovery protocol.

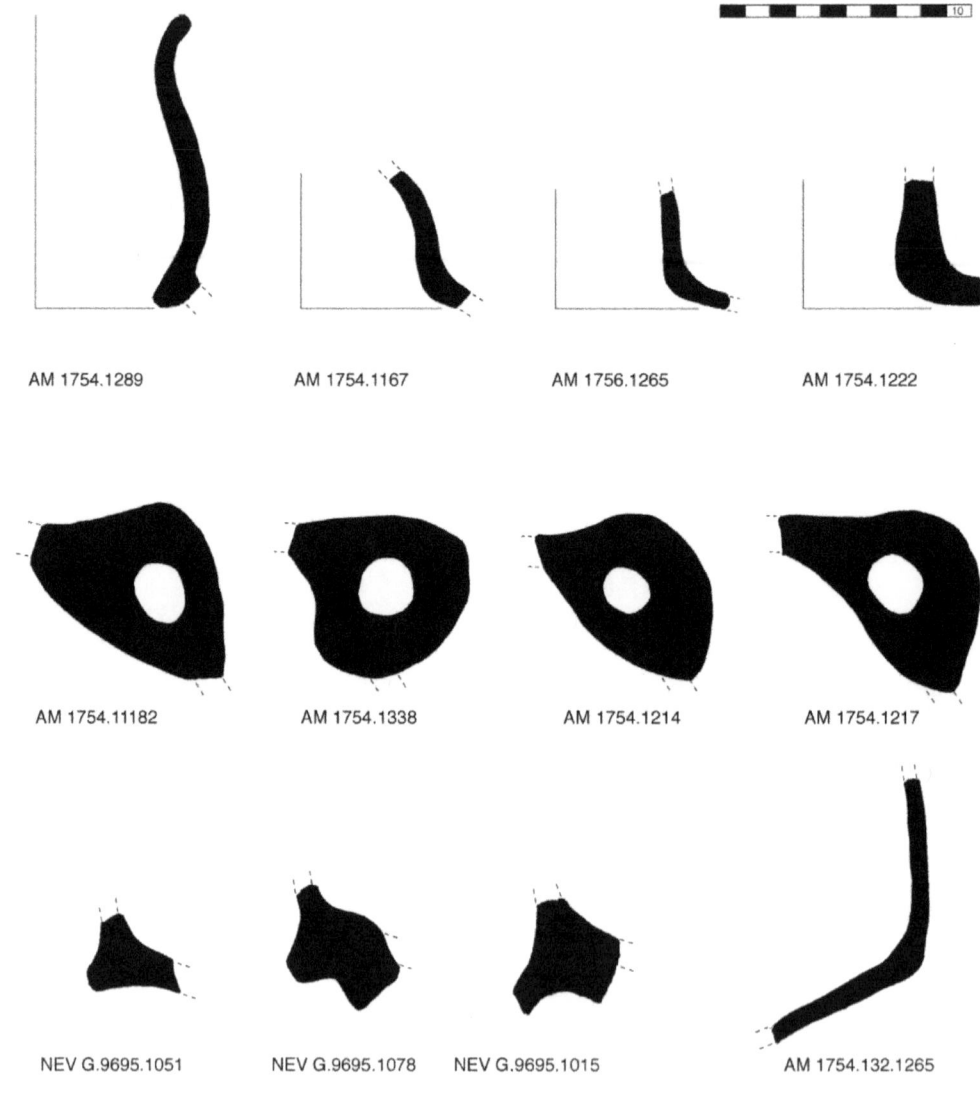

Figure A.1.8.1
Twelve of 18 pottery fragments from the sites of Abu Matar and Nevatim had diagnostic profiles that could be associated with Chalcolithic 'churns'.

Appendix A.2
Detailed description of the microwave-assisted liquid chromatography procedures used in the recovery of organic residues from pottery fragments examined in this study. These procedures were adapted from a protocol for the extraction, isolation and tranesterification of free fatty acids from marine sediments developed by Eglinton/Hughen Laboratories at Woods Hole Oceanographic Institution (Hughen et al. 2004).

1. Sample pottery fragments by grinding ~ 2 mm of the ceramic matrix from interior surfaces into a fine powder with a high-speed modeling drill fitted with an abrasive tungsten bit. Collect ~ 5g of the fine powder on sterilized sheets of aluminum foil.

2. Place the 5g of ceramic powder in a pressurized Teflon vessel that has been successively prerinsed (3X) with DCM, MeOH and hexane.

3. Extract samples in a microwave-accelerated reaction system (MARS) in 25 ml of dichloromethane and methanol organic solvents (DCM:MeOH, 90:10 v/v) using the Greenchem DDT method (100°C and 180 psi of pressure).

4. After extraction, solvent exchange into 0.5mL of DCM.

5. If any moisture is suspected to be present in the sample, elute through a Na_2SO_4 column (see step 16).

6. Concentrate each sample to a volume of 0.5mL. Split off and archive an aliquot for GC/TOF analysis if desired.

7. Silica Gel Columns in Pasteur pipettes
   a. Plug the bottom of each pipette with a piece of pre-combusted glass wool.
   b. Load 4 cm of fully activated SiO_2 into the pipette.
   c. Rinse the column with two bed volumes of hexane.
   d. Charge each sample onto the top of the column using a Pasteur pipette.
   e. Elute the F1 fraction using 4mL of hexane (yielding alkanes).
   f. Elute the F2 fraction using 4mL of 1:1 toluene/hexane (yielding PAHs).
   g. Elute the F3 fraction using 4mL of 2% formic acid in DCM (yielding fatty acids).
   h. Elute the F4 fraction using 4mL of 2% formic acid in MeOH (yielding the most polar compounds).

8. Blow down the F3 fraction to virtual dryness under N_2, and archive the remaining fractions in 4mL vials.

9. Re-animate the F3 fraction with ~ 0.5mL DCM.

10. Aminopropyl columns in Pasteur pipettes:
    a. Plug the bottom of each pipette with a piece of pre-combusted glass wool and rinse with MeOH, DCM and Hexane three times.
    b. Wet 0.5g of LC-NH_2 stationary phase with hexane and transfer it to the column using a Pasteur pipette.

11. Charge each sample onto the top of the column using a Pasteur pipette until the solvent level is just above the top of the stationary phase. Rinse the original vial with a small amount of DCM twice, and transfer these rinses to the column as well.

12. Elute the column with 7 mL of 9:1 (v/v) DCM/acetone to retrieve the less polar F1 fraction. Collect it in a clean storage vial for archival.

13. Elute the column with 8 mL of 2% (v/v) formic acid in DCM to extract the free fatty acid F2 fraction. Collect it in another vial and evaporate solvent completely.

14. Transerification of the F2 fraction from step 13
    a. Prepare a solution of 95:5 (v/v) MeOH/HCl. The MeOH must have a known isotopic ($\delta^{13}C$) composition if isotopic characterization of the corresponding methyl esters is to be performed. The MeOH must be completely anhydrous.
    b. Transfer 10mL of the MeOH/HCl solution to each fatty acid sample (the F2 fraction from step 13), purge the headspace with N_2, cap quickly, and heat at 70°C for 12-15 hours.

15. Add 20mL of Milli-Q water and 10mL of Hexane to each sample. Sonicate vials for 5 minutes. (This step employs a liquid/liquid extraction to partition the fatty acid methyl esters from the aqueous phase into hexane.) Allow the phases to separate completely after sonication.

16. Na_2SO_4 Columns in Pasteur pipettes
    a. Plug the bottom of each pipette with a piece of pre-combusted glass wool.
    b. Fill each pipette about halfway up with pre-combusted Na_2SO_4.
    c. Rinse the column with hexane.

17. Transfer the hexane (top) phase from step 15 to the top of the Na_2SO_4 column using a Pasteur pipette. Avoid taking the aqueous phase. Elute the sample with hexane and collect in a clean vial.

18. Add 5mL of hexane to each residual aqueous phase (from step 15) and sonicate again for 5 minutes. Then repeat step 17.

19. Repeat step 18.

20. Concentrate each dried sample to a volume of 0.5mL.

21. Silica Gel Columns in Pasteur pipettes
    a. Plug the bottom of each pipette with a piece of pre-combusted glass wool.
    b. Load 4 cm of 5% deactivated SiO_2 into the column.
    c. Rinse the column with two bed volumes of hexane.
    d. Using a Pasteur pipette, charge each sample onto the top of the column.
    e. Elute the F1 fraction using 4mL of hexane.
    f. Elute the F2 fraction using 4mL of 5% Ethyl acetate in hexane.
    g. Elute the F3 fraction using 4mL of MeOH.

22. Solvent exchange the F2 fraction into 1.5 ml of 100% hexane in preparation for GC/MS analysis.

www.ingramcontent.com/pod-product-compliance
Lightning Source LLC
Chambersburg PA
CBHW041708290426
44108CB00027B/2892